LIBRARY OF HEBREW BIBLE/
OLD TESTAMENT STUDIES

423

Formerly Journal for the Study of the Old Testament Supplement Series

JEREMIAH, ZEDEKIAH, AND THE FALL OF JERUSALEM

Mark Roncace

t&t clark

NEW YORK • LONDON

T & T Clark International, Madison Square Park, 15 East 26th Street, New York,
NY 10010

T & T Clark International, The Tower Building, 11 York Road, London SE1 7NX

T & T Clark International is a Continuum imprint.

Library of Congress Cataloging-in-Publication Data
Roncace, Mark.
Jeremiah, Zedekiah, and the Fall of Jerusalem / Mark Roncace.
   p. cm. — (Journal for the Study of the Old Testament. Supplement Series; 423)
Includes bibliographical references and index.
ISBN 0-567-02671-X
   1. Bible. O.T. Jeremiah XXXVII, 1–XL, 6—Criticism, Narrative. I. Title. II.
Series.
BS1525.52.R66 2005
224'.206—dc22
                         2005006786

Typeset and edited for Continuum by Forthcoming Publications Ltd
www.forthcomingpublications.com

Printed in the United States of America

ISBN 0-567-02671-X (hardback)

CONTENTS

ACKNOWLEDGMENTS

An earlier version of this book was submitted as a dissertation to the faculty at Emory University. I thank Martin Buss, Vernon Robbins, and especially Carol Newsom for their expert guidance. This book would have been impossible without them. I also thank my student-colleagues at Emory—Megan Moore, Amy Cottrill, Brad Kelle, Tamara Yates, and David Casson—for offering substantive feedback in the early stages of the project.

Jeff Shade provided important technical assistance in preparing the final draft. My mother, Paula Roncace, edited the manuscript; it is much better because of her efforts. Finally, I thank my wife, Michelle, who supported me in so many ways throughout the process. I dedicate the book to her.

Introduction

The book of Jeremiah features several fascinating narratives about the life of the prophet, one of which is found in Jer 37–44. This text is by far the longest continuous narrative in all the prophetic books. It is a lively and sophisticated account, contains complex characters and vivid dialogue and action, and participates in an intertextual network with a variety of other stories. This study offers a narratological and intertextual analysis of Jer 37:1–40:6, roughly the first half of the story which depicts the dynamic interactions between Jeremiah and Zedekiah as they attempt to negotiate the inevitable destruction of Jerusalem, a deeply complex social and religious watershed. The study follows them through the vicissitudes of their personal lives and the public tragedy.

A broad overview of 37:1–40:6 gestures toward its richness. After a short introduction (37:1–2), Zedekiah sends a delegation to consult Jeremiah who delivers a message of unconditional defeat to the emissaries (37:3–10). Jeremiah is then arrested as he attempts to leave Jerusalem and is incarcerated (37:11–16). Zedekiah calls a meeting with Jeremiah who again renders a word of destruction to the king (37:17–20). Nonetheless, the king honors Jeremiah's request not to be sent back to the life-threatening prison into which the officials had placed him and commits him instead to the court of the guard (37:21). The officials subsequently approach Zedekiah and demand that Jeremiah be killed because of his seditious message; the king yields and the officials throw the prophet into a cistern (38:1–6). Sanctioned by Zedekiah, Ebed-melech rescues Jeremiah from the pit (37:7–13). Zedekiah again summons Jeremiah and a long, intricate conversation ensues (38:14–28). Next the narrative reports the fall of Jerusalem, the blinding of Zedekiah, and the slaughtering of the king's sons and nobles at the hands of the Babylonians (39:1–10). Jeremiah, however, is rescued by Babylonian officials and entrusted to Gedaliah (39:11–14). An interlude reports an oracle delivered to Ebed-melech when Jeremiah had been imprisoned (39:15–18). The section concludes with a Babylonian official's monologue addressed to Jeremiah as the prophet is released and remains in the land under Gedaliah (40:1–6).

Scholars who have closely studied Jer 37–44 consider it to be among the finest of biblical narratives.[1] Despite the artistry of this story, there has been little

---

1. Gunther Wanke, for instance, observes that these stories are "von hohem dichterischen Rang" and are unparalleled by any other Hebrew Bible narrative (*Untersuchungen zur sogenannten Baruchschrift* [BZAW 122; Berlin: de Gruyter, 1971], 144). Else Holt analyzes "the literary tools of the author of this fine novella" and describes the story as a "skillfully composed narrative" ("The Potent Word of God: Remarks on the Composition of Jeremiah 37–44," in *Troubling Jeremiah* [ed. A. R. P. Diamond, K. M. O'Connor, and L. Stulman; JSOTSup 260; Sheffield: Sheffield Academic

sustained, detailed analysis of its literary features. Recent major commentaries have devoted minimal in-depth attention to it apart from text-critical observations, identification of major themes, and a few comments on its overall structure. Several important monographs on the subject have been published, namely those by Gunther Wanke,[2] Karl-Friedrich Pohlmann,[3] Herbert Migsch,[4] Christopher Seitz,[5] Axel Graupner,[6] and Hermann-Josef Stipp.[7] Building on the classic work by Bernard Duhm, Sigmund Mowinckel, and Wilhelm Rudolph, these studies employ some combination of historical-critical, source-critical, or redaction-critical approaches; they address questions of provenance, authorship, and the ideological nature of the various sources. In general, these works presume that there are layers within the text which can be unraveled. Their objective is to separate the original narrative from secondary insertions and then to determine how the redactor edited these hypothetical sources. While the weaknesses of these traditional methods have been well documented, their valuable contributions to the understanding of Jer 37–44 should be recognized.[8] It is misguided to deny the presence of multiple layers in the text or to challenge the importance and validity

Press, 1999], 161–70). See also Herbert Migsch, *Gottes Wort über das Ende Jerusalems* (Klosterneuburg: Österreichisches Katholisches Bibelwerk, 1981), 268.

2.   Wanke, *Untersuchungen zur sogenannten Baruchschrift*.

3.   Karl-Friedrich Pohlmann, *Studien zum Jeremiabuch: Ein Beitrag zur Frage nach der Entstehung des Jeremiabuches* (Göttingen: Vandenhoeck & Ruprecht, 1978).

4.   Migsch, *Gottes Wort*.

5.   Christopher Seitz, *Theology in Conflict: Reactions to the Exile in the Book of Jeremiah* (BZAW 176; Berlin: de Gruyter, 1989).

6.   Axel Graupner, *Auftrag und Geschick des Propheten Jeremia: Literarische eigenart, Herkunft und Intention vordeuteronomistischer Prosa im Jeremiabuch* (Neukirchen–Vluyn: Neukirchener Verlag, 1991).

7.   Hermann-Josef Stipp, *Jeremia im Parteienstreit: Studien zur Textentwicklung von Jer 26, 36–43 und 45 als Beitrag zur Geschichte Jeremias, seines Buches und judäischer Parteien im 6. Jahrhundert* (Frankfurt am Main: Anton Hain, 1992).

8.   For example, it seems unlikely that one can make such precise separations between the "original" layer and secondary insertions. One could easily point to the different conclusions of these studies as evidence of the difficulty of this task. After all, the redactor's goal is to blend earlier materials with his own stories so as to leave behind as few fingerprints as possible. Cf. John Barton, *Reading the Old Testament: Method in Biblical Study* (Philadelphia: Westminster, 1984), 56–58. One wonders how much editing redactors can do before they become authors. Redactional studies also assume that different viewpoints within the text are indicators of different levels of tradition. This assumption demands too much consistency. Rather, various ideas and views can be held by the same individual, whether it be the author/editor or Jeremiah himself. Furthermore, tensions and contradictory perspectives may be part of the overall literary or rhetorical nature of the text. It seems quite possible that a final editor/author was strategically making use of, or at least was aware of, such discrepancies. Finally, these redaction-critical readings appear to be guilty of the "intentional fallacy." They calculate that the author/editor is speaking from a specific viewpoint which can be determined from evidence offered in the text. Not only does this assume that the redactor's motivations and intentions can be identified, a notion that has been challenged by literary critics, but it also tends toward circular reasoning. Features in the text reconstruct the author's viewpoint which is then used to find evidence in the text for that perspective. Cf. Gail Streete, "Redaction Criticism," in *To Each its Own Meaning* (ed. S. L. McKenzie and S. R. Haynes; Louisville, Ky.: Westminster John Knox, 1999), 105–21 (116).

of diachronic approaches. It is clear that the narrative material in the book of Jeremiah has been through several hands; studies which attempt to separate those layers and to demonstrate the nature of the redactional work provide a deeper understanding of the text. Redaction critics, however, need not claim that the inconsistencies, tensions, and seams in the text preclude an integrated reading of the final form. Likewise, literary critics would do well not to dismiss the kinds of incongruities and disparities which lead a redaction critic to propose a composite text and which provide the clues for reconstructing the text's sources. Indeed, synchronic and diachronic approaches each have something to contribute to the interpretation of the narrative.[9]

Quite tellingly, in David Gunn's 1987 prediction of the future proliferation of poetic-literary studies of Hebrew Bible narratives, he anticipated that there would be a growing number of works on Genesis through 2 Kings, with special focus on Joshua, Judges, and Kings, as well as an interest in Chronicles, and Ezra and Nehemiah. He mentions nothing of work on narratives found in the Prophets.[10] Gunn was right. While there are numerous narrative-critical and intertextual studies of many texts in the Hebrew Bible, there are very few such studies on the prose material in Jeremiah.[11] This is a somewhat curious phenomenon. Perhaps it is because so many of the stories in Genesis through Kings deal with the "family" unit and are marked with sex, love, lies, jealousy, violence, anger, and other elements that modern readers tend to find intriguing and entertaining. Many of the biblical texts that have been the subject of extensive analysis by literary critics are often the same texts that could serve as scripts for box office hits—and, of course, have served as such.[12] They make for stimulating productions, in part, because of their focus on the "personal" face of history, which engages modern audiences. To be sure, Jer 37:1–40:6 has its share of intrigue, deception, personal suffering, and violence, but it is set against a backdrop of national and international politics. It is one in which all the main characters are men, and women appear only in visions and even then only to provoke male action (38:22–23). If contemporary readers relish stories of love, sex, and war, the one under consideration here is mainly a story of war. Furthermore, one

---

9. Brian Boyle also stresses that both synchronic and diachronic approaches are necessary for a fuller appreciation of Jer 37–38. See his two short articles, "Ruination in Jerusalem: Narrative Technique and Characterisation in Jeremiah 37–38," *Compass* 12 (1998): 38–45; and "Narrative as Ideology: Synchronic (Narrative Critical) and Diachronic Readings of Jeremiah 37–38," *Pacifica* 12 (1999): 293–312.

10. David Gunn, "New Directions in the Study of Biblical Hebrew Narrative," *JSOT* 39 (1987): 65-75 (72).

11. A striking attestation of the accuracy of Gunn's forecast is seen in Leo Perdue's *The Collapse of History* (OBT; Minneapolis: Fortress, 1994). Perdue analyzes Jer 37–44 in his discussion on "narrative theology." What is remarkable about his eleven-page treatment of this text is that there is not one footnote on these pages. Although nearly all other pages in Perdue's book contain footnotes (some quite extensive), here Perdue has multiple consecutive un-footnoted pages. He had no one to cite when doing a narrative reading of these chapters. His analysis, incidentally, is little more than a summary of the story.

12. One thinks of the films and plays featuring Joseph, Moses, David and Bathsheba, Samson and Delilah, and Esther.

of the two main characters in the text is a prophet, a type of character with whom identification is perhaps more challenging. Whatever the reason, the fact remains that much work remains to be done on the prophetic narratives in the book of Jeremiah.

Scholars have longed recognized Jer 37–44 as a unified narrative describing Judah's last days. The narrative is framed by chs. 36 and 45, both of which are dated to the fourth year of Jehoiakim's reign, and it is evident that 37:1–2 serves as an introduction to a new section. The present study, however, concludes at Jer 40:6, the point at which Gedaliah becomes the main character and Jeremiah, in fact, disappears from the story (until ch. 42). There are a number of structural clues, outlined in the study, which suggest that 40:6 represents an appropriate breaking point. Most notable and easily identifiable are the six similar recurring phrases which indicate where Jeremiah remained (יֵשֶׁב), the last of them appearing in 40:6. Perhaps a future project will examine the remainder of the story.

The present study will proceed as follows. Chapter 1 lays the theoretical groundwork by discussing narratological and intertextual analysis. Characterization and point of view receive special attention; the discussion of intertextuality outlines this study's understanding and employment of the concept and addresses the interconnected nature of the book of Jeremiah as a whole, as well as of Jer 37:1–40:6. Chapters 2, 3, and 4 represent the heart of this study. These three chapters are better seen as a single unit with three divisions—hence each chapter has the same title, distinguished only by the subtitles. The division into three chapters has been made strictly for logistical reasons (i.e. to prevent footnote numbers from becoming too cumbersome). Chapter 2 opens with an overview of Jer 37–44, and then more specifically of 37:1–40:6, observing some of the structural features of both units. The remainder of Chapter 2 and all of Chapters 3 and 4 closely examine each of the ten episodes in 37:1–40:6, beginning with a translation of the MT.[13] The narratological analysis does not apply rigidly a given set of categories to each episode; instead, it addresses issues as they arise. For instance, some episodes require a consideration of the setting, while for others the development of the plot or the rhetoric of the characters' speech will need to be assayed. Each section concludes with an examination of the intertextual features of the episode. I hope that this multi-faceted approach will illuminate the text's sophistication and richness, which in turn can shed new light on the understanding of the book of Jeremiah and promote fresh ways to study the prose material in the prophetic books. Chapter 5 develops the intertextual aspect of the study by exploring the portrayals of Jeremiah and Zedekiah and their relationship in terms of other prophet–king narratives in the Hebrew Bible, particularly those of Samuel and Saul, Nathan and David, and the anonymous man of God from Judah and Jeroboam. A conclusion summarizes the main findings and offers a few reflections on the import of the study.

---

13. See William McKane, *A Critical and Exegetical Commentary on Jeremiah XXVI–LII* (ICC; Edinburgh: T&T Clark, 1996) for a thorough discussion of the text-critical problems for each episode.

Chapter 1

CHARACTER, PERSPECTIVE, AND INTERTEXTUALITY

In the last several decades narrative criticism has been broadly and successfully applied to many texts in the Hebrew Bible. Due to its widespread acceptance and employment, a thorough explanation and defense of a narratological method is unnecessary. There are, however, a couple of issues for which a short discussion may be helpful, namely, characterization and point of view. The same is true for intertextual studies: the approach is well established in biblical studies, so detailed theoretical discussion is not needed. Nevertheless, I want to outline the specific nature of the intertextual approach taken here and to make some general remarks about the intertextual features of the book of Jeremiah as a whole and of the narratives in particular.

Characterization

The stories in Jer 37:1–40:6 are about people. Ten different named characters have roles in the narrative, five of whom have speaking parts, including the officials collectively. Jeremiah and Zedekiah, both of whom are complex figures, are of obvious significance. Quite simply one cannot study the stories in Jer 37:1–40:6 without giving close attention to the development of the characters.

As many others have observed, however, character can be difficult to discuss and define and it is especially difficult to separate from other aspects of the work.[1] Shlomith Rimmon-Kenan writes, "Any element in the text may serve as an indicator of character and, conversely, character-indicators may serve other purposes as well."[2] Similarly, as another theorist states, "it is in the nature of literary character to be dependent for its very existence on other parts and to cohere, ultimately inextricably, with plot and with every other part."[3] Consequently, "it is not possible to face a text and announce, 'I shall now talk about character' in the

---

1. See, for example, Baruch Hochman, *Character in Literature* (Ithaca, N.Y.: Cornell University Press, 1985), 13–27; Charles C. Walcutt, *Man's Changing Mask: Modes and Methods of Characterization in Fiction* (Minneapolis: University of Minnesota Press, 1966), 5–6.

2. Shlomith Rimmon-Kenan, *Narrative Fiction: Contemporary Poetics* (London: Metheun, 1983), 59. Cf. also James Phelan, *Reading People, Reading Plots: Character, Progression and the Interpretation of Narrative* (Chicago: University of Chicago Press, 1989), ix.

3. Mary Springer, *A Rhetoric of Literary Character* (Chicago: University of Chicago Press, 1978), 12.

same way that one might say, 'I shall now talk about plot' or 'metaphor.'"[4] Because it is intertwined with all other aspects of the text, at some level one is always discussing characterization, for "without personification there can be no storytelling."[5] Thus, there is not a separate section for "characterization" in the analysis of each episode.

The portraits of biblical characters are achieved through a variety of techniques which are generally the same as those found in non-biblical literature: statements, descriptions, and evaluations by the narrator, the characters' inward and outward speech and their actions, what other characters say about them, and how characters compare and contrast with other characters.[6] Of course, these techniques of characterization occur in combination in biblical texts, but the different types of characterization need not always be in harmony. As Rimmon-Kenan observes, one must examine "the interaction among the various means of characterization. The result, as well as the reading process, will be different according to whether the indicators repeat the same trait in different ways, complement each other, partially overlap, or conflict with each other."[7] This study will pay attention to these different modes of characterization.

The dialogue between characters, particularly between Jeremiah and Zedekiah, is especially important for characterization in the Jeremianic narratives. In fact, over half of chs. 37–38 is presented as direct speech. The narrator creates suspense and deepens tension in the story by dwelling on the intricate personal interactions between prophet and king. The audience watches them and listens to them, perceiving their inner life (or, in some cases, becomes frustrated in the attempt to do so). Characters cannot be studied in isolation, but rather one must "examine the respects in which the impression of individual character rises from the relationships among and between characters."[8] What the characters say to and about each other can be considered alongside what the narrator says about the characters, how point of view is constructed by the narrator, and how analogous figures respond in similar situations (intertextuality).

When careful attention is given to these various elements of characterization, both Jeremiah and Zedekiah emerge as complex and ambiguous figures—"round" to use Forster's classic terminology.[9] Other interpreters have recognized the

---

4. Rawdon Wilson, "The Bright Chimera: Character as a Literary Term," *Critical Inquiry* 7 (1979): 725–49 (726).

5. J. Hillis Miller, "Narrative," in *Critical Terms for Literary Study* (ed. F. Lentricchia and T. McLaughlin; Chicago: University of Chicago Press, 1995), 66–79 (75).

6. Cf. Robert Alter, *The Art of Biblical Narrative* (New York: Basic Books, 1981), 30, 114; Adele Berlin, *Poetics and Interpretation of Biblical Narrative* (Bible and Literature Series 9; Sheffield: Almond, 1983), 33–42; Shimon Bar-Efrat, *Narrative Art in the Bible* (JSOTSup 70; Sheffield: Almond, 1989), 47, 92; David Gunn and Dana N. Fewell, *Narrative in the Hebrew Bible* (Oxford: Oxford University Press, 1993), 46–89; Jan Fokkelman, *Reading Biblical Narrative* (Louisville, Ky.: Westminster John Knox, 1999), 55–72.

7. Rimmon-Kenan, *Narrative Fiction*, 70.

8. Bert O. States, *Hamlet and the Concept of Character* (Baltimore: The Johns Hopkins University Press, 1992), xix.

9. Edward M. Forster, *Aspects of the Novel* (New York: Penguin Books, 1962), 67–78.

depth of Zedekiah's depiction, even if they have not analyzed it in close detail. For example, Gerald Keown, Thomas Smothers, and Pamela Scalise write that Zedekiah is a "gray figure, neither fully positive or fully negative."[10] Similarly, Mary Callaway concludes that no other figure throughout the Hebrew Bible is depicted more poignantly than Zedekiah;[11] others have referred to Zedekiah's image as a tragic one.[12] Zedekiah's complexity is no different from many other characters in the Hebrew Bible, including that of the most prominent Judean king, David. In fact, Charles Conroy's description of David's characterization could also be said of Zedekiah's portrayal, although the stories about them vary in length and kind: "It seems that the narrator wants the reader to sympathize with the king but, at the same time, not to ignore the flaws of character and errors of political judgment that were largely responsible for the pain and disasters both within the king's family and within his kingdom. The narrator's presentation of David, then, is sympathetic but not uncritical."[13] Given David's obvious importance and centrality in the Hebrew Bible, it is quite significant that Zedekiah's characterization is akin to his, for at first glance, most readers would not put these two kings in the same category. Rather, even those who see Zedekiah as a complex character ultimately label him a "weak figure." Keown, Smothers, and Scalise, for example, despite their appreciation of Zedekiah's ambiguous nature, conclude that Zedekiah is "consistently weak." A recent work by Stuart Lasine, however, offers a different and helpful lens through which one can view Zedekiah's characterization and the narrative dynamics surrounding its development. It is helpful to introduce very briefly his work here since it will be explored further in the study.

Using a variety of methods—psychological, literary, and social-scientific—Lasine demonstrates the way in which information management functions in the maintenance and exercise of monarchical power. While his focus is on biblical kings and kingship, he also considers royal power and information management in the ancient Near East (Rameses II, Esarhaddon) and Greece (Homer's Achilles, Sophocles's King Oedipus), as well as those of European kings. A main purpose of Lasine's study is to illuminate the paradoxical nature of the king's position—a position that must constantly monitor information management, gossip, the private–public distinction, loyalty, and scapegoating. He writes: "While the king may seem to be totally independent and powerful, he is utterly dependent upon his courtiers to demonstrate their loyalty by sharing information with him. The paradoxical nature of the king's situation became more and more evident to me.

10. Gerald Keown, Thomas Smothers, and Pamela Scalise, *Jeremiah 26–52* (WBC 27; Dallas: Word Books, 1995), 214.

11. Mary Callaway, "Telling the Truth and Telling Stories: An Analysis of Jeremiah 37–38," *USQR* 44 (1991): 253–65 (265).

12. Bernard Duhm, *Das Buch Jeremia* (KHC; Tübingen: J. C. B. Mohr, 1901), 301; John Thompson, *The Book of Jeremiah* (NICOT; Grand Rapids: Eerdmans, 1980), 631; and Wilhelm Rudolph, *Jeremia* (3d ed.; HAT; Tübingen: J. C. B. Mohr, 1958), 203.

13. Charles Conroy, *Absalom, Absalom! Narrative and Language in 2 Sam 13–20* (Rome: Biblical Institute, 1978), 112.

He is simultaneously powerful and helpless, knowledgeable and ignorant, an idol and a potential scapegoat."[14] Lasine's study features insightful analyses of the reigns of Saul, David, and Solomon. Yet it is clear that the topics that Lasine mentions are also germane to Zedekiah's kingship. Lasine observes Jer 37–38 as a text where "royal knowledge and information management" are key—but he devotes barely one page to studying it. Lasine's work sheds light on Zedekiah's character by helping one see that Zedekiah's situation and his handling of it are characteristic of not only other biblical kings, but also of monarchs throughout history. Rather than being a "weak" figure, Zedekiah is enmeshed in the game of information management in which all kings must participate. Zedekiah is, in fact, at times presented as a powerful figure because he controls the flow of information in his kingdom. Like all kings, however, Zedekiah is a paradox, as will be shown.

Jeremiah's portrayal in these narratives is equally sophisticated, although surprisingly few commentators have considered his depiction in these stories specifically. If Zedekiah can be called a tragic figure, so too can Jeremiah. The observations of Gerhard von Rad capture much of Jeremiah's portrayal:

> Jeremiah's sufferings are described with a grim realism, and the picture is unrelieved by any divine word of comfort or any miracle. The narrator has nothing to say about the guiding hand of God; no ravens feed the prophet in his hunger, no angel stops the lion's mouth. In his abandonment to his enemies Jeremiah is completely powerless—neither by his words nor his sufferings does he make any impression on them. What is particularly sad is the absence of any good or promising issue. This was an unusual thing for an ancient writer to do, for antiquity felt a deep need to see harmony restored before the end. Jeremiah's path disappears in misery, and without any dramatic accompaniments. It would be completely wrong to assume that the story was intended to glorify Jeremiah and his endurance. To the man who described these events neither the suffering itself nor the manner in which it was borne had any positive value; he sees no halo of any kind round the prophet's head.[15]

It is safe to say that this is not the typical image of a Hebrew prophet. Jeremiah's sufferings and the absence of divine assistance, as was promised in Jer 1, create a pathetic and simultaneously dubious image. Jeremiah's ambiguity arises from consideration of the details in the text, as the analysis will show. His motives and intentions remain obscure; there are discrepancies between his words and events as they unfold; and he is concerned for his personal safety to the point of being willing to prevaricate to preserve his security. Jeremiah is a prophet of Yahweh, but he is a human being too.

---

14. Stuart Lasine, *Knowing Kings: Knowledge, Power, and Narcissism in the Hebrew Bible* (Atlanta: Society of Biblical Literature, 2001), xiv.

15. Gerhard von Rad, *Old Testament Theology* (2 vols.; New York: Harper & Row, 1965), 2:207–8. It is interesting that von Rad is reading intertextually (the references to Elijah and Daniel) in order to sketch his portrayal of Jeremiah. John Goldingay notes that "our last sight of Jeremiah is his back as he turns his feet wearily south, his ministry apparently fruitless, his future apparently only death, far away from the inheritance that he had promised that he and his brethren would repossess in Palestine" (*God's Prophet, God's Servant* [Greenwood, S.C.: Attic, 1984], 17).

Both Jeremiah and Zedekiah, then, are ambiguous and complex figures—ones who cannot be easily defined. Robert Alter speaks of an "abiding mystery" in biblical characters because their "unpredictable and changing nature" prevents one from being able to assign to them "fixed Homeric epithets." Instead, "only relational epithets determined by the strategic requirements of the immediate context" can be applied to them.[16] Likewise, Meir Sternberg states that "reading a character becomes a process of discovery," whereby the reader must perform "progressive reconstruction, tentative closure of discontinuities, frequent and sometimes painful reshaping in the face of the unexpected," and must accept that there may exist "intractable pockets of darkness to the very end."[17] Because of the "mystery" and "darkness" that surrounds characters, the reader's ability to make a final or fixed judgment is not always possible. In this vein, Peter Miscall maintains that the analysis of biblical characters will often "end in undecidability."[18] In his analysis of Abraham, for instance, Miscall writes that "he is either faithful and obedient or cunning and opportunistic." Miscall prefers, however, to leave both options open: "it is not a matter of choosing either one or the other, but of choosing both at the same time." For him characterization is not a matter of deciding between various alternatives, but of seeing them on a "continuum." Accordingly, he concludes that "the two Abrahams are not two distinct possible characters, but positions at either end of the continuum of the person Abraham which are already merging into other possible characters and are moving towards each other."[19]

Something of the sort can be said of the characters in Jer 37:1–40:6. They can be read in various and contrasting ways, but one need not decide between the alternatives. Rather, the interpretations can be permitted to exist on a continuum in which the various possibilities interact with each other. In other words, the various actions and speeches of the characters are susceptible to wide-ranging interpretations with each interpretation making more undecidable a portrayal that is already complex and undecidable.[20] The goal of this study to draw out the "complex and undecidable" features of the characters, mainly of Jeremiah and Zedekiah. One, however, can only arrive at tentative conclusions because both king and prophet "end in undecidability," shrouded in "mystery" and "darkness."

A final note on characterization remains. While Zedekiah and Jeremiah are clearly the main actors in the story, there are "minor characters" who also contribute in substantive ways to the plot. As David Galef remarks, "understanding how an author deploys minor characters helps one understand how the work is

---

16. Alter, *Art of Biblical Narrative*, 64.

17. Meir Sternberg, *The Poetics of Biblical Narrative: Ideological Literature and the Drama of Reading* (Bloomington: Indiana University Press, 1985), 323–24.

18. Peter Miscall, *The Workings of Old Testament Narrative* (Philadelphia: Fortress, 1983), 21.

19. Miscall, *The Workings of Old Testament Narrative*, 21.

20. Cf. Gerald Prince (*Narratology: The Form and Function of Narrative* [New York: Mouton, 1982], 71), who observes that because of the many "presuppositions, implications and connotations to a set of propositions (about a character), different readers' descriptions of a given character may vary: the readers will all isolate the same set . . . but they will think of different connotations."

put together."[21] Minor characters give the story "depth" by providing "a contrasting, shifting background against which the major figures play out the drama of their lives."[22] Accordingly, it will be necessary to consider not only such figures as Irijah, Ebed-melech, and the officials, but even more peripheral characters who have no speaking parts, such as the emissaries sent by the king (37:3) and the poor people who remain in the land (39:10). The importance of some of these characters is derived from their patronymic, which links with other minor players in the book of Jeremiah. Indeed, "the analysis of minor figures will inevitably reveal the painstaking construction of the work; how the author intends to get from alpha to omega, or what contrast he has in mind, or what thematic principles he is stressing."[23] Similarly, concerning minor characters in biblical narrative, Uriel Simon observes their "great importance to the biblical narrator" as they frequently "provide the key to the message of the story" by "furthering the plot . . . and the characterization of the protagonist."[24]

Point of View

Characterization is difficult to discuss apart from other narratological features of the text, one of which is point of view. Here biblical critics have most often appropriated the works by literary theorists Boris Uspensky and Seymour Chatman.[25] Chatman distinguishes between the interest point of view—the object of the story's interest—and perceptual point of view—the perspective through which the events of the story are perceived. The object of the story's interest in Jer 37–40 is obviously Jeremiah; the audience watches what he says and does and what happens to him. Although the narrative's focus is clearly on Jeremiah, his perceptual point of view is noticeably absent. The reader does not know what he is thinking or feeling, or how events appear from his perspective. Chatman's categories help one to see that the object of the story is not always the same character from whose point of view the story is related.

Somewhat similar to Chatman's categories, Uspensky distinguishes four different levels of point of view. The ideological point of view is a "general system of viewing the world conceptually," and therefore "least accessible to formalization." It is the view through which the events of the story are evaluated. The

21. David Galef, *The Supporting Cast: A Study of Flat and Minor Characters* (University Park: Pennsylvania State University Press, 1993), 1.

22. Galef, *The Supporting Cast*, 22.

23. Galef, *The Supporting Cast*, 22.

24. Uriel Simon, *Reading Prophetic Narratives* (trans. L. J. Schramm; Bloomington: Indiana University Press, 1997), 269.

25. Boris Uspensky, *Poetics of Composition* (Berkeley: University of California Press, 1973); and Seymour Chatman, *Story and Discourse: Narrative Structure in Fiction and Film* (Ithaca, N.Y.: Cornell University Press, 1978). See also, Mieke Bal, *Narratology: An Introduction* (Toronto: University of Toronto Press, 1997); and Gérard Genette, *Narrative Discourse: An Essay in Method* (Ithaca, N.Y.: Cornell University Press, 1980). In biblical studies, see Berlin, *Poetics and Interpretation*, 43–82; Fokkelman, *Reading Biblical Narrative*, 123–55.

phraseological plane consists of "the strictly linguistic means of expressing point of view,"[26] that is, how different points of view are syntactically and grammatically signaled. The spatial and temporal levels represent the location in time and space of the narrator (the "describing subject") in relation to the narrative (the "described event").[27] The psychological level refers to the perspective from which events are described or perceived. The viewpoint may be objective (external) or subjective (internal). Included in this plane are the voices of the characters and the voices of those who are quoted, such as the prophets who opposed Jeremiah (37:19). While speeches and quotations are "a basic device of expressing changes of point of view on the level of phraseology,"[28] the actual content of the speech or quotation reflects the psychological point of view of the one who utters it.

In Jer 37:1–40:6, the narrator expresses his ideological point of view most clearly in the introduction in 37:1–2 (the king and people did not listen to the voice of Yahweh). The reader is to understand, however, that the narrator continues to shape and mold the story, indeed, to tell the story. Standing quietly behind every ויהי ("and it happened") and ויאמר ("and he said"), the narrator mediates all descriptions and quotations in the story; he constantly holds this intermediary position between the narrative and the reader. Temporally and spatially the narrator's view in 37:1–2 is external to the characters in the story. The narrator stands outside the story and after its conclusion (presumably in the exilic or early post-exilic period). As the reader moves into the story, however, one encounters the dialogue of the different characters. As Berlin says, "direct speech . . . is the most dramatic way of conveying the characters' internal psychological and ideological points of view." Furthermore, "it also tends to internalize the spatial and temporal viewpoint," so that readers are situated with the character as the character speaks.[29] Because over half of Jer 37–40 is direct speech, the reader is often invited to stand with the different characters and perceive events from their perspective.

Beyond the introduction in 37:1–2, the narrator minimizes his presence, making no further explicit evaluative statements.[30] The narrator's minimal intrusion creates space for the multiple and contrasting perspectives of the characters presented in their direct speech, in the dialogue among them. Bar-Efrat observes that although a characters' "speech is always embedded in that of the narrator, who gives them the floor,"[31] "whenever characters use direct speech in the narrative, their point of view is, naturally, reflected."[32] The importance of this observation lies in the recognition that "this way of narration expresses the narrator's empathy for the character whose point of view is adopted," which "is not the same as

26. Uspensky, *Poetics of Composition*, 15.
27. Uspensky, *Poetics of Composition*, 57.
28. Uspensky, *Poetics of Composition*, 32.
29. Berlin, *Poetics and Interpretation*, 64.
30. The only other place where the narrator's voice is clearly heard is in 37:4–5.
31. Bar-Efrat, *Narrative Art in the Bible*, 42.
32. Bar-Efrat, *Narrative Art in the Bible*, 41.

identification and may even include criticism."[33] Similarly, Jose Sanders observes that "the material within a perspective space is interpreted as valid or factual to the person to whom the space is bound, while only *possibly* valid outside this space."[34] In other words, the narrator allows space for a character to express a perspective and for the implied audience to evaluate the validity of this stance. This is precisely what is taking place in Jer 37–40. Whenever a narrator relinquishes space to a character, that character is permitted to become the ideological center of the text. Thus, it is crucial to examine those instances in which the point of view is handed over from the narrator to the character, from external to internal, in order to establish the existence of sympathy for any ideological position staked within the text.[35] In this way, the narrator of Jer 37–40 provides space for multiple and competing ideologies to express themselves. The competing perspectives and ideologies prevent readers from siding too facilely with the views of one character against those of another. Instead, one must watch the characters carefully and listen to their speech, to their point of view, before making tentative decisions about them and their perspectives.

Readers find themselves on the same temporal and spatial level as the characters in the story, seeing matters from their ideological and psychological perspectives. Instead of standing outside the narrated events with the narrator, readers are inside with the characters and must negotiate with them various opinions, multiple perspectives, and missing logical connections which are natural and characteristic of human existence.[36] As readers work through the text, they shift from one perspective to another—a process that Wolfgang Iser calls the "wandering viewpoint."[37] Further, Raymond Person, in his conversational analysis, shows how readers assume the viewpoints of the different speakers in a conversation—which is germane since much of the direct speech in the Jeremianic narratives is, in fact, in the form of conversation.[38] A major result of the use of multiple points of view is ambiguity, about which Lotman observes: "The relations between them [different points of view] contribute additional layers of meaning. . . . Every one of the points of view in a text makes claims to be the truth and struggles to assert itself in the conflict with opposing ones."[39]

---

33. Bar-Efrat, *Narrative Art in the Bible*, 39.

34. Jose Sanders, *Perspective in Narrative Discourse* (Tilburg: Proefschrift Katholieke Universiteit Brabant, 1994), 37 (italics in original).

35. Cf. Benjamin Berger, "Picturing the Prophet: Focalization in the Book of Jonah," *SR* 29 (2000): 55–68 (64–65).

36. See Lyle Eslinger, "Viewpoints and Point of View in 1 Samuel 8–12," *JSOT* 26 (1983): 61–76 (69). Eslinger argues that if readers seek meaning and order, they "must submit to the creator . . . the omniscient narrator." Otherwise, "without the narrator's guidance" readers are "quickly bewildered . . . lost in diverse details and opinions."

37. Wolfgang Iser, *The Act of Reading: A Theory of Aesthetic Response* (Baltimore: The Johns Hopkins University Press, 1978), 108–18.

38. Raymond Person, *Structure and Meaning in Conversation and Literature* (Lanham, Md.: University Press of America, 1999), 44–46.

39. Jurij Lotman, *The Structure of the Artistic Text* (trans. R. Vroon; Ann Arbor: University of Michigan Press, 1977), 266, 279.

The question then arises how the narrator's point of view relates to those of the various characters. Here one can point to the work of Robert Polzin on the Deuteronomistic History (DH). Polzin considers the issue of where a work's "ultimate semantic authority" lies.[40] By "ultimate semantic authority" Polzin, following Mikhail Bakhtin, means "the basic ideological and evaluative point of view of a work . . . the unifying ideological stance of a work's 'implied author.'" Is the "ultimate semantic authority" to be found in the "reliable" speech of the narrator? Or is it in the words of a specific character, such as Jeremiah or Yahweh or Zedekiah? Polzin has demonstrated that in the DH it is found in the intersection of the voices, in the dialogue that takes place throughout the work. The "ultimate semantic authority" thus does not lie in one voice/perspective, but rather arises in the conversation of all the voices, including that of the reader. The same can be said for Jer 37:1–40:6. The narrator's view articulated in 37:1–2 must be evaluated alongside the other (ideological and psychological) viewpoints in the story, namely, those of the characters, and alongside the events that unfold (the plot). When read with a sensitivity to this multi-voicing, one finds, as will be demonstrated, that chs. 37–38 challenge the narrator's ideological position expressed in 37:1–2. The events as they unfold in the narrative prove to be more complex than the narrator's view voiced in v. 2.[41]

Polzin's observations are strongly influenced by Bakhtin's idea of a dialogic work, as opposed to a monologic one. Bakhtin developed these notions to describe what he perceived in the novels of Dostoevsky, but they can be fruitfully appropriated for biblical texts.[42] Briefly, unlike a monologic work, a dialogic one "requires a plurality of consciousness" that "cannot be fitted within the bounds of a single consciousness."[43] It contains multiple consciousnesses—unmerged voices—that intersect, that are in conversation. Texts, of course, are

---

40. See Robert Polzin, *Moses and the Deuteronomist* (Bloomington: Indiana University Press, 1980), 20–28, 66–69. Polzin takes this phrase from Uspensky.

41. See Robert Polzin's three works: *Moses and the Deuteronomist; Samuel and the Deuteronomist* (Bloomington: Indiana University Press, 1989); and *David and the Deuteronomist* (Bloomington: Indiana University Press, 1993). Most commentators fail to consider how the following narratives challenge v. 2. Robert Carroll (OTL; *Jeremiah: A Commentary* [Philadelphia: Westminster, 1986], 671) is exemplary: "This title [v. 2] summarizes the content of 37–39 and anticipates by way of explanation the fall of Jerusalem. It opens the final part of the book (G order) with a clear statement to the effect that even a change of king did not avert the nations fate (sealed in 36). Zedekiah continues his predecessor's policy of ignoring the words of Jeremiah. All that follows will unfold the consequences of that attitude. . . . As the fall of Jerusalem comes into focus, it is sufficient to know that the Babylonian replacement on the throne proved to be no more receptive to the divine word mediated through the agency of Jeremiah than all the other kings." Similarly, Brian Boyle, claiming to take a narratological approach, argues that the stories are a simple development of the theme outlined in 37:2.

42. Barbara Green offers a very helpful summary of how biblical scholars have employed Bakhtin. See her *Mikhail Bakhtin and Biblical Scholarship* (Atlanta: Society of Biblical Literature, 2000). See also Carol A. Newsom's "Bakhtin, the Bible, and Dialogic Truth," *JR* 76 (1996): 290–306.

43. Mikhail Bakhtin, *Problems of Dostoevsky's Poetics* (trans. C. Emerson; Minneapolis: University of Minnesota Press, 1984), 81.

not conversations, but, according to Bakhtin it is possible to produce in a literary work something that approximates an authentic dialogue. This mode of writing he called polyphonic.[44] In a polyphonic work, unlike a monologic one, the author creates several consciousnesses that are genuinely independent of one another and of the author's perspective. In such a text, the dialogic play of these consciousnesses and their expressed ideas calls the reader to participate in the conversation. As a descriptive category, then, polyphony is a useful model for understanding what is taking place in Jer 37–40. This is not to claim that Jer 37–40 is a polyphonic writing; rather polyphony is a concept that can be employed heuristically to explore the ways in which point of view and characterization are developed.

The narrator of Jer 37–40 does not guide readers through the maze of opinions and perspectives. Instead, he contributes to the multitude of voices and views. Polzin explains that the Deuteronomist

> uses his characters' and his narrator's efforts at securing the success of their own enterprise as the starting point for a meditation upon the limitations of explanatory and predictive ideologies. . . . [T]hese characters and their narrator sometimes succeed and sometimes not. Ultimately, the Deuteronomist is calling attention to the narrator himself and asks his readers to apply the same evaluative criteria to that narrator as to the characters he introduces.[45]

The same can be said of Jer 37–40. Readers are invited to consider not only the narrator's explicit evaluation voiced in v. 2, but also the narrator's perspective as he shapes the stories. Likewise, one is called to apply the same evaluative criteria to Jeremiah's viewpoint that is applied to his opponents and the narrator.

Carroll asserts that "the modern exegete would be well advised not to side with one or the other ideology too easily."[46] The implied author writes after the events have unfolded; this temporal point of view makes it easy to cast the story in simple terms of black and white. Jeremiah was right and the officials were wrong. The officials, however, also voice their view of the situation and they do so on their own terms. Their voice stands in dialogue with that of Jeremiah, the narrator, and the other characters in the story. Carroll's advice to the modern interpreter is right on target, but Bakhtin and Polzin can sharpen the point: it is the dialogic nature of the text which invites all readers not to side too facilely with any ideological position. Rather, readers are called upon to consider the various voices, each from its own spatial, temporal, psychological, and ideological point of view. The voice of the narrator does not subordinate all others to it. The commentators, including Carroll himself, end up siding with Jeremiah and denouncing the officials and the king. But the point is that the dialogic, polyphonic nature of the text calls the reader to listen to the dialoguing of different

---

44. Although he does not refer to Bakhtin, Mark Biddle discusses the "polyphony" in other portions of Jeremiah. See his *Polyphony and Symphony in Prophetic Literature: Rereading Jeremiah 7–20* (Macon: Mercer University Press, 1996).

45. Polzin, *Moses and the Deuteronomist*, 199.

46. Carroll, *Jeremiah: A Commentary*, 680.

views and to enter that debate with the various temporal, psychological, and ideological perspectives.[47]

Contextual Analysis

As has been made clear, the literary features of Jer 37–44 have not been closely investigated. One of the most basic of such components is the way that certain themes and motifs are developed throughout the story, mainly by the repetition of words and phrases. Accordingly, a contextual analysis of many of the episodes discusses how the different scenes in Jer 37:1–40:6 are connected to each other— how the scenes work in context to create the sense of a unified whole (which is not to say that the narrative is consistent and unambiguous).[48] There are a number of such repeating words and phrases in the text in question—words that are used with different nuances. There are also variations on words and phrases. However, the significance which one draws from verbal repetition and variation depends on the individual reader. In discussing this phenomenon in biblical narrative, Jonathan Magonet observes that some readers will conclude that a particular repetition or variation has no particular significance.[49] Others will attribute it to stylistic features of the narrative—for example, an author may choose not to use the exact same word in a short span of text for aesthetic reasons. Still other readers may observe the same "fact" in the text and derive an important meaning from it. A reader's overall interpretation of a story or character can depend in large part on the significance one attributes to such details. For instance, Magonet illustrates how Dana Fewell and David Gunn understand Naomi's character very differently from Coxon based on the way that each interprets the verbal nature of the text.[50] In short, the "contextual analysis" of the episodes will call attention to the verbal

47. It should not be argued that the perceived polyphonic nature of the text is an intentional strategy by the (implied) author. Perhaps it is. In general, the compositional style of ancient Israelite writing does tend to create less "controlled" texts. That is, the style of biblical narration is one that undercuts or challenges the narrator's intents and claims, as Polzin has shown. It is possible, too, that, influenced by deconstructionist readings, one may be a resistant reader who imposes suspicions on the text by reading "against the grain." Of course, one first must know which way the grain goes— which is difficult to determine—in order to read against it. Therefore, the three possibilities for the polyphonic nature of the text—intentional strategy by the author, style of biblical story-telling in general, or a resistant reading—are best left open.

48. Contextual analysis as it is defined here is not unlike rhetorical criticism which pays careful attention to the verbal nature of the text. Understanding how the narrative develops key themes and ideas is crucial for an overall interpretation of the passage. Contextual analysis differs, of course, from intertextual analysis which examines how aspects of the text are linked to other passages in the Hebrew Bible (see below).

49. Jonathan Magonet, "Character/Author/Reader: The Problem of Perspective in Biblical Narrative," in *Literary Structure and Rhetorical Strategies in the Hebrew Bible* (ed. L. J. Regt, J. de Waard, and J. P. Fokkelman; Winona Lake, Ind.: Eisenbrauns, 1996), 3–12.

50. Dana Fewell and David Gunn, "'A Son is Born to Naomi!': Literary Allusions and Interpretation in the Book of Ruth," *JSOT* 40 (1988): 99–108; Peter Coxon, "Was Naomi a Scold? A Response to Fewell and Gunn," *JSOT* 45 (1989): 25–37; Fewell and Gunn, "Is Coxon a Scold? On Responding to the Book of Ruth," *JSOT* 45 (1989): 39–43.

features of the text—noting the repetition of theme words such as שמע, יד, יצא, and שוב—and attempt to draw out their contribution to the richness of the narrative.

Intertextual Theory

As with narratological analyses, intertextual readings of biblical texts have proliferated dramatically in recent years, so that it is no longer necessary to provide a lengthy explanation and defense of such an approach. It will be beneficial, nonetheless, to indicate how intertextuality is understood for this study and to introduce how scholars have applied the concept of intertextuality to the book of Jeremiah.

First, the theories of intertextuality that inform this project can perhaps best be explained by mentioning some now well-known quotes, which is, of course, a very intertextual exercise in itself.[51] The term "intertextuality" is typically credited to Julia Kristeva (if it is not a paradox to say who "first" coined the term "intertextuality") who used the word to describe Bakhtin's concept of dialogism. She discusses

> the 'literary word' as an *intersection of textual surfaces* rather than a *point* (a fixed meaning) . . . as a dialogue among several writings: that of the writer, the addressee (or the character) and the contemporary or earlier cultural context. . . . [A]ny text is constructed as a mosaic of quotations; any text is the absorption and transformation of another. The notion of *intertextuality* replaces that of intersubjectivity, and poetic language is read as at least *double*.[52]

For Kristeva, all writing is interdependent on other writing—everything is a mosaic of quotations. Roland Barthes expresses similar ideas in his description of a text:

> The intertextual in which every text is held, it itself being the text-between of another text, is not to be confused with some origin of the text: to try to find the 'sources', the 'influences' of a work, is to fall in with the myth of filiation; the citations which go to

---

51. While the "original" (in English translation) of all of these quotes has been consulted, they are also cited in Patricia Tull, "Intertextuality and the Hebrew Scriptures," *CRBS* 8 (2000): 59–90; or in Robert Carroll, "The Book of J: Intertextuality and Ideological Criticism," in *Troubling Jeremiah* (ed. A. R. P. Diamond, K. M. O'Connor, and L. Stulman; JSOTSup 260; Sheffield: Sheffield Academic Press, 1999), 220–43. To demonstrate the intertextual nature of talking about intertextuality, Carroll notes that he found some of the citations in other "secondary" works on these theorists. Tull's article is an excellent summary of intertextual theory generally and as it relates more specifically to Hebrew Bible studies. See also Dana Fewell, ed., *Reading Between Texts: Intertextuality and the Hebrew Bible* (Louisville, Ky.: Westminster John Knox, 1992); Robert Carroll, "Intertextuality and the Book of Jeremiah: Animadversions on Text and Theory," in *The New Literary Criticism and the Hebrew Bible* (ed. J. C. Exum and D. J. A. Clines; JSOTSup 143; Sheffield: JSOT Press, 1993), 55–78; and Patricia Tull, "Rhetorical Criticism and Intertextuality," in *To Each its Own Meaning* (ed. S. McKenzie and S. Haynes; Louisville, Ky.: Westminster John Knox, 1999), 156–80.

52. Julia Kristeva, "Word, Dialogue and Novel," in *The Kristeva Reader* (ed. T. Moi; Oxford: Basil Blackwell, 1986), 34–61 (36–37 [emphases in original]). See also Kristeva's *Desire in Language: A Semiotic Approach to Literature and Art* (ed. L. S. Roudiez; trans. T. Gora, A. Jardine, and L. S. Roudiez; New York: Columbia, 1980), 66.

make up a text are anonymous, untraceable, and yet *already read*: they are quotations without inverted commas.[53]

Similarly, Barthes says,

> We know that a text is not a line of words releasing a single 'theological meaning' (the 'message' of the Author-God) but a multi-dimensional space in which a variety of writings, none of them original, blend and clash. The text is a tissue of quotations . . . the writer can only imitate a gesture that is always anterior, never original. His only power is to mix writings, to counter the ones with the others, in such a way as never to rest on any of them.[54]

Texts are so completely interwoven that attempting to trace lines among them becomes a meaningless exercise. Michel Foucault writes, "The frontiers of a book are never clear-cut; beyond the title, the first lines, and the last full-stop, beyond its internal configuration and its autonomous form, it is caught up in a system of references to other books, other texts, other sentences: it is a node within a network."[55]

The present study understands intertextuality along the lines of Kristeva, Barthes, and Foucault. All writers are readers of other texts; boundaries between texts are fluid; every text intersects with other texts; all writing is a node within a complex network of quotations. Literature can be conceived "in terms of space instead of time, conditions of possibility instead of permanent structures, and 'networks' or 'webs' instead of chronological line or influence."[56] This approach enables one to consider the various elements in a text that derive additional significance from their relation to another text, unhindered by questions of historical development and influence. Willem Vorster has observed that proponents of biblical intertextuality "focus on texts as networks pointing to other texts. . . . In the place of an object which has meaning has come a network calling for reaction by the reader."[57] Ellen van Wolde's comments are also germane here: "It is not the chronology of texts that should occupy the centre of attention, but the logical and analogical reasoning of the reader in interaction with the text."[58] Van Wolde not only de-emphasizes chronological questions, thus pointing to a network model of intertextuality, but she also observes the importance of the reader in making the connections, a point which can be developed a bit further.

---

53. Roland Barthes, *Image–Music–Text* (Glasgow: Fontana, 1977), 160 (emphasis in original).

54. Barthes, *Image–Music–Text*, 146.

55. Michel Foucault, *Language, Counter-Memory, Practice: Selected Essays and Interviews* (ed. D. Bouchard; Ithaca, N.Y.: Cornell University Press, 1977), 3.

56. Thais Morgan, "The Space of Intertextuality," in *Intertextuality and Contemporary American Fiction* (ed. P. O'Donnell and R. C. Davis; Baltimore: The Johns Hopkins University Press, 1989), 239–79 (274).

57. Willem Vorster, "Intertextuality and Redaktionsgeschichte," in *Intertextuality in Biblical Writings: Essays in Honor of Bas van Iersel* (ed. S. Draisma; Kampen: Kok, 1989), 15–26 (22). Vorster discusses how types of texts, such as birth stories or apocalyptic texts, invite the reader to consider the text in light of the intertext.

58. Ellen van Wolde, "Trendy Intertextuality," in *Intertextuality in Biblical Writings: Essays in Honor of Bas van Iersel* (ed. S. Draisma; Kampen: Kok, 1989), 43–49 (43).

The concept of intertextuality includes a wide range of possibilities, from the traditional notions of echoes, allusions, and direct quoting to the more complex and subtle "references" or connections between texts and texts' participation in a range of cultural discourses and genres.[59] Given this broad conception of intertextuality, it is understandable that different readers will hear or see various connections, for each have their own repertoire of texts. It is impossible, then, to formulate a complete list of a given text's intertextual connections. Some readers may miss allusions "intended" by the author and see others that are not. No one actually reads the text exactly the way that the author "intended." Indeed, "slippage is simply inevitable."[60] Thus one must allow room for the agency of the reader in the production of meaning.

Accordingly, this study does not pretend to offer an exhaustive intertextual analysis of Jer 37:1–40:6, for that would be a potentially endless process. Instead, it endeavors to follow the text's lead, but ultimately the reader is the one who makes connections between texts.[61] By "following the text's lead" is meant that through its use of parallel plots, themes, words, motifs, and so forth, the text forms a "network of analogies" by which "the text itself is trying to show how it should be read."[62] However, it is quite arduous to determine what the text provides and what the reader supplies. In the end it is the reader who establishes the analogous texts.[63] Miscall explains that "the reader decides which textual threads to pick up and follow, how far to follow each one and whether to tie them all together at some end or center or just leave them lying on the page."[64] Similarly, as Owen Miller has put it, the intertextual link is made "by the reader making, in his engagement with that text, connections with his own repertoire." But he also observes that a text can "demand" an intertext when the reader perceives the text as "incomplete, in need of some 'supplementary', text."[65]

The significance of these intertextual relations lies in their mutual illumination of texts. Two passages that have common themes, motifs, images, vocabulary, analogous structures, or parallel characters will inevitably each take on added depth and richness when examined in light of one another. Sometimes, too, one of the two texts will echo a third; in this way all three texts enter a web of relations. The network of such relations is theoretically endless, which contributes to

59. Cf. Jonathan Culler, *The Pursuit of Signs* (Ithaca, N.Y.: Cornell University Press, 1981), 103.

60. Tull, "Intertextuality and the Hebrew Scriptures," 63.

61. A major challenge in writing this book was to determine which intertextual threads to follow and how far to follow them—how many nodes in the network to explore in some detail. Since the network is in theory limitless, much is necessarily left unexamined.

62. Miscall, *Workings of Old Testament Narrative*, 13–14, 29.

63. Cf. Tull, "Intertextuality and the Hebrew Scriptures," 63–64; Miscall, *Workings of Old Testament Narrative*, 3, 141.

64. Peter Miscall, "Isaiah: The Labyrinth of Images," *Semeia* 54 (1991): 103–21 (107).

65. Owen Miller, "Intertextual Identity," in *Identity of the Literary Text* (ed. M. J. Valdes and O. Miller; Toronto: University of Toronto Press, 1985), 19–40 (33). Richard Hays (*Echoes of Scripture in the Letters of Paul* [New Haven: Yale University Press, 1989], 29–32) has formulated seven criteria to assist in identifying and interpreting intertextual connections: availability, volume, recurrence, thematic coherence, historical plausibility, history of interpretation, and satisfaction. This approach may be helpful on some level, but the criteria are too rigid and limiting.

textual instability and gives rise to an inexhaustible number of readings. The following study will begin to explore that network in which Jer 37:1–40:6 participates, with attention given to the ways in which the various nodes illuminate the stories of Jeremiah and Zedekiah.

Intertextuality and Jeremiah

One can begin within the book itself. It is easy to see many connections within the book of Jeremiah as a whole. In fact, Geoffrey Parke-Taylor has devoted a whole volume to cataloguing its doublets and recurring phrases.[66] The book's complex and difficult arrangement of material opens the way for a study of the development of various phrases, themes, and images as they are interwoven throughout the book. One does not have to look outside of Jeremiah to demonstrate its intertextual nature; it is itself already intertextually generated. The many instances of repeated use of the same texts (6:13–15 = 8:10–12; 11:20 = 20:12; 16:14–15 = 23:7–8; 23:19–20 = 30:23–24) indicate "the highly intertextual reflectivity going on in the book of Jeremiah."[67] A specific example that reveals the intertextual engagement involved in the book's formation is the *leitwörter* in 1:10. The terms "pluck up," "break down," "destroy," "overthrow," "build," and "plant" appear again in various combinations (12:14–17; 18:7, 9; 24:6; 31:28, 38, 40; 42:10; 45:4) thereby guiding the reader.

Intertextual features are also found in the narratives of the book of Jeremiah. An examination of these texts demonstrates how intertextuality forces the reader into encountering other texts within the book itself. This combination of intertextuality and narrativity "mov[es] the discussion away from more traditional textualist issues to more modern narratological matters in relation to the biblical text."[68] For example, Jeremiah's so-called Temple Sermon appears in 7:1–15. Here the reader finds only the content of the speech. In ch. 26, however, part of the sermon reappears with much more contextualization, namely, with a story about how it was received; thus chs. 7 and 26 are connected. Chapter 26, in turn, is linked to ch. 36. In ch. 26 various groups react to Jeremiah's declarations, to his point of view; some reject the message and the prophet while others accept them. The prophet's life is endangered and he eventually escapes through the assistance of the Shaphan family. In ch. 36, set a few years later, Jeremiah again attempts to influence the community. This time he does not verbally preach to the people as he did in the Temple Sermon, but rather his words are dictated to Baruch and read to various groups of people. Symbolized by the fate of the scroll which was burned by King Jehoiakim, Jeremiah's message is rejected, which connects with the issue that was left open in ch. 26.

In addition to the many intertextual elements identifiable within the book of Jeremiah itself, there are numerous ties between it and the Pentateuch and the

---

66. Geoffrey Park-Taylor, *The Formation of the Book of Jeremiah: Doublets and Recurring Phrases* (Atlanta: Society of Biblical Literature, 2000).

67. Carroll, "Book of J," 228.

68. Carroll, "Intertextuality and the Book of Jeremiah," 67–68.

DH.[69] Perhaps the most obvious feature is that the last chapter in Jeremiah (52) is the same as the last chapter of 2 Kings (25). This shared material points to the close relationship between the two works, which is not surprising since, as is widely known, many have proposed a Deuteronomistic edition of Jeremiah. The language, the *topoi*, and other concerns of the authors of the DH are also present in the book of Jeremiah, and it may be said that there is a stronger element of Deuteronomistic writing in Jeremiah than in any other prophetic book. In addition to the superscription (1:1–3), many of the narratives show Deuteronomistic traces (7:1–8:3; 11:1–13; 25:1–14; 26; 44), as does the collection of material on the kings of Judah in 21:11–23:6. Here the poems are accompanied by prose commentaries that are closely linked to the DH. The poems about anonymous people receive a new and specific context by the associated commentaries. The poetry, then, intersects with the DH's list of the last kings of Judah to produce an intertextual account of their fates.

A different brand of intertextual connections with the Pentateuch and the DH can be seen in the links between the person Jeremiah and Moses. Holladay has argued that the historical Jeremiah self-consciously modeled his career after Moses. One need not subscribe to Holladay's historical reading to appreciate the parallels that he points out, for instance, in the calls of Jeremiah and Moses or the verbal connections between the Song of Moses and various texts in Jeremiah.[70] Others have argued that the Deuteronomistic depiction of Moses as the first prophet among the wilderness generation supplies the primary thematic force at work on the final editors of the book of Jeremiah.[71] Moses is presented as a prophet who intercedes for the people and prevents their complete destruction, even if they still must wander in the wilderness for forty years. In the book of Jeremiah, the prophet is forbidden to intercede. If the prophetic office originated in Egypt, the land out of which Moses led the children of Israel, Jeremiah represents the return to Egypt. Thus, Israel's occupation of the land is framed by the stories of Moses and Jeremiah; exodus and exile are connected by these two prophets. In fact, making a number of observations regarding the return to Egypt and the vocabulary of intercession found in Jeremiah and Deuteronomy, Alonso Schökel has referred to Jeremiah as an "anti-Moses."[72] One can also note connections between Jeremiah's laments and Moses' conversations with Yahweh— both are prophets who talk back to the deity. Further, both Jeremiah and Moses

---

69.   There are, of course, links between Jeremiah and other prophetic literature. For a good discussion of the common material, see William Holladay, *Jeremiah 2: A Commentary on the Book of the Prophet Jeremiah, Chapters 26–52* (Philadelphia: Fortress, 1989), 44–53. Holladay does not employ the intertextual approach taken here, however; instead he talks of "borrowing" and "dependence."

70.   See William Holladay, "The Background of Jeremiah's Self-Understanding: Moses, Samuel, and Psalm 22," *JBL* 83 (1964): 153–64; and "Jeremiah and Moses: Further Observations," *JBL* 85 (1966): 17–27.

71.   Christopher Seitz, "The Prophet Moses and the Canonical Shape of Jeremiah," *ZAW* 101 (1989): 3–27.

72.   Alonso Schökel, "Jeremías como anti-Moisés," in *De la Tôrah au Messie: Etudes d'exégèse et herméneutique bibliques offertes à Henri Cazelles pur ses 25 années d'enseignement à l'Institut Catholique de Paris* (ed. M. Carrez, J. Doré, and P. Grelot; Paris: Desclée, 1981), 245–54.

die outside the land of Israel. These discernible parallels in the presentations of Moses and Jeremiah can shed light on the portrayal of each of them; they also invite the reader to look for other characters in the Hebrew Bible who are analogous to Jeremiah.

In Jer 26, which is strongly connected to other parts of the book of Jeremiah, the characters themselves point to a figure who is analogous to Jeremiah. Specifically, the elders of the land who come to Jeremiah's defense cite the case of Micah, who, like Jeremiah, prophesied destruction for Jerusalem, but yet was not killed by Hezekiah. In the process the elders quote Mic 3:12 and refer to the salvation of the city during Hezekiah's reign, which intersects with the DH. Thus, a network of intertexts among the book of Jeremiah, other prophetic texts, and the DH is formed. Another example of analogous texts can be found in the story of Jehoiakim in Jer 36 and the story of Josiah finding the law book in 2 Kgs 22. Ernest Nicholson suggests that Jer 36 "was consciously composed as a parallel" to 2 Kgs 22 and that "there appears to be a very deliberate contrast drawn between Josiah's penitence on hearing the Book of the Law and Jehoiakim's attitude and reaction to Jeremiah's scroll."[73] Both ch. 36 and 2 Kgs 22 reflect one another and represent contrasting ways to hear and read prophetic words.

In addition to analogous texts which may trigger an intertextual link, sometimes one word makes the connection.[74] When readers consider the occurrences of a word in other biblical texts, all the connotations of that word in the other texts and all the words with which it is associated in those texts intersect with its meaning in the text under consideration.[75] There are several such instances of this kind of intertextuality in Jer 37–40. Furthermore, beyond the linguistic level, common images—which are created by words—call for intertextual consideration. Miscall writes that "a particular image can entail rhetorical or logical development." He offers an example from the book of Isaiah: "Light includes fire by synecdoche since the fire produces a type of light; the same applies to sun, moon and stars which produce light."[76] Thus, once a mental image is formed, it interacts with other mental pictures, forming a network of images. These types of intertextual connections—linguistic and imaginary—add to the richness of Jer 37–40, as will be demonstrated.

Mary Callaway, in two short articles, has made some helpful observations concerning the intertextual nature of Jer 37–38.[77] What is particularly insightful

---

73. Ernest Nicholson, *Preaching to the Exiles: A Study of the Prose Tradition in the Book of Jeremiah* (New York: Schocken Books, 1970), 42–43. Here Nicholson cites Paul Volz, *Der Prophet Jeremia* (Leipzig: Deichert, 1928), 329, and Martin Kessler, "Form Critical Suggestions on Jer. 36," *CBQ* 28 (1966): 389–401 (396) as also having made a similar observation. This strengthens the validity of seeing a relationship between Jer 36 and 2 Kgs 22.

74. Cf. Robert Alter, *The World of Biblical Literature* (New York: Basic Books, 1992), 111.

75. Cf. Mark Love, *The Evasive Text: Zechariah 1–8 and the Frustrated Reader* (JSOTSup 296; Sheffield: Sheffield Academic Press, 1999), 45.

76. Miscall, "Isaiah: The Labyrinth of Images," 104.

77. Callaway, "Telling the Truth," 253–65; and "Black Fire on White Fire: Historical Context and Literary Subtext in Jeremiah 37–38," in *Troubling Jeremiah* (ed. A. R. P. Diamond, K. M. O'Connor, and L. Stulman; JSOTSup 260; Sheffield: Sheffield Academic Press, 1999), 171–78.

is that she basis her argument on narratological analysis; namely, she finds the repetitive nature of Jer 37–38 as the key indicator to read the text intertextually. Specifically, she perceives that there are two distinct "narrative modes" or "voices" in the text. One mode or voice is that of a chronicler reporting the events of the last days of Jerusalem. The other is present, not in the details provided by the chronicler, but in the narrative structure. It is the "sound of silence" in the spaces between the scenes of the narrative. This second voice is what makes the narrative unreadable by disrupting linear chronology. In other words, Callaway argues that the plot of the story in Jer 37–38 falters. Each of the episodes in the narrative has a plot, but the episodes taken together do not form a plot. These stories, she argues, exhibit all the problems of a cycle of stories that have been redacted into a continuous story. The narrative is comprised of alternating vignettes depicting Jeremiah being arrested by the officials and then having a secret interview with Zedekiah. Because the narrator provides few chronological clues, the reader is unable to determine how much time elapses between the episodes. This loose connection between episodes is most salient at 38:1–6 where it is unclear how Jeremiah could be arrested for his treasonous message if he were already confined to the court of the guard (37:21). Callaway suggests that rather than presenting a linear progression of events, the narrative is composed in a cyclical fashion—scenes united by repeating themes. This type of story is based on principles different from those of the linear narrative or the historical chronicle where the temporal or causal link between scenes is of primary importance. In the stories of Jeremiah and Zedekiah, these links have been loosened. Lacking the temporal relation of the episodes and of a plot driving the episodes toward a denouement, the reader must find a different way to shape the scenes into a coherent narrative. Repetition is the device that guides the reader through the story.

Callaway too quickly forgets about the "voice" of the chronicler and thus her argument that the narratives cannot be understood in a linear fashion is suspect. Nonetheless, her observation that the stories have a cyclical quality to them is helpful. Indeed, the composition of the book of Jeremiah as a whole is more circular than linear. The narratives in chs. 26–45 are clearly out of order chronologically, as the dates in the text indicate. This feature of the book directs the reader toward a more intertextual mode of reading. The lack of temporal relation or connection of the narratives in chs. 26–45 and specifically of the episodes in chs. 37–38 invite one to read the stories in light of one another, in a spatial mode, to let them bump up against each other.

Callaway's insight can be strengthened by pointing to the work of Michael Riffaterre. He calls attention to what he refers to as "ungrammaticalities" which serve as clues for the reader to look for intertextual significance. Ungrammaticalities are textual patterns that are incomprehensible with the sole help of context, grammar, lexicon, and descriptive systems. They are conflicts that form obstacles to making sense of the text—as if they were a grammatical anomaly or

---

Her later article is a revision of the earlier one. Interestingly, in neither of these two articles does she mention the term intertextuality.

deviation from normal conventions. Specifically, Riffaterre discusses the tension between a linear and non-linear reading, precisely the situation that confronts the reader of Jer 37–38. He writes that "the reader who shares the author's culture will have a richer intertexture. But he will be able to draw on that wealth only when semantic anomalies in the text's linearity force him to look to non-linearity for a solution."[78] Likewise, he contends that "the result or effect of the nonlinear, paragrammatic reading is perceptible only through the ungrammaticalities or gaps that disrupt the linear sequence." The ungrammaticalities in Jer 37–38 created by the lack of explicit linearity call the reader to construct meaning through intertextual connections.[79]

Concerning how one may read Jer 37–38 in such a fashion, Callaway observes that the repeated encounters between king and prophet establish a framework for the story. She asserts that "stories of such encounters were almost a standard literary form" and points to the confrontation between Moses and Pharaoh as the longest such story; she also cites (with no discussion) three instances in the books of Samuel (1 Sam 13; 15; 2 Sam 12) and a series of stories in Kings (1 Kgs 18:17–46; 21:1–29; 22:1–38; 2 Kgs 3:13–20; 20:1–11, 12–19).[80] The material in Jer 38, she notes, is particularly reminiscent of the encounter between an unnamed king of Israel, presumably Ahab, and Micaiah in 1 Kgs 22. Thus, the stories in Jer 37–38 have been narrated "so that they tell a story whose form can be recognized. . . . As they are narrated the events become encoded so that the listener can recognize the lineaments of a prophet–king story. Such a framework guides the way the listener hears the story and invites comparison with similar stories."[81] As is well known, the Hebrew Bible is filled with such encoded material—the tale of the wise young courtier in the court of a foreign king, the story of the struggle of the beloved but barren wife, the hero who meets his bride at a well, just to name a few.[82]

Callaway concludes that the organizing principle of Jer 37–38 is not plot, but rather the repeated use of a well-known story form. The circular rather than linear structure leads readers to "re-visit the scene and to compare it with the others." The dominant story form of prophet–king encounter influences one's

---

78. Michael Riffaterre, *Text Production* (trans. T. Lyons; New York: Columbia University Press, 1983), 87; and *Semiotics of Poetry* (Bloomington: Indiana University Press, 1978), 5–6. Riffaterre seems to go too far here when he says that a reader can draw on intertextual wealth "only" when signaled by an ungrammaticality. To be sure, many other factors can trigger intertextual recognition.

79. A few others have employed Riffaterre in the analysis of biblical texts. See Robert Brawley, *Text to Text Pours Forth Speech: Voices of Scripture in Luke–Acts* (Bloomington: Indiana University Press, 1995).

80. Callaway, "Telling the Truth," 263.

81. Callaway, "Telling the Truth," 264. Here she cites Hayden White, *Tropics of Discourse: Essays in Cultural Criticism* (Baltimore: The Johns Hopkins University Press, 1978), 81–100, for a discussion of this phenomenon in literature.

82. This, of course, is what Alter has called a "type-scene." He observes: "The reading of any literary text requires us to perform all sorts of operations of linkage, both small and large, and at the same time to make constant discriminations among related but different words, statements, actions, characters, relations, and situations" (*Art of Biblical Narrative*, 188). Similarly, Bal refers to the "frame of reference" that guides a reader's expectations (*Narratology*, 80–85).

reading of all the episodes. The narrative's structure also "calls readers back into Israel's story." Sometimes it will remind them of Joseph in the pit, at other times of Ahab and Micaiah, or of Isaiah and Hezekiah. "To hear Zedekiah's story," Callaway suggests, "is to be reminded of a dozen other stories of kings and prophets before him." Similarly, she says, "The narrative not only doubles back on itself, but it doubles back on Israel's history and invites us to hear those old stories again in light of this new one."[83] Callaway—with the aid of Riffaterre—has pointed in the right direction: the ungrammaticalities in the text—long observed by redaction critics—force the reader to search for a solution, which can be found by moving into a network of intertextual relationships from which meaning emerges.

As Callaway has shown, prophet–king stories provide the framework against which the stories of Jeremiah and Zedekiah can be read. Callaway also claims that because prophet–king narratives in the Hebrew Bible are "varied," it is difficult to determine what that story form would have meant to the reader. It is possible, however, to make some general assessments of the nature of these stories. This enables one to identify a rough (not neat) template or grid—a model in the Israelite and Judean cultural and literary tradition of what occurred when prophets and kings met. As John Darr asserts, "awareness of . . . convention (character types and typical situations) and intertextual linkage . . . is necessary for full interpretation of . . . characters." Accordingly, "it is imperative that we reconstruct the framework of literary and social conventions that constrained the ancient reader's understanding of characters."[84] While a substantive analysis of all the prophet–king stories in the Hebrew Bible is beyond the focus of this study, there are about thirty of them, it will be beneficial to consider the "framework of literary and social conventions" of prophet–king stories in order to understand more fully the encounters between Jeremiah and Zedekiah. Thus, in the process of the study those general conventions can be examined as they shed light on features of Jer 37–40; the fifth chapter will also devote attention to the stories of Jeremiah and Zedekiah as they relate to several other prophet–king narratives.

In sum, the seminal works of Polzin and Alter, among others, over two decades ago paved the way for numerous "close readings" of biblical texts. Since then, countless literary analyses have invigorated the study of Hebrew Bible narratives. The close attention to intertextual issues is likewise well-established among biblical scholars. Although narratological and intertextual readings have proven quite fruitful, they have not been applied to the narratives in the book of Jeremiah, even though it is evident that the stories lend themselves to this kind of reading. This chapter has provided a theoretical base for a narratological reading, specifically discussing issues of characterization and point of view, and for intertextual analysis, outlining a network model for such a reading.

---

83. Callaway, "Telling the Truth," 264–65.

84. John Darr, *On Character Building: The Reader and the Rhetoric of Characterization in Luke–Acts* (Louisville, Ky.: Westminster, 1992), 48. Similarly, Darr observes that one understands characters by "inferring from the repertoire of indices characteristics not immediately signaled in the text, but familiar from other texts and from life" (48).

Although this study is guided by these approaches, interpretation should always be flexible, incorporating imagination, intuition, and joy into the process. These elements, of course, are much more difficult to discuss methodologically. In other words, this study has not taken a theory and applied it rigidly to a given text to see what might surface. Rather, it employs certain strategies to help articulate what one "senses and feels" when reading the text, to assist expression of imagination. I hope these chosen tools provide an adequate means to construct an interesting, insightful, and persuasive reading of this story.

It is, however, only "a reading" of Jer 37:1–40:6. The indefinite article "a" suggests the indefiniteness of the interpretation presented. Readers are invited to probe the text carefully, to analyze, and to disagree with the arguments made here. Although it is only one reading, it is one that I hope will provoke thought and discussion about this story, which can in turn create space for reflection on human life.

Chapter 2

OF PROPHETS, KINGS, AND DESTRUCTION: PART 1

Overview

In order to study the narratives in Jer 37:1–40:6, it is necessary first to consider the overall shape and content of chs. 37–44.[1] Although these chapters offer a sustained narrative, few have considered the structural features of the story as a whole.[2] The proposal here is that after a short introduction in 37:1–2, chs. 37–44 break into two sections, each consisting of ten episodes.[3] The first ten episodes, the subject of this study, are in 37:1–40:6 and relate events leading up to and surrounding the fall of Jerusalem; the second ten episodes found in 40:7–44:30 narrate events after the fall.[4] The following diagram illustrates:

1. Chapters 36 and 45 both are set "in the fourth year of King Jehoiakim." Thus they frame, but do not belong to, the continuous narrative in chs. 37–44.

2. Holladay (*Jeremiah 2*, 282) divides 37:1–44:30 into eight sections, but only after shifting portions of the text which he thinks are dislocated. He calls 43:4–44:30 an "appendix." H. Kremers ("Leidensgemeinschaft mit Gott im Alten Testament: Eine Untersuchung der 'biographischen' Berichte im Jeremiabuch," *EvT* 13 [1953]: 122–40) proposed that the text divides into ten sections (37:11–16; 37:17–21; 38:1–6; 38:7–13; 38:14–28a; 38:28b–40:6; 40:7–12; 40:13–41:9; 41:10–15; 41:16–43:7). Kremers identifies these units on the basis of form-critical analysis, specifically the terminating phrases in 37:16b, 21b; 38:6b, 13b, 28; 39:14b; 40:6; 43:7. Wanke follows Kremers and divides 37:11–43:7 into ten sections; he considers 37:1–10 an introduction (*Untersuchungen zur sogenannten Baruchschrift*, 94–95). Perdue (*The Collapse of History*, 249) divides the text very much as is done here, with the exception that he makes 41:9–10 a separate episode and divides ch. 44 into three episodes, which seems unnecessary. It also disrupts the correspondences between the two sections. José M. Abrego (*Jeremías y el Final del Reino: Lectura sincrónica de Jer 36–45* [Valencia: Institución san Jerónimo, 1983], 62) puts a break at 40:1, and he calls 40:1–6 a "scene bridge" between chs. 37–39 and 40–43.

3. An episode can be defined as a unit of action or speech which has a clear beginning and end. By way of contrast, a scene can be defined as a unit of action or speech in which there is no change in the characters present, the location, or the continuity of time. An episode may be comprised of more than one scene. Cf. Meyer H. Abrams, *A Glossary of Literary Terms* (5th ed.; Chicago: Holt, Rinehart & Winston, 1985), 2, 62. Similarly, concerning specifically biblical narrative, Jacob Licht states that a "scene presents the happenings of a particular place and time, concentrating the attention of the audience on the deeds and the words spoken" (*Storytelling in the Bible* [Jerusalem: Magnes, 1978], 29).

4. In a very brief article on chs. 37–44, Sean McEvenue ("The Composition of Jeremiah 37.1 to 44.30," in *Studies in Wisdom Literature* [ed. W. C. van Wyk; Pretoria: Society for the Study of the Old Testament, 1972], 59–67) sets out "to search for the clues and structural elements which were evident to the editor." He discovers literary unity in chs. 37–44 on two levels: its organization into eleven sections and the editorial organization according to the theme of not listening to the voice of Yahweh. Before the fall of the city, it is the king and servants who do not listen; and after the fall, the Palestinian community does not obey. Thus, according to McEvenue, the text has both a narrative and rhetorical structuring, expressive of theological content.

Section 1	*Section 2*
Episode 1: Jeremiah receives emissaries from Zedekiah and announces that the Babylonians will return and conquer Jerusalem (37:3–10)	Episode 1: Gedaliah receives those who remain in the land and instructs them to serve the Babylonians (40:7–12)
Episode 2: Jeremiah attempts to go to Benjamin, but Irijah does not believe that he is not deserting and arrests him; Jeremiah is imprisoned by the officials (37:11–16)	Episode 2: Leaders of the people come to Gedaliah and apprise him of Ishmael's plan; Johanan suggests that he kill Ishmael, but Gedaliah does not believe their report about Ishmael (40:13–16)
Episode 3: Zedekiah meets with Jeremiah, and the prophet announces a word of defeat for Zedekiah; Jeremiah is moved to the court of the guard (37:17–21)	Episode 3: Ishmael meets with Gedaliah and the Judeans and kills them (41:1–3)
Episode 4: The officials charge Jeremiah with undermining morale and propose that he be killed; the king turns the prophet over to them and they throw Jeremiah into a pit (38:1–6)	Episode 4: Ishmael kills pilgrims coming to Jerusalem, throws them and the other dead into a pit; he takes others captive and flees to the Ammonites (41:4–10)
Episode 5: Ebed-melech hears what the officials have done and he approaches the king; he is authorized to rescue Jeremiah from the pit (38:7–13)	Episode 5: Johanan hears what Ishmael has done and he pursues Ishmael and rescues the remnant; Johanan intends to go to Egypt (41:11–18)
Episode 6: Zedekiah meets with Jeremiah and expresses fear of obeying the prophet's word; the king advises Jeremiah on answering the officials should they question him and Jeremiah follows his orders (38:14–28)	Episode 6: Johanan and the commanders of the forces meet with Jeremiah and promise to obey his word (42:1–6)
Episode 7: The fall of Jerusalem; Zedekiah is blinded and taken to Babylon; all others, besides the poor, are also taken into captivity (39:1–10)	Episode 7: After ten days, Jeremiah advises them to stay in the land and warns of the consequences if they disobey (42:7–22)
Episode 8: Nebuchadrezzar gives commands to treat Jeremiah well and to permit him to do what he wishes; Jeremiah is entrusted to Gedaliah (39:11–14)	Episode 8: Johanan and the leaders reject Jeremiah's message; Jeremiah goes to Egypt with them (43:1–7)
Episode 9: Flashback to Jeremiah's oracle of salvation to Ebed-melech before the destruction of Jerusalem (39:15–18)	Episode 9: Jeremiah's oracle predicting Nebuchadrezzar's defeat of Egypt serves to condemn the Judean refugees (43:8–12)
Episode 10: A Babylonian captain delivers a prophetic message to Jeremiah; Jeremiah is allowed to do what he pleases and he remains in the land with Gedaliah (40:1–6)	Episode 10: Jeremiah speaks against the remnant community in Egypt for infidelity and for leaving their homeland (44:1–30)

These two sets of ten episodes have some thematic and verbal parallels which make the division into two sections of ten episodes more compelling.[5] For instance, in the first episodes, Gedaliah and Jeremiah essentially offer the same word when approached by people seeking guidance—serve the Babylonians. The second episodes are connected by the notion of deception (שֶׁקֶר), as both Irijah and Gedaliah refuse to trust the words spoken to them. In the fourth episodes, Jeremiah is thrown into a cistern (בּוֹר), as are those whom Ishmael has killed. The fifth episodes detail a rescue—Jeremiah is saved by Ebed-melech, and the people taken captive by Ishmael are delivered by Johanan's forces. Jeremiah's advice is sought in each of the sixth episodes. The seventh episode is the pivotal one in each section; in the first Jerusalem falls, and in the second Jeremiah lays out the two options for the remnant community (stay in the land and prosper or go to Egypt and die). In the eighth episode in the first section, Jeremiah is allowed to stay in the land; in the second section he is compelled by Johanan's group to go to Egypt. Both the ninth and tenth episodes in each section begin with nearly the same formula, "The word of Yahweh came to Jeremiah." Further, the ninth episode in the first section represents a flashback to an oracle spoken previously, while in the second section, the word is a prediction of what will happen to the Egyptian community. There certainly is not perfect symmetry between the two sections, but there is enough to suggest an overall design to the final form of chs. 37–44.

Looking more specifically at the first ten episodes, one discovers a loose chiastic structure—not a rigid one.[6] This provides additional support for the proposed divisions. The structure can be illustrated as follows:

---

5.   Others have observed parallel structures in other sections of narrative in Jeremiah. Elmer Martens, for instance, interprets the recurring themes and structures in chs. 34–38 as deliberate parallel structuring ("The Narrative Parallelism and Message in Jeremiah 34–38," in *Early Jewish and Christian Exegesis: Studies in Memory of William Hugh Brownlee* [ed. C. Evans and W. F. Stinespring; Atlanta: Scholars Press, 1987], 33–49). For other examples of parallelism in Jeremiah, see Kenneth T. Aiken, "The Oracles against Babylon in Jeremiah 50–51: Structures and Perspectives," *TynBul* 35 (1984): 25–63; Winfried Thiel, *Die deuteronomistische Redaktion von Jeremia 1–25* (Neukirchen–Vluyn: Neukirchener Verlag, 1973), 219–29, who sees the phenomenon in Jer 18–20; and Thomas Overholt, *The Threat of Falsehood: A Study in the Theology of the Book of Jeremiah* (Naperville, Ill.: Alec R. Allenson, 1970), 29–30, on chs. 27–29.

6.   While this structure generally follows the division of each episode into two scenes (see below), it is to be noted that the first and tenth scenes each represent three lines in the structure (A, B, C, A', B', C') and that the eighth and ninth scenes only receive one line. Observations on formal patterning do not lead easily to pronouncements about meaning; further, there have been so many studies of chiastic structures that it has been said that any decent literary critic could fake a chiasm. Cf. David Gunn, "Narrative Criticism," in *To Each its Own Meaning* (ed. S. McKenzie and S. Haynes; Louisville, Ky.: Westminster John Knox, 1999), 201–29 (228). Abrego (*Jeremías y el Final del Reino*, 65–87) presents the following chiastic structure for Jer 37–39:

A.   Introduction (37:1–2)
B.   Freeing of Jerusalem and imprisonment of the prophet (37:3–16)
C.   Interview between Zedekiah and Jeremiah (37:17–21)
D.   Accusation of the prophet (38:1–13)
C'. Interview between Zedekiah and Jeremiah (38:14–28a)
B'. Fall of Jerusalem and liberation of prophet (38:28b–39:14)
A'. Conclusion (39:15–18).

A   Delegation sent to Jeremiah (37:3)

  B Jeremiah is free (37:4–5)

    C Jeremiah proclaims message (37:6–10)

      D Jeremiah's encounter with Irijah (37:11–14)

        E Jeremiah confined by officials (37:15–16)

          F Jeremiah proclaims message (37:17–20)

            G Jeremiah put in court of the guard (37:21)

              H Jeremiah proclaims message (38:1–3)

                I Jeremiah confined in pit (38:4–6)

                  Ebed-melech intercedes on Jeremiah's behalf (38:7–10)

                I' Jeremiah released from pit (38:11–13)

              H' Jeremiah proclaims message (38:14–27)

            G' Jeremiah put in court of the guard (38:28)

          F' Fulfillment (?) of message (39:1–10)

        E' Jeremiah released by Babylonians (39:11–14)

      D' Jeremiah's oracle for Ebed-melech (39:15–18)

    C' Message proclaimed to Jeremiah (40:1–3)

  B' Jeremiah is freed (40:4–5)

A' Jeremiah goes to Gedaliah (40:6)

This structure demonstrates not that there is a perfect chiasm in this section, but that repeating themes, motifs, and images provide both literary cohesiveness and an overarching structure. In addition, other notable features can be observed within the first ten episodes themselves (section 1). The first six episodes and the last three can be grouped together, with the climactic seventh episode—the fall of Jerusalem—separating them. The first six episodes each have dialogue in which two different people or parties speak in direct discourse; the seventh episode is the only one without direct speech; and in the last three episodes only one party speaks. The following outlines the first six episodes based on the direct discourse (the conversations) in the dialogues:

Episode	First Speaker	Second Speaker	Episode	First Speaker	Second Speaker	Continuing Dialogue
1. 37:3–10	Zed/emissaries[7]	Jeremiah	4. 38:1–6	Officials	Zedekiah	
2. 37:12–14	Irijah	Jeremiah	5. 38:7–13	Ebed-mel	Zedekiah	(Ebed-mel)[8]
3. 37:17–21	Zedekiah	Jeremiah	6. 38:14–28	Zedekiah	Jeremiah	Zedekiah Jeremiah Zedekiah Jeremiah Zedekiah

7.   Zedekiah instructs the emissaries what to say to Jeremiah, but the story does not record the emissaries actually repeating the king's message to the prophet (which is common in biblical narrative). The actual reported speech in the narrative is attributed to Zedekiah, but the conversation is between Jeremiah and the emissaries.

8.   Here Ebed-melech is speaking to Jeremiah, not the king; and Jeremiah does not respond. It is the one instance in these stories where one party speaks and the other does not reply (i.e. it is not a dialogue).

There is a certain symmetry in these six conversations. The third and sixth dialogues feature direct conversation between Jeremiah and Zedekiah. The first and second involve Jeremiah and two different parties (emissaries and Irijah), just as the fourth and fifth have Zedekiah and two different parties (officials and Ebedmelech). In the first and second episodes Jeremiah is spoken to and then responds, just as in the fourth and fifth Zedekiah is spoken to and then answers; both Jeremiah and Zedekiah have the last word. In the first episode Jeremiah converses with a group (emissaries) which is sent from the king to Jeremiah; in the fourth Zedekiah speaks with a group which has heard Jeremiah and comes to the king (i.e. there is a reversal of movement). In the second episode Jeremiah converses with an individual (Irijah); in the fifth Zedekiah talks with one person (Ebed-melech). The third and sixth conversations (between prophet and king) take place in "secret" (סתר) and in houses (the king's and Yahweh's); the second and fifth occur at the Benjamin gate; and in the first and third no particular location is mentioned. Moreover, the main topic of the first and last conversations is the fate of the nation, while the intervening four dialogues pertain to the fate of Jeremiah. In addition, these middle four episodes alternate between those hostile to Jeremiah (Irijah and the officials) and those more benevolent to him (Zedekiah and Ebed-melech).

Each of the first six episodes are connected insofar as each can be divided into two scenes based on the characters involved and the setting of the events:

	Scene 1		Scene 2	
1.	Zedekiah sends emissaries	(37:3–5)	Jeremiah responds to emissaries	(37:6–10)
2.	Jeremiah and Irijah at the gate	(37:11–14)	Officials detain Jeremiah	(37:15–16)
3.	Jeremiah and Zedekiah converse	(37:17–20)	Jeremiah sent to court of guard	(37:21)
4.	Officials confront king	(38:1–5)	Officials throw Jeremiah in pit	(38:6)
5.	Ebed-melech goes to king	(38:7–10)	Ebed-melech rescues Jeremiah	(38:11–13)
6.	Jeremiah and Zedekiah converse	(38:14–26)	Officials confront Jeremiah	(38:27–28)

The final three episodes are also linked together. Jeremiah's two releases in the eighth and tenth episodes frame a flashback episode in which Jeremiah utters an oracle to Ebed-melech. Jeremiah, accordingly, is the speaker in the middle (ninth) episode while Babylonian officials speak in the two framing episodes. Additionally, episode nine, the middle one, is linked to both eight and ten. It is connected to eight in that in the eighth episode Nebuchadrezzar offers a word of salvation through his servant to Jeremiah—apparently since Nebuchadrezzar considered Jeremiah "faithful" to his cause. Similarly, in episode nine Yahweh offers a word of salvation through Jeremiah to his servant (Ebed-melech) because Ebed-melech has been faithful. Episodes nine and ten are also hooked together by the word of Yahweh which is spoken in both of them—once *by* Jeremiah (ninth) and once *to* Jeremiah (tenth).

In short, the narrative in chs. 37–44 appears to have a general design and structure which features an introduction (37:1–2) followed by two sections each consisting of ten episodes. The first ten episodes also contain a number of unifying elements which invites closer analysis of them.

Introduction: 37:1–2[9]

(1) Zedekiah son of Josiah, whom King Nebuchadrezzar of Babylon made king in the land of Judah, reigned as king[10] in place of Coniah son of[11] Jehoiakim. (2) Neither he nor his servants nor the people of land listened to the words of Yahweh that he spoke through the prophet Jeremiah.

The narrator's introduction in vv. 1–2 provides important information and an over-arching ideological perspective on the events that are about to be narrated. However, as Polzin has demonstrated, the events of biblical narrative frequently offer a commentary on introductory and summary statements, such as the one that is found in vv. 1–2. That is, what the narrator tells the reader in a summary evaluation may or may not be in harmony with what is shown in the preceding or following stories. Events and views presented by the characters in the subsequent stories may challenge the narrator's observations. The narrator's perspective in vv. 1–2, then, is only one of several possible perspectives—or ways to interpret —the occurrences in the story.

In this introduction, the narrator also presents one of the two key foci of the plot: how or why it is that Zedekiah will not listen to the words of Yahweh. The other main element is the personal fate of Jeremiah. These two plot lines, of course, interweave throughout the story. The narrated sections focus mainly on Jeremiah's circumstances, but Zedekiah is the primary focus of the dialogue scenes. Accordingly, the final episode before the fall of Jerusalem contains almost entirely direct speech regarding Zedekiah.

Language Analysis

A consideration of the grammar and syntax of vv. 1–2 provide several insights into the complex nature of Zedekiah's position. A literal translation of v. 1 reads: "And Zedekiah son of Josiah reigned as king in place of Coniah son of Jehoiakim, whom King Nebuchadrezzar of Babylon made king in the land of Judah."[12] The primary difficulty is that the placement of the אֲשֶׁר clause ("whom King Nebuchadrezzar of Babylon made king in the land of Judah") at the end makes its antecedent unclear. Grammatically, Coniah (Jehoiachin) would be the most logical referent, but this is problematic because it is known that Nebuchadrezzar made Zedekiah king, not Coniah, after the first deportation (2 Kgs 24:17). Thus, most commentators safely assume that the אֲשֶׁר clause refers to Zedekiah and move it in the translation to follow his name.[13] However, the peculiar grammatical

---

9. All translations are my own unless otherwise noted.

10. The word מֶלֶךְ is not represented in the Greek and is regarded by some as a title.

11. The Greek omits "Coniah son of."

12. Many have argued that vv. 1–2 are from a later redactor. See Pohlmann, *Studien zum Jeremiabuch*, 51; Wanke, *Untersuchungen zur sogenannten Baruchschrift*, 98; Migsch, *Gottes Wort über das Ende Jerusalems*, 50–51.

13. Not all move the clause, however. Holladay (*Jeremiah 2*, 265), for instance, leaves it at the end but makes no comments as to its ambiguous referent.

construction points to the ambiguity of Zedekiah's relationship to Nebuchadrez-zar and the Babylonians and his identity as king in Judah.[14]

First, Zedekiah is both king of Judah ("and he reigned as king in place of Coniah"), and thus must be loyal to Yahweh, and he is a vassal of Nebuchadrez-zar ("whom King Nebuchadrezzar made king"), and thus has obligations to him as well. Zedekiah's predicament should be understood against this complicated backdrop. Secondly, perhaps the text is playing on the notion of kingship—a form of the word "king" appears four times in the verse. Is Zedekiah really the "king" or is he simply a vassal of Nebuchadrezzar, with whom the real power lies? Is Zedekiah "king" only from his own perspective? Or is he "king" in the narrator's view as well?[15] The text offers no answers and how readers supply them affects how they interpret Zedekiah's actions in the ensuing stories.[16]

Intertextuality

The very fact that Zedekiah has already appeared numerous times in the book (chs. 21; 32; 34) suggests that the significance of these verses lies other than in the simple conveying of information; thus, one can consider their relation to other texts. The narrator's introduction recalls both previous narratives within the book itself and stories in the books of Kings. Thus, from the very beginning the reader is invited to consider the narrative in light of its intertextual connections; in the case of v. 1 the connections draw additional attention to the complexity of per-spectives present in this short introduction.

Verses 1–2 echo the Deuteronomistic style by introducing a king's reign followed by a summary evaluation of his rule. Yet both verses differ in content and structure from the Deuteronomistic formula. Verse 1 differs by not giving Zedekiah's age, the length of his reign, or his mother's name (cf. 2 Kgs 24:18); instead, it mentions the three preceding kings—Josiah, Jehoiakim, and Jehoia-chin—and a foreign king. Verse 1 does not focus on chronology, but on the fact that Nebuchadrezzar, not a Judean king, is in control of Judah. Verse 2 contrasts by omitting the phrase "he did evil in the eyes of Yahweh" (cf. 2 Kgs 24:19), and stating that "neither he nor his servants nor the people of the land listened (שמע) to the words of Yahweh that he spoke through the prophet Jeremiah." The infor-mation contained in these divergences from the Deuteronomistic style—the mention of three previous kings and the evaluation in v. 2—is precisely the same material that connects chs. 36 and 37.

The very mention of Jehoiakim in 37:1 points to ch. 36 where Jehoiakim is the main character. Verse 1 also links Zedekiah and Jehoiakim by observing that

---

14. Given the abundance of names in v. 1, even the "he" at the beginning of v. 2 is ambiguous due to the fact that its presumed referent, Zedekiah, is the name farthest from the pronoun.

15. In a similar vein, the identification of Nebuchadrezzar as "king of Babylon" (which is deleted in the Greek) contrasts with the identifications of Zedekiah and Coniah as the "the son of." The titles remind the reader that Zedekiah and Coniah are the sons of dead and defeated kings (Josiah and Jehoiakim) while Nebuchadrezzar is the reigning king of Babylon.

16. See Abraham Malamat, "Jeremiah and the Last Two Kings of Judah," *PEQ* 83 (1951): 81–87, for a discussion of who was considered "king," Jehoiachin or Zedekiah.

Zedekiah was appointed king by Nebuchadrezzar; they were the only two Judean kings who were installed in office by a foreign ruler—Jehoiakim having been placed on the throne by Pharaoh Neco (2 Kgs 23:34). By identifying Zedekiah as the son of Josiah, v. 1 also reminds the reader that Zedekiah and Jehoiakim were brothers, both sons of Josiah. This invites comparison between the two kings, which the additional connections develop.

The primary intertextual link is with 36:30–31, an oracle of Jeremiah against Jehoiakim:

> (30) Therefore, thus says Yahweh concerning King Jehoiakim of Judah: He will have no one to sit upon the throne of David, and his dead body will be thrown out to the heat of day and the frost of night. (31) And I will punish him and his offspring and his servants for their iniquity. I will bring on them and on the inhabitants of Jerusalem and on the people of Judah all the disasters which I have spoken to them, for they did not listen.

This text connects in three ways with vv. 1–2. First, the evaluation of Zedekiah's reign in 37:2 is the same one given of Jehoiakim, his servants, and the people, namely, that they too did not listen (לֹא שָׁמְעוּ) to Yahweh.[17] Although their reigns are judged similarly by the narrator, there are striking contrasts in the depiction of the two kings. Jehoiakim cuts up the scroll containing the words of the prophet; Zedekiah persistently seeks his guidance. Jehoiakim is hostile to Jeremiah, ordering his arrest; Zedekiah ameliorates the prophet's conditions. Jehoiakim never meets Jeremiah face to face; Zedekiah has two intimate encounters with him.[18] Given that the two kings receive the same evaluation—which is hard to miss due to the proximity of 36:31 and 37:2—the reader is surprised to see Zedekiah as much more receptive of the prophet and the prophetic word.

Second, the mention of Jehoiachin in 37:1 informs (or reminds) the reader that Jehoiakim did in fact have a successor (i.e. Jehoiachin);[19] it was Jehoiachin who "had no one to sit on the throne of David"—his successor was his uncle, Zedekiah.[20] Although Jehoiachin is king for only three months (2 Kgs 24:8), there is an apparent discrepancy between Jeremiah's word (Jer 36:30) and the events that unfold (37:1). Jehoiakim had arrogantly ignored the words on Jeremiah's scroll and yet did not suffer the penalty announced by Jeremiah.[21] This is not the only

---

17. Cf. Abrego, *Jeremías y el final del Reino*, 66. See also Seitz, *Theology in Conflict*, 237: "37:1–2 are an obvious attempt to link chapters 36 and 37."

18. Jeremiah, however, is treated well by some of Jehoiakim's officials (36:19), which contrasts with Zedekiah's officials' treatment of the prophet.

19. Jehoiachin is conspicuously absent from most of the book of Jeremiah, appearing only here and in 22:24–30, an oracle spoken against him.

20. The Greek omits "Coniah son of Jehoiakim" so that 37:1 is then a fulfillment of 36:20—namely, that Zedekiah becomes king in place of Jehoiakim.

21. Others have pointed out that inaccurate predictions may cast doubt on the prophetic role. For example, Paul Kissling notes that errors in Elisha's forecasts question his reliability (*Reliable Characters in the Primary History* [JSOTSup 224; Sheffield: Sheffield Academic Press, 1996], 174–76, 189, 199). Similarly, Wesley Bergen observes that Huldah's failed prediction about a peaceful death for Josiah (2 Kgs 22:20; 23:29) serves to "increase any skepticism the reader may have concerning the importance of prophecy," and, further, that a discrepancy between Elisha's word and subsequent events in 2 Kgs 3 "acts as a wrecking ball, knocking down the image of Elisha that I have carefully

such instance of the prophet being inaccurate. Furthermore, in light of Jeremiah's persistent counsel to surrender to the Babylonians (38:2, 17, 21), the mention of Jehoiachin in v. 1 may be important for another reason. According to 2 Kgs 24:12, Jehoiachin had surrendered to the Babylonians (in 598); nonetheless, he was taken into exile as a prisoner and the temple was looted. The mention of the deported Jehoiachin, therefore, may raise the question of whether or not capitulation was the best policy.

The third connection develops sympathy for Zedekiah by showing that his reign was doomed from the start. The oracle in 36:31 claims that the city's fate is sealed by Jehoiakim's failures; thus Zedekiah's actions (whether or not he listens to the prophet) have no bearing on the outcome. It would seem that Zedekiah could prove more receptive to Jeremiah's words than his predecessor, but apparently this still would not avert the destruction. This connection with 36:31 casts a fateful and ominous shadow over the events about to be narrated.

These specific links between 37:1–2 and ch. 36 are complemented by a more general structural resemblance between chs. 36 and 37–38. The scroll in ch. 36 is proclaimed three times—first to all the people (vv. 5–10), then to the officials (vv. 11–20), and finally to the king (vv. 21–26). This parallels Zedekiah's three interviews with Jeremiah, resulting in the prophet's three proclamations to Zedekiah (37:3–10, 17–21; 38:14–28).[22] The multiple productions of the word of Yahweh not only join chs. 36 and 37–38 but they also mirror the story of Moses, forming an intricate intertextual nexus. In 36:1–4 Yahweh instructed Jeremiah to take a scroll and to write on it all the words that he had commanded him to speak. When the scroll was read to Jehoiakim, he destroyed it piece-by-piece by throwing it into the fire. In response to Jehoiakim's destruction of the scroll, Yahweh commanded Jeremiah to dictate a second scroll to replace the original. The prophet obeyed the deity's instructions and a second scroll was produced. This sequence of events is reminiscent of the stories of Moses on Mount Sinai and his encounter upon descending from the mountain with the golden calf constructed by Aaron. Both Jeremiah and Moses were instructed to write the words of Yahweh; both characters experience the destruction of the original document; both are commanded to rewrite the documents.[23] This similarity between Moses

---

constructed" and that this "shattering of an important image is a significant event in a story, for I lose faith not only in the particular character, but also in the class of characters of which this image is a representative" (*Elisha and the End of Prophetism* [JSOTSup 286; Sheffield: Sheffield Academic Press, 1999], 46, 82). David Marcus points out the satire present in the story of the "lying prophet" in 1 Kgs 13 (*From Balaam to Jonah: Anti-Prophetic Satire in the Hebrew Bible* [Atlanta: Scholars Press, 1995], 67–91). For a different approach to failed prophecies, see Robert Carroll, *When Prophecy Failed: Cognitive Dissonance in the Prophetic Tradition of the Old Testament* (New York: Seabury, 1979).

22. Cf. Martens, "Narrative Parallelism and Message," 43–45. Martens also sees several other parallel features in chs. 36 and 37–38.

23. In conjunction with these similarities in plot sequence, there is a syntactical connection in Yahweh's instruction to Moses and Jeremiah to make a second copy. In Exod 34:1, Yahweh says, "Cut two tablets of stone like the former ones (רִאשֹׁנִים), and I will write on the tablets the words that were on the former tablets, which you broke. In Jer 36:28, the deity says, "Take another scroll and write on it all the former (הָרִאשֹׁנִים) words that were on the first scroll, which King Jehoiakim

and Jeremiah is strengthened by the uniqueness of this sequence in the Hebrew Bible.[24]

Finally, although there is no specific verbal repetition, vv. 1–2 recall Jeremiah's word in ch. 27. There, the prophet expressed his view concerning Zedekiah's precarious position of being "king" of Judah and a vassal to Babylon. According to the prophet (speaking in the name of Yahweh), Zedekiah could successfully navigate his dual role by submitting to the Babylonians, for this was the will of Yahweh. Consequently, he could be simultaneously loyal to both Yahweh and Nebuchadrezzar. This was a novel perspective, and one that Zedekiah would understandably struggle to enact, especially since the destruction of the city was apparently inevitable, as the link with 36:31 indicated.

First Episode: 37:3–10

(3) King Zedekiah sent Jehucal son of Shelemiah and the priest Zephaniah son of Maaseiah to the prophet Jeremiah saying, "Please pray for us to Yahweh our God." (4) Now Jeremiah came and went among the people, for they had not put him in prison. (5) And the army of Pharaoh had come out from Egypt; and when the Chaldeans who were besieging Jerusalem heard report of them, they withdrew from Jerusalem. (6) Then the word of Yahweh came to the prophet Jeremiah saying: (7) Thus says Yahweh God of Israel: Thus you all will say to the king of Judah who sent you all[25] to me to inquire of me: Look, the army of Pharaoh who came out to help you, will return to its land, to Egypt. (8) And the Chaldeans will return and fight against this city, and they will capture it and burn it with fire. (9) Thus says Yahweh: Do not deceive yourselves saying, "The Chaldeans will surely go away from us," for they will not go away. (10) Even if you struck down all the army of the Chaldeans who are fighting against you and there remained among them only wounded men, each in his tent, they would rise up and burn this city with fire.

This episode consists of two scenes (v. 3 and vv. 6–10) separated by a parenthetical note (vv. 4–5). The two scenes are distinguished by their setting, although neither location is specified, and by the characters involved—Zedekiah and the emissaries in the first scene and Jeremiah and the emissaries in the second.

An important preliminary observation is just how striking it is for the king to send a delegation to Jeremiah when the narrator's immediately preceding statement (v. 2) had declared that Zedekiah and his servants did not listen to Yahweh.[26] Zedekiah's action causes the reader to pause over the tension. Why does a

destroyed." Both statements begin with an imperative, refer to the original document with the word ראשנים, and end with an אשר clause that indicates how the first text was destroyed.

24. Others have pointed out that Jer 36 is connected to Jer 26 and 2 Kgs 22–23. See Martin Kessler, "Jeremiah Chapters 26–45 Reconsidered," *JNES* 27 (1968): 81–88; Charles Isbell, "2 Kings 22:3–23:4 and Jer 36: A Stylistic Comparison," *JSOT* 8 (1978): 33–45; and Norbert Lohfink, "Die Gattung der 'Historischen Kurzgeschichte' in den letzten Jahren von Juda und in der Zeit des Babylonischen Exils," *ZAW* 90 (1978): 319–47.

25. The Greek has two second-person singulars (ἐρεῖς . . . πρὸς σὲ).

26. Redaction-oriented commentators typically account for the tension by attributing vv. 2 and 3 to different sources. Although a surprising number of commentators do not address the significance of this incongruity in the text as it stands, there are several who do. See Walter Brueggemann, *To Build, to Plant: A Commentary on Jeremiah 26–52* (ITC; Grand Rapids: Eerdmans, 1991), 139–40;

king who does not listen to Yahweh send for a prophet of Yahweh? While no one answer presents itself (and certainly not at this point in the story), it is crucial to recognize the tension. Indeed, the very first sentence of the story suggests that Zedekiah's actions be considered alongside the narrator's evaluation of him.

The "Dialogue"
The first episode is the only one in which there is an absence of any recorded dialogue—that is, when one party speaks and the other responds (hence the quote marks around "dialogue" in the sub-heading). When Zedekiah addresses the emissaries, he tells them what to say to Jeremiah, but the story does not record their relaying the message to the prophet. This is of consequence because of the apparent miscommunication that occurs in this episode. Perhaps, however, it is not miscommunication, but an indication of the nature of the relationship between Jeremiah and Zedekiah at the time. The issue here is that Jeremiah says that Zedekiah sent emissaries to him to "inquire" (דרשׁ) of Yahweh (v. 7), when the king, instead, is seeking intercessory "prayer" (התפלל) from the prophet (v. 3). Some interpreters have pointed out this tension, but have not discussed its literary significance.[27] As Alter and other biblical narrative critics have shown, however, the alteration of a single term is often quite significant in biblical narrative.[28]

To address this verbal discrepancy, one must distinguish between a prophet's "praying" (התפלל) and "seeking an oracle" (דרשׁ). For an answer, the use of these terms in other contexts can be examined. When one asks a prophet to "pray" on one's behalf, one is seeking salvation from suffering or death. For instance, in the first interaction between a prophet and king in the Hebrew Bible, Abraham (in the sole reference to him as a prophet) prays for Abimelech king of Gerar and Abimelech is saved from death (Gen 20:17). Likewise, when the people of Israel complained in the wilderness and provoked Yahweh to send a plague of fire, Moses "prayed" for the people and the fire abated (Num 11:1–2). Later, when the Israelites speak against God and Moses, Moses "prays" to Yahweh who provides the bronze serpent (Num 21:4–9). Moses also reports that his prayer delivered Aaron and the people from God's wrath after they had built the golden calf (Deut 9:20). Similarly, the Israelites ask Samuel to "pray" for them so that they do not die on account of all their sins (1 Sam 12:19). In 1 Kgs 13:6 Jeroboam asks an unnamed man of God to "pray" for him so that his withered hand may be restored. In all these cases, the prophet offers intercessory prayer for the salvation (healing, restoration) of a certain group or individual who is facing suffering or death.[29]

McEvenue, "The Composition of Jeremiah 37.1 to 44.30," 62; Keown, Smothers, and Scalise, *Jeremiah 26–52*, 214; and Timothy M. Willis, " 'They Did Not Listen to the Voice of the Lord': A Literary Analysis of Jeremiah 37–45," *ResQ* 42 (2000): 65–84 (82–83).

27. See Hetty Lalleman-deWinkel, *Jeremiah in Prophetic Tradition* (Leuven: Peeters, 2000), 220–22; and George Macholz, "Jeremia in der Kontinuität der Prophetie," in *Probleme biblischer Theologie* (ed. H. W. Wolff; Munich: Kaiser, 1971), 314–15.

28. Alter, *Art of Biblical Narrative*, 180.

29. Similarly, Elisha prays for healing for the Shunammite's son (2 Kgs 4:33), and Job (though not a prophet) offers intercessory prayer to save his friends (Job 42:8, 10).

By contrast, "to inquire" (דרשׁ) of Yahweh occurs in a different context. It involves seeking an answer about future events and/or counsel about what to do in a specific situation. The parenthetical note, "when one went to inquire of God," in the story of Saul and his lost donkeys in 1 Sam 9:9 demonstrates the nature of "inquiring": Saul was seeking a specific answer to a specific problem about his donkeys. In 1 Kgs 22, Ahab and Jehoshaphat "inquire" of Yahweh through Micaiah before going to war against Aram. The same two kings again "inquire" of the deity through Elisha before battling Moab in 2 Kgs 3. Further, Ben-Hadad sends Hazael to Elisha "to inquire" whether he would recover from his illness (2 Kgs 8:8). When the law book is found during Josiah's reign, he sends a delegation to the prophetess Huldah with instructions "to inquire" of Yahweh about what to do in view of the discovery (2 Kgs 22:13). Within the book of Jeremiah itself, there is one other instance of Jeremiah's "inquiring" of Yahweh. In 21:2 Zedekiah sent two men to Jeremiah to "inquire of Yahweh on our behalf, for King Nebuchadrezzar of Babylon is making war against us." The prophet responds with an oracle of defeat. This use of דרשׁ is consistent with its function elsewhere. The king seeks a word from Yahweh about what to do in a crises. In short, a word of prayer is addressed *to* Yahweh while an inquiry expects a word *from* Yahweh.

In the passage at hand, Zedekiah asks Jeremiah to "pray for us," but the prophet does not pray *to* Yahweh, but offers an oracle *from* Yahweh instead.[30] In light of the שׁמע in v. 2, one can note that "praying" involves speaking rather than listening, which may reduce the tension between the narrator's evaluation in v. 2 and the king's request in v. 3. At any rate, the king's request for prayer is apparently ignored by the prophet.[31] It is conspicuous that Jeremiah not only does not pray, but he himself asserts that the king had "inquired" (דרשׁ) of Yahweh (37:7), which he had not. Ironically, in one sense it is Jeremiah who does not listen to the words of the king.

There is, however, an explanation for Jeremiah's apparent disregard of the king's petition. In other places the prophet is commanded not to pray for the people because Yahweh will not listen (Jer 7:16; 11:14; 14:11–12).[32] Yahweh and Jeremiah are only willing to engage in one-way communication with the king. Yahweh will speak to the king through the prophet, but neither Yahweh nor the prophet will listen to the king's request for prayer—which, again, seems ironic in light of v. 2. In this scene, then, nobody is listening: Zedekiah does not want to listen—he wants prayer spoken to Yahweh; Jeremiah does not listen to the king; and Yahweh will not listen to the king. With intercessory prayer an impossibility since Yahweh would not listen, Zedekiah seemingly had no hope

---

30. Against Henning G. Reventlow (*Liturgie und prophetisches Ich bei Jeremia* [Gütersloh: Gütersloher, 1963], 145) and Samuel Balentine ("The Prophet as Intercessor: A Reassessment," *JBL* 103 [1984]: 161–73), the Jeremiah tradition is not collapsing the distinction between "inquiring" and "praying." Rather, it is playing on well-established ideas.

31. Cf. Walter Brueggemann, *A Commentary on Jeremiah: Exile and Homecoming* (Grand Rapids: Eerdmans, 1997), 355.

32. In 7:16 Yahweh says that he will not hear "you" (Jeremiah); in 11:14 and 14:12 Yahweh will not listen "when they call" and will not hear "their cry" (the people's).

for salvation. Indeed, the word from Yahweh that Jeremiah delivers is an unconditional message of defeat; there are no specific instructions on how that fate might be avoided.[33] Thus there is nothing for the king to obey, only a message to hear (which may be a play on the different meanings of שׁמע; see below).

Narrative Time and Doubling

The contents of vv. 4–5 break the temporal flow of the story, but they provide information that is crucial for both vv. 6–10 and 11–16. Verse 4 serves as a flashforward telling the reader that Jeremiah would be imprisoned, as he will be in the next episode in vv. 11–16.[34] Verse 5 functions as a flashback indicating that the Babylonians had withdrawn from the city because the Egyptians were advancing; this helps to set the context for vv. 6–10. Thus a loose chiastic structure is created: a (v. 4), b (v. 5), b' (vv. 6–10), a' (vv. 11–16). More important is the unusual shift in time; the juxtaposition of a flashforward and flashback forces the reader simultaneously to anticipate events (Jeremiah's imprisonment) and to look back on events (the lifting of the siege). Furthermore, because of the arrangement of material in the book of Jeremiah, v. 4 can function both as a flashback, recalling earlier stories that took place while Jeremiah was in prison (32:2; 33:1) and a flashforward, anticipating his imprisonment in the next episode. The head-twirling sequence in vv. 4–5 serves as a guide to readers, directing them to look for significance in intertextual links.

In addition to all the temporal movement, there is also a tremendous amount of spatial movement contained in vv. 4–5—the Babylonians, the Egyptians, and Jeremiah are all in motion. Fittingly, this activity is inserted into an episode that tells of the journey by the emissaries from the king to Jeremiah and back to the king. This physical movement in vv. 4–5 depicts the city of Jerusalem as a double for Jeremiah. Just as Jeremiah is permitted to "come and go" (v. 4) so too the people in Jerusalem are able to come and go because of the lifting of the siege (v. 5). Both freedoms, however, are momentary, if not completely illusory—the city's because of the returning Babylonian army and the prophet's because of his detainment by Irijah when he attempts to "go out . . . among the people" (v. 13). Neither the city nor the prophet truly has any freedom. There is a certain irony, then, in the prophet telling the people that their freedom will be short-lived, for his will be as well.

On another level, Jeremiah's role mirrors that of the Egyptians in that from Zedekiah's perspective both of them can offer a form of intervention—Jeremiah

---

33. Pohlmann (*Studien zum Jeremiabuch*, 52–69) cites Jeremiah's message in 37:7–10 as part of the "golah-oriented" redaction to declare Yahweh's word on the inevitable destruction of Jerusalem. Pohlmann claims the golah-oriented redactors had a number of already existing stories about Jeremiah and the last days of Jerusalem, but these stories—specifically the ones in which Jeremiah offers Zedekiah a chance to save himself and in which the prophet makes the same offer to those remaining in Judah after the fall of Jerusalem—were not always in line with the view they wished to express. Since they could not simply exclude these accounts, the "golah-oriented" editors corrected them by interpolations in order to bring them into conformity with their views.

34. The traditional language of flashforward and flashback is employed, although narratologists such as Bal use more complicated terminology to distinguish finer nuances of temporal shifts.

by praying to Yahweh on behalf of the king and people, and the Egyptians by deterring the Babylonian siege. Neither form of assistance materializes, however, as Jeremiah does not pray and the Egyptians return home.

Point of View

In contrast to the use of narrative summary in vv. 4–5 to convey relevant information, vv. 6–10—the second scene describing the encounter between Zedekiah's delegation and Jeremiah—employs direct discourse. Thus there is a shift from the narrator's point of view to the characters' perspective. However, one difficulty is to determine whose point of view is being presented in the oracle. This question arises because of the peculiar nature of Jeremiah's speech in vv. 7–8. Much as the text is playing on the distinction between "pray" and "inquire," there seems to be a play on commonly accepted forms of prophetic speech. Specifically, the messenger formula, "thus says Yahweh," appears to be misplaced. When one examines other forms of prophetic speech, the messenger formula always follows the instructions to the emissaries. The expected phrasing is, "This is what you will say to the king: thus says Yahweh . . . " This is precisely the sequence used in all other instances in which emissaries from a king consult a prophet (cf. 1 Kgs 14:7; 2 Kgs 1:6; 19:6; 22:18; Jer 21:3).[35] Therefore the reversal ("Thus says Yahweh . . . this is what you will say . . . ") in 37:7 is striking. The result is that there is some doubt about who is speaking, about whose perspective is being presented.

To elaborate, in the phrase, "This is what you (pl.) will say to the king of Judah who sent you (pl.) to me to inquire of me," there is ambiguity concerning the referent of the two first-person pronouns.[36] One possible interpretation is that both first-person pronouns refer to Yahweh. On this reading, Jeremiah is making himself transparent to the divine voice. It is the words/view of Yahweh spoken/ presented by the prophet. Another reading, however, focuses on the fact that Zedekiah sent the delegation to Jeremiah, not directly to Yahweh (v. 3). Accordingly, the initial first-person pronoun ("to me") appears to refer to Jeremiah. This would then suggest that the second "me" also points to Jeremiah since it would be awkward to switch voices in mid-sentence. Jeremiah, then, would be claiming that the king has sent to inquire of him rather than of Yahweh. This would have implications for Jeremiah's portrayal since, as competent readers know, kings inquire of Yahweh through prophets; they do not inquire of prophets themselves.[37] Furthermore, if read this way, the word of Yahweh is mixed with the

35. Of particular importance is that 2 Kgs 19 and Jer 21, two texts which are echoed here in Jer 37, illustrate the much more natural sequence. Isaiah says to Hezekiah's emissaries: "Say to your master: thus says Yahweh . . . " And earlier Jeremiah said to Zedekiah's delegation: "Thus you will say to Zedekiah: thus says Yahweh . . . "

36. The Greek eliminates these problems by reading "Thus you (sing.) will say to the king of Judah who sent to you (sing.) to inquire of me." Here it is Yahweh speaking to Jeremiah and it is clear that the "me" is Yahweh (the divine first-person pronoun).

37. There is no other instance in the Hebrew Bible when someone inquires of a prophet; they always inquire of the deity, either directly or through a prophet. One possible exception occurs in 1 Sam 28:6–7 where Saul inquires of the medium at Endor expressly because when he had inquired

word of Jeremiah, for the prophet's voice is heard after the messenger formula. Because of this unusual form of prophetic speech the reader is not sure where the divine voice begins and ends. If the prophet has said, "thus says Yahweh," and then reverted to his own voice ("me"), when, if at all, does he return to declaring the deity's message?

Thus, uncertainty exists regarding whose view is being expressed. It is well known that prophets can speak for themselves, not only for Yahweh, and Jeremiah does speak in his own voice and on his own behalf in future scenes, which raises further questions about whose perspective is being voiced here. In fact, in the sixth episode, it is possible that Jeremiah exploits his oracular powers to secure his own safety. These observations interplay with the fact that in this episode the narrator twice (vv. 3, 6) names Jeremiah as a "prophet."[38]

There are other issues regarding point of view in each of Jeremiah's two oracles. First, it is Jeremiah, or Yahweh, not the narrator or Zedekiah, who interprets the significance of the Egyptian advance by saying that the Egyptians had come out "to help you." The narrator (v. 5) had simply reported that the Egyptians had "come out from Egypt," and Zedekiah had requested prayer but given no specific reason for the petition. As a result, the reader never knows the king's point of view regarding the Egyptian advance—did he see it expressly as (divine) action on behalf of Jerusalem or not? Neither does the narrative indicate Zedekiah's motivation for sending the delegation—and indeed it is not clear why he would request intercessory prayer precisely when salvation appeared to be underway in the form of the Babylonian withdrawal. Rather it is Jeremiah's oracle (with the phrase "to help you") that attributes motivation to Zedekiah, namely, suggesting that the king was hoping that the Egyptians would assist them in battle against the Babylonians.

This attribution fits well with the fact that Jeremiah interpreted the emissaries as "inquiring" of Yahweh, for by "inquiring" Jeremiah must address a specific situation. So he in a sense creates the context for the inquiry—would the Egyptians help Jerusalem? Of course, from Zedekiah's point of view, he had asked for prayer, not for an inquiry of Yahweh. Thus, Zedekiah's point of view is refracted through Jeremiah's speech on several levels.

If in the first oracle Jeremiah's voice expresses Zedekiah's perspective, in the second oracle Jeremiah, or Yahweh, explicitly assumes the people's point of view when he says, "Do not deceive yourselves, saying, 'the Babylonians will surely go away from us.'" This is an example of quoted direct speech, that is, one speech quoted within another. As will be seen, this technique is a recurrent feature in these episodes, and it is not unusual in biblical narratives. What is noteworthy here, however, is that it is quoted internal speech—words that Zedekiah and the people of Jerusalem were, according to Jeremiah's report, thinking

---

of Yahweh, the deity did not answer. Does Jeremiah think that Zedekiah has inquired of him directly because Yahweh will not answer the king?

38. See Berlin, *Poetics and Interpretation*, 60–62, for a discussion of "naming" as it relates to point of view.

or saying to themselves. According to George Savran's terms, this reported speech is "unverifiable" because the scene in which it occurred is lacking.[39] There is no narrative in the book of Jeremiah where the king or people express hope that the Babylonians will withdraw or, for that matter, that the Egyptians will assist them. The reported speech, however, is believable, for one has no reason to suspect that this is not the king's and people's view. Here again the prophet's words attribute to the king and people a certain perspective that is not stated by them or by the narrator. The general effect of this is a certain complexity that arises from hearing one character's point of view voiced by another.[40] Furthermore, Jeremiah's approach here seems somewhat pre-emptive, for he has put words into the mouth of another and then told them not to say those words. This is all the more ironic given that Jeremiah had ignored, or reinterpreted, what the king had actually requested (i.e. prayer). If Jeremiah previously put words into Zedekiah's mouth (saying that the king had "inquired"), one wonders if he is doing the same thing here with the king and people.

In this particular instance, the potential complexity of the communicative situation is considerably greater because Jeremiah is not only presenting the king's and people's point of view, but Jeremiah himself is also speaking in the name of Yahweh. Indeed, all prophetic speech which follows the messenger formula is quoted direct speech. Here the prophet is presenting Yahweh's view, which is expressing Zedekiah's and Jerusalem's view.

Rhetoric

The rhetoric of Jeremiah's two oracles is enhanced by several instances of artful word-play on the multiple connotations of יצא, שוב, and שמע. The message cleverly depicts the Egyptians and the Babylonians carrying out the actions that Jerusalem should have followed. According to Jeremiah, the Egyptian army that came out (יצא) from Egypt would return (שוב) to Egypt, allowing the Babylonians to return (שוב) and fight against the city. Thus, the double "turning back" of ally and foe would lead to the city's fall. Jeremiah had counseled Jerusalem to "repent" (שוב) and surrender (יצא) to the Babylonians in order to be saved. But because the city had not followed his advice, the Egyptian advance (יצא) and return (שוב) would result in the destruction of the city by the Babylonians. Similarly, the Babylonians "hear" (שמע) about the Egyptians (v. 5) and subsequently "return" (שוב) to besieging Jerusalem because it had refused to listen (שמע) to Jeremiah and repent (שוב). The people's punishment, then, results from the Babylonians "hearing" and "returning," precisely the actions that the king and people had not done.

Jeremiah's second oracle in vv. 9–10 also includes smart word-play. Verse 9 reads: "Thus says Yahweh, Do not deceive (נשא) yourselves, saying, 'The Chaldeans will surely go away from us,' for they will not go away." The words תשאו נפשתיכם ("deceive yourselves") appear nowhere else in the Hebrew Bible,

39. George Savran, *Telling and Retelling* (Bloomington: Indiana University Press, 1988), 7.
40. Cf. Berlin, *Poetics and Interpretation*, 97.

and they are clearly a play on the expected נשׂאו נפשׁתיכם, which literally means "to lift up your spirit" and can thus be rendered "to get your hopes up."[41] This word-play is particularly apt because in the previous oracle Jeremiah had told the king not to rely on Egyptian assistance because it would not materialize—that is, not to get their hopes up. The prophet, however, employs the word נשׁא, which means "deceive."[42] Thus, the play suggests that "getting one's hopes up" (נשׂא) was, in truth, "deceiving oneself" (נשׁא).[43]

Intertextuality

This first episode, much like the introduction in vv. 1–2, is tied both to other texts within the book of Jeremiah and to the Deuteronomistic History (DH). The intertextual connections between 37:3–10 and 21:1–10, long pointed out by scholars, serve, conveniently enough, to underscore some of the observations made concerning point of view. In 21:1–10 Zedekiah sent emissaries to Jeremiah "to inquire" (דרשׁ) of Yahweh for the king and the people because "King Nebuchadrezzar of Babylon is making war against us; perhaps Yahweh will perform a wonderful deed for us, as he has often done, and will make him withdraw from us." According to 37:5, the Babylonians had withdrawn from the city. Thus it appears that Zedekiah's hopes for divine intervention were in the process of being fulfilled. If Zedekiah did interpret the withdrawal of the Babylonians precisely as Yahweh's intervention which he expressed hope for in 21:2, then it is noteworthy that he would call on Jeremiah when the siege was lifted. Surely it seemed as if the prophet had been wrong; the mass destruction foretold in 21:3–7 appeared to be diverted. Thus, when read in conjunction with ch. 21, Zedekiah's consulting Jeremiah at this time seems particularly commendable.[44]

---

41. The phrase נשׂא נפשׁ occurs nine times: Deut 24:15; 2 Sam 14:14; Pss 24:4; 25:1; 86:4; 143:8; Jer 22:27; 44:14; Hos 4:8.

42. Several commentators are duped by this switch, attesting to its shrewdness. Thompson (*The Book of Jeremiah*, 632), for instance, incorrectly explains that "The expression *do not deceive yourselves* in the translation renders the idiomatic Hebrew expression 'do not cause your souls to rise (lift up).'" Similarly, Lawrence Boadt (*Jeremiah 26–52, Habakkuk, Zephaniah, Nahum* [Wilmington, Del.: Michael Glazier, 1982], 94) says, "The RSV's 'Do not deceive yourselves,' literally means 'Don't get your hopes up!'" Both are obviously reading נשׁא instead of נשׂא.

43. The word נשׁא itself has certain connotations and echoes in the book of Jeremiah where it appears four other times (4:10; 23:39; 29:8; 49:16). In 4:10 the prophet accuses Yahweh of deception (נשׁא) by promising peace and then bringing destruction. Thus, one could, as John Calvin suggested, see the withdrawal of the Babylonians as "God for a time permit[ting]" the people "to be deceived by a fortunate event" (*Commentaries on the Book of the Prophet Jeremiah and the Lamentations* [ed. and trans. John Owen; 5 vols.; Grand Rapids: Eerdmans, 1950], 4:367). In fact, in 23:39 Yahweh declares, "I will deceive (נשׁא) you and cast you away from my presence." One wonders if deception originates within oneself, as 37:9 suggests, or with Yahweh?

44. Ronald Clements, *Jeremiah: A Bible Commentary for Teaching and Preaching* (IBC; Atlanta: John Knox, 1988), 218, writes: "Supposing that the most serious threat of which Jeremiah had spoken had now passed, his sending to Jeremiah (v. 3) would have been intended as a move towards reconciliation." Clements, however, concludes on a different note: "The situation and his sending to Jeremiah serve to highlight very clearly the weakness, indecision, and facile clutching at every straw of political advantage which marked Zedekiah's years on the throne of Judah" (219).

In contrast to ch. 37, Zedekiah in 21:2 does reveal his hopes, his point of view, that the deity would "perform a wonderful deed for us." This line recalls Jerusalem's miraculous salvation from the Assyrians a century earlier during the reign of Hezekiah.[45] The story of Hezekiah, Isaiah, and the Assyrian crisis provides the backdrop for this episode, as will be seen. According to Jeremiah, however, the only miraculous deed that would be performed during the Babylonian siege is the wounded remnant of the Babylonian army destroying Jerusalem (37:10). If previously the angel of the Yahweh had killed 185,000 of the enemy, now only a few Babylonians could destroy all of Jerusalem. The verbal connections between 37:3–10 and 21:1–10 underscore this idea. In 21:5–7 Jeremiah declared to Zedekiah's delegation that Yahweh himself would fight against the city and that the remnant (שׁאר) who survived Yahweh's attacks would be handed over to Nebuchadrezzar who would "strike them down (נכה) with the edge of the sword." By contrast, in ch. 37 the prophet announces that even if those in Jerusalem "strike down" (נכה) the Babylonian army, there will remain a "remnant" (שׁאר), albeit, a wounded one, that will destroy the city.[46]

There are similar verbal connections between 37:3–10 and the narrative in ch. 34, a story which is linked to the present episode because it transpired during the temporary lifting of the siege. In 34:21–22 Jeremiah had stated that Yahweh would cause the Babylonian army, which had temporarily withdrawn from Jerusalem, to return (שׁוב) to fight against, capture, and burn the city.[47] This was to be punishment for Zedekiah's and the people's freeing their Hebrew slaves, but then recanting and taking them back. The people's treatment of the slaves parallels God's treatment of the people: momentary freedom followed by re-imprisonment. The implication in ch. 34 is that if the people had allowed the slaves to remain free, they themselves would have retained freedom. There the people "listened" (שׁמע) to Yahweh and entered into a covenant to release the slaves (v. 10); but they "turned" (שׁוב) and secured the slaves (v. 11). Just as the Babylonian's "hearing" (שׁמע) about the Egyptian advance provided momentary freedom for Jerusalem (37:5), so too the people's "listening" (שׁמע) to the words of Yahweh provided temporary respite for the slaves. Because the people "turned away" (שׁוב) from the covenant and caused the slaves to return (שׁוב), Yahweh is causing the Babylonians to return (שׁוב) and terminate the people's freedom too. Thus, the

---

45. Cf. A. R. Pete Diamond, "Portraying Prophecy: Of Doublets, Variants and Analogies in the Narrative Representation of Jeremiah's Oracles—Reconstructing the Hermeneutics of Prophecy," *JSOT* 57 (1993): 99–119 (112); John Bright, *Jeremiah: A New Translation with Introduction and Commentary* (AB 21; New York: Doubleday, 1965), 215; Helga Weippert, *Die Prosareden des Jeremiabuches* (BZAW 132; Berlin: de Gruyter, 1973), 71; Thompson, *Jeremiah*, 467; McKane, *A Critical and Exegetical Commentary on Jeremiah I–XXV*, 496.

46. All the other uses of "remnant" in chs. 37–44 refer to the Jerusalem community (38:4, 22; 39:9, 10; 40:6; 41:10; 42:2), so its reference here to the Babylonian army enhances the word-play.

47. Most scholars would argue that historically the events in ch. 34 occur during the same Babylonian withdrawal referred to in ch. 37. Regardless of the historical scenario, the suggestion here is that the report of the Babylonian withdrawal in v. 5 and Jeremiah's proclamation of their return in v. 7 recalls ch. 34.

recollection of ch. 34 prompted by v. 5 anticipates the prophet's word of judgment.

Concerning the intertextual links with the DH, this first episode clearly points to the stories in 2 Kgs 19 in which Hezekiah sends a delegation to Isaiah asking him to pray for the remnant.[48] In both episodes, Jerusalem was threatened by a foreign power and Egypt represented possible assistance. Furthermore, in both instances, the prophet offers an oracle using the messenger formula ("thus says Yahweh") in response to the king's request for "prayer"—a unique scenario in biblical narratives.[49] The text's invitation to compare these two episodes contributes to the portrayal of prophet and king. Specifically, there are several verbal echoes between the two stories that emphasize Jeremiah's reversal of Isaiah's message. Hezekiah implores Isaiah to pray for the "remnant" (19:4), while Jeremiah declares that even a "remnant" of the Babylonian army would destroy Jerusalem (37:10). Isaiah asserts that the king of Assyria will "hear a report and return" (שׁמע שׁמועה ושׁב) to his own land where he will be killed (19:7), while Jeremiah declares that although the Babylonians had "heard a report" (. . . שׁמעו שׁמעם, 37:5) and withdrawn, they would "return" (שׁב, 37:8) to Jerusalem and destroy the people in their own land. For Isaiah, the Assyrian withdrawal was divine intervention that brought salvation. For Jeremiah, the Babylonian withdrawal was only temporary and the divine plan was to return the Babylonians to Jerusalem in order to bring destruction. If the angel of Yahweh slew the Assyrians while they were "in the camp" (2 Kgs 19:35), Jeremiah claims that injured Babylonians would each rise "in his tent" and burn the city.

In addition, the words "this city" referring to Jerusalem are used in 37:8 and 10; they also appear five times in the stories of Hezekiah and Isaiah in 2 Kings (18:30; 19:32, 33, 34; 20:6) and in the parallel text in Isaiah (36:15; 37:33, 34, 35; 38:6). Only one other place, in fact, in the DH does this phrase occur in reference to Jerusalem (2 Kgs 23:27) and it does not occur at all in the book of Isaiah outside these stories.[50] The uniqueness of this expression highlights that Isaiah's message for "this city" was salvation, while Jeremiah's was destruction.

The Rabshakeh enjoins the people not to allow Hezekiah to deceive (נשׁא) them by compelling them to rely on Yahweh (2 Kgs 18:29); and in a second speech, the Rabshakeh encourages Hezekiah not to let Yahweh deceive (נשׁא) him (Hezekiah) by promising to deliver the city (19:10). Similarly, Jeremiah tells Zedekiah not to deceive (נשׁא) himself by thinking that the city would be saved.[51] Jeremiah

---

48. Holladay (*Jeremiah 2*, 287) and Robert Carroll ("The Book of J," 227) comment that the Hezekiah–Isaiah stories stand in the background to the Zedekiah–Jeremiah narratives, but they make no specific links.

49. The only other similar situation is in Jer 42:1–8 where Jeremiah responds with an oracle to the remnant's request for prayer. The community, however, specifically requested advice about what to do after Gedaliah's death (v. 3), so it was appropriate for Jeremiah, after prayer to Yahweh, to deliver an oracle using the messenger formula.

50. The phrase appears several other times in DH, but not in reference to Jerusalem (Josh 6:26; Judg 19:11; 1 Sam 9:6; 2 Kgs 2:19).

51. The relative infrequency of נשׁא strengthens the connection. Six of the total thirteen occurrences of נשׁא are in these two stories (cf. 2 Chr 32:15; Isa 36:14; 37:10).

proclaims that the Egyptians will be of no help to Jerusalem, while the Rabshakeh compares Egypt to a broken reed that pierces all who rely on them (2 Kgs 18:21). The Rabshakeh mocks the weakness of Hezekiah and Jerusalem by indicating he will supply them horses if they have enough men to ride them (2 Kgs 18:23–24); likewise, Jeremiah employs a tone of mockery when he proclaims that even a weak and wounded remnant of the Babylonian army would destroy Jerusalem. Jeremiah, in short, delivers the same message as the enemy: do not be deceived, for there is no escape from inevitable destruction.[52]

These correspondences between Jer 37:3–10 and the Hezekiah–Isaiah narrative cast Jeremiah in the role of the Rabshakeh as one who spoke a message of defeat against Jerusalem. As Diamond observes, this comparison with the Rabshakeh "risks undermining Jeremiah's authority, for on the surface it enables the reader to view Jeremiah as an agent of the enemy king and a blasphemer."[53] Diamond asserts, however, that "the association of Zedekiah with the impiety of Jehoiakim (who has already been constituted as anti-Josiah by analogy with 2 Kgs 22–23) firmly underlines the contrast with the circumstances of Hezekiah's reign." Thus, given Jehoiakim's impiety, Diamond argues that "Jeremiah's role in Zedekiah's day is justified and the prophet is defended from the charge of dereliction of prophetic duty—in failing to intercede as Isaiah had done for the community's protection." For Diamond, although the narrator "risks undermining Jeremiah's authority," ultimately, the narrator eschews this by demonstrating that the situation was different in Jeremiah's day, thus he is not to be understood as an anti-Isaiah or Rabshakeh figure.

Diamond's argument seems contrived—especially since Zedekiah is contrasted, not likened, to Jehoiakim in several crucial ways. However, to illustrate that the "risk of undermining" Jeremiah's authority remains, one needs simply to note the work of Christof Hardmeier, who has also assayed closely these two prophet–king stories, has drawn the opposite conclusion.[54] Hardmeier argues that the Hezekiah–Isaiah narratives were composed as polemic against Jeremiah, so he proposes that the connection between the Rabshakeh and Jeremiah was meant to undermine Jeremiah's role. While Hardmeier takes a very different methodological approach, his point is that the intertextual connections (although he does not refer to them as such) do, in fact, depict Jeremiah in a negative light by paralleling him to the Rabshakeh. While the method employed in the present study is certainly closer to Diamond's, the interpretation is more akin to Hardmeier's. The intertextual ties do "risk undermining Jeremiah's authority." Because the risk persists, Jeremiah's role, and thus his characterization more generally, remain ambiguous.

---

52. If here the prophet delivers the enemy's message, then after the fall of the city it will be the enemy (the Babylonians) who deliver the prophet's message (40:2–3).

53. Diamond, "Portraying Prophecy," 114.

54. Christof Hardmeier, *Prophetie im Streit vor dem Untergang Judas: Erzählkommunikative Studien zur Entstehungssituation der Jesaja- und Jeremiaerzählungen in II Reg 18–20 und Jer 37–40* (BZAW 187; Berlin: de Gruyter, 1990), 307–20.

Not only does the narrative "enable the reader to view Jeremiah as an agent of the enemy king and a blasphemer," as Diamond says, but also—and more importantly—it enables Zedekiah to view Jeremiah as such. Even if the reader resists a negative perception of Jeremiah, the comparisons with the Rabshakeh make it easier to understand how Zedekiah could conclude the prophet to be a traitor. Of course, if Yahweh's intentions during the Babylonian crisis are not what they were during the Assyrian crisis, then what was once blasphemous (surrendering) is now fidelity. Jeremiah's analogous role to the Rabshakeh is a challenge both to Zedekiah and the reader to determine just how far the analogy is to be extended.

Finally, like Jeremiah, Zedekiah's portrayal in relation to the Hezekiah–Isaiah stories is complex. On the one hand, Zedekiah's consulting Jeremiah reveals that he recognized Jeremiah to be a true prophet of Yahweh—just as Hezekiah consulted Isaiah.[55] On the other hand, unlike Hezekiah, Zedekiah does not pray directly to Yahweh. Hezekiah appears more earnest in his seeking the deity than does Zedekiah. However, if Yahweh has refused to hear Zedekiah's prayer, what options did the king have?

In addition to the Hezekiah–Isaiah narratives, this first episode also contains other allusions to texts in the DH. The prophet declares that the Babylonians will return (שׁוב), fight against (נלחם), capture (לבד), and burn (שׂרף) Jerusalem with fire (אשׁ) (v. 8). These series of verbs echo Judg 1:8, the only other text (other than Jer 34:22) in the Hebrew Bible where "fight" (נלחם), "capture" (לבד), and burn with "fire" (אשׁ) occur together. This verse reports the initial capture of Jerusalem by the tribe of Judah. Jeremiah is utilizing the same words and images to proclaim, ironically, the end of Israelite control of Jerusalem. The city would be defeated by the Babylonians in the same manner that the Israelites first took it. These verbal echoes might seem to form only a tenuous link were it not for the end of Jeremiah's second oracle, which also plays ironically on images of the initial conquest of Jerusalem.[56] In 2 Sam 5:6–8, David, immediately after being anointed king of all Israel, marches against Jerusalem which is held by the Jebusites who say to David: "You will not come in here, even the blind and the lame will turn you back" (2 Sam 5:6). David, of course, is able to penetrate the stronghold and capture the city (2 Sam 5:7–10). Jeremiah reverses these images. Now it is the Babylonian troops who are outside the city trying to force their way in, and if the Jebusites mistakenly thought that even their blind and lame men could fend off the Israelites, now the Israelites will be unable to fend off even the wounded Babylonian soldiers. The echoes of traditions about Jerusalem's capture contrast Zedekiah's failure with David's success.[57]

---

55. One may also draw a line between Josiah consulting Huldah to interpret the law book and Zedekiah consulting Jeremiah to interpret the events of the day.

56. Cf. John Bracke (*Jeremiah 26–52 and Lamentations* [Louisville, Ky.: Westminster John Knox, 2000], 64), but he does not point out the link of v. 7 to Judg 1.

57. Perhaps also v. 10's hint of the initial occupation of Jerusalem creates an ironic reversal in view of Zedekiah's being blinded and taken into captivity (39:7). The lame (i.e. the wounded) Babylonians could capture Jerusalem and lead out its king blind. If the blind and lame could not keep David out, Zedekiah is led out blinded by the lame enemy.

Second Episode: 37:11–16

(11) When the army of the Chaldeans withdrew from Jerusalem because of the army of Pharaoh, (12) Jeremiah went out from Jerusalem to go to the land of Benjamin, slipping out of the city among a crowd of other people.[58] (13) But when he was at the Benjamin gate, an officer of the guard there named Irijah son of Shelemiah son of Hananiah arrested the prophet Jeremiah saying, "You are deserting to the Chaldeans." (14) Jeremiah said, "That is false. I am not deserting to the Chaldeans." But he would not listen to him. And Irijah arrested Jeremiah and brought him to the officials. (15) The officials were enraged at Jeremiah and they struck him and they put him in jail, in the house of Jonathan the scribe, which they made into a prison. (16) So Jeremiah came to the cistern-house, in the cells, and he remained there many days.

The second episode also consists of two scenes. In the first, Jeremiah is detained and questioned by Irijah (vv. 11–14a), and in the second the officials beat the prophet and imprison him (vv. 14b–16). The episode has minimal direct discourse unlike all the other episodes, but the speech between Jeremiah and Irijah is highlighted by its place at the center of the episode. Its importance is further accentuated by the shift from narrative time in vv. 11–12 to narration time in vv. 13–14 (the dialogue) and then back to narrative time in vv. 15–16.[59] That is, the narrator slows the pace of the story, focusing the reader's attention on the dialogue. Further, these first two episodes are the only two that are linked temporally. Verse 11 sets the context during the time of the Babylonian withdrawal (cf. v. 5) and v. 12 explains that Jeremiah "went out" "among the people" which illustrates the freedom he was said to possess (v. 4).

Point of View
The presentation of diverging points of view is central to this episode. Each of the three different characters—Jeremiah, Irijah, and the officials—as well as the

---

58. This follows McKane's rendering of the phrase, לחלק משם בתוך העם (*Jeremiah XXVI–LII*, 922, 926–28). The difficulty is caused not only by לחלק, but also by משם. Most understand לחלק as meaning "to divide" or to "receive a portion" and render "to take his portion of property from among the people," which they then connect with Jeremiah's purchase of family land in Benjamin in ch. 32. In ch. 32, however, Jeremiah purchased the land while he was a prisoner in Jerusalem, so it is not immediately clear how it relates to the present episode in which the prophet attempts to journey to Benjamin. The Greek renders τοῦ ἀγοράσαι ἐκεῖθεν ἐν μέσῳ τοῦ λαοῦ ("to buy there in the midst of the people"). McKane, however, points out that the root with which Kimchi associates חלק is not "divide," but "be smooth or slippery" (Pss 5:10; 36:3; Prov 2:16; 7:5; 28:3). He also notes that this understanding is in agreement with a Greek miniscule which translates חלק as ἀποδρᾶσαι ("to escape"). McKane also cites Gesenius on this verse who argues that "slipping away" or "escaping" is an easy semantic advance from "slipperiness." Accordingly Gesenius translates, "so that he might be lost in the middle of the crowd of people." Finally, John Calvin (who McKane does not mention) reads חלק as "separate" (i.e. divide), but he understands the sense to be that Jeremiah wanted to "separate himself"—because he was tired of his prophetic duties (*Commentaries on the Book* 4:373–74). Even the more common understanding of לחלק can take on a metaphorical sense indicating that Jeremiah is trying to "escape" or "slip out." In short, McKane makes a good case for following a tradition of interpretation that makes the move from "smoothness" to "slipperiness," which yields the sense of חלק as "slip away."

59. For narrative time and narration time, see Bar-Efrat, *Narrative Art in the Bible*, 143–44.

narrator offer their own perspectives on the events. However, none of the viewpoints are fully and clearly divulged. The primary question here is: What is Jeremiah doing when he attempts to leave the city and journey to the land of Benjamin? The narrator's viewpoint is presented first in v. 12: "And Jeremiah went out (יצא) from Jerusalem to go to the land of Benjamin . . . לחלק משם בתוך העם." Given that Jeremiah has just uttered an oracle of destruction against Jerusalem and that he advised surrendering (יצא) to the Babylonians (21:9) and will do so again later (38:2, 17), the image of Jeremiah "יצא-ing" from Jerusalem must, initially at least, carry connotations of surrendering. These connotations may remain depending on how one interprets the narrator's explanation regarding Jeremiah's activity. The narrator's view is unclear because of the difficult phrase לחלק משם בתוך העם. As it is rendered here, Jeremiah is trying to "slip away" in a crowd of people (בתוך העם) who are exiting Jerusalem.[60] Thus, one might very well perceive Jeremiah's action as deserting to the enemy, even though he denies such an allegation. As will be seen in the sixth episode, Jeremiah is not averse to lying to protect himself. At any rate, the point here is that the narrator makes an (intentionally?) ambiguous statement about Jeremiah's actions and the reader must decide what the prophet's intentions are.

The story then switches to Irijah's point of view. Although he is a minor figure, by identifying Irijah by name and having him speak, the audience is offered another important perspective. It is reported that Irijah arrested (תפש) Jeremiah and accused him of deserting (נפל) to the Babylonians (v. 13). Given the circumstances, Irijah has good reason to suspect that Jeremiah is deserting (of course, he is not privy to the narrator's statement). In fact, Irijah's perspective may be the one most comprehensible in this episode. When he is detained by Irijah, Jeremiah, in turn, states his position: "That is false (שקר). I am not deserting to the Chaldeans." The prophet's reticence here is striking, for he does not disclose his intentions. The reader may be puzzled by such taciturnity, for a complete and rigorous defense would have included what his plans were—rather than simply gainsaying that he was deserting. Similarly, one may wonder why Jeremiah is silent—giving no explanation—when he is confronted by the officials.[61] Jeremiah does not expressly affirm or clarify the narrator's view regarding his reasons for leaving. Thus the reader, assuming the narrator is to be trusted, knows more than Irijah—Jeremiah is going to Benjamin לחלק משם בתוך העם—but less than Jeremiah himself, whose motives remain unexpressed.

After Jeremiah denies the allegation, the narrative reports, "and he did not listen to him." This is typically understood as Irijah did not listen to Jeremiah, but there is nothing grammatically that prevents one from reading that Jeremiah did not listen to Irijah.[62] Jeremiah tried to disregard Irijah's charge—not unlike in

---

60. See the discussion of textual issues in the notes on the translation above.

61. Alexander Rofé comments that Jeremiah's "behavior during that particular incident at the Benjamin gate is altogether pathetic; he is no more than a ne'erdo-well" (*The Prophetical Stories* [Jerusalem: Magnes, 1988], 108).

62. This reading has the advantage of maintaining the same subject: "Jeremiah said . . . and he did not listen."

the previous episode where Jeremiah appeared to dismiss Zedekiah's request for prayer. On this reading, it is again the prophet, ironically, who does not listen, rather than the king and the people. While this is not crucial for an overall interpretation of the episode, perhaps the ambiguity is designed to suggest that neither Jeremiah nor Irijah listened to the other—a mutual dismissing of each other's point of view.

The final point of view is that of the officials. They were "enraged" (קָצַף)[63] with Jeremiah, beat him, and imprisoned him. While their ideological perspective is apparently contrary to Jeremiah's, it is unclear why they are angry with him or why they treat him as they do. In fact, one may wonder why they would not have been content to let him leave the city so that he would not have a negative influence on morale (cf. 38:4). It is one thing to detain a political enemy, but it is quite another to be enraged—especially since this is the only instance of attributed emotion in these episodes—and to harm him physically. The officials' behavior here is more perplexing when contrasted with the officials' benevolent actions toward Jeremiah in 36:19 (though they are not necessarily the same officials). Thus, like Jeremiah's motives and intentions, theirs too remain opaque. Jeremiah, then, represents the narrative's interest point of view, but the story is told from the officials' perceptual point of view. The narrative stresses the emotions and actions of the officials, not Jeremiah. Consequently, the reader's degree of identification with the prophet is limited.[64]

The four different perspectives each vie for validity, which, in part, is what makes this episode so compelling for the reader. The ambiguity resulting from the multiple and incomplete perspectives draws readers into the story as they must develop their own view, their own ideological perspective which will enable them to evaluate the characters and events. The conclusion to this scene functions to make precisely this invitation to the reader. By ending with a specific and detailed account of where Jeremiah is imprisoned (vv. 15–16), which contrasts with the lack of clarity in the narrator's statements about why Jeremiah was going to Benjamin, the narrator focuses attention on the prophet's plight, perhaps increasing sympathy for him, thereby prompting readers to formulate their own opinions.

Contextual Analysis

Careful attention to the verbal nature of the text reveals its depth and complexity. Irijah's "not listening" to Jeremiah (if read this way) recalls the narrator's introductory statement that no one listened to the words of Yahweh spoken through

---

63. The intensity of their feeling toward Jeremiah is underscored when one observes that קָצַף is almost always used to describe Yahweh's "wrath." Cf. James Montgomery, *A Critical and Exegetical Commentary on the Books of Kings* (New York: Scribner, 1951), 364.

64. Cf. Berlin, *Poetics and Interpretation*, 49. Here she cites Susan S. Lanser, *The Narrative Act: Point of View in Prose Fiction* (Princeton: Princeton University Press, 1981), for a fuller discussion of this notion. Lanser writes: "Affinity with a character thus depends to some extent on the degree to which that character is 'subjectified'—made into a subject, given an active human consciousness" (206).

Jeremiah (37:2). In this episode, however, Jeremiah is not speaking a word of Yahweh; he is arguing his own personal case. There is no mention of Yahweh, no divine command to go to Benjamin, and no word of defense from Yahweh. Jeremiah is on his own. Therefore, although the phrase "he did not listen" points to the introduction, its setting and context do not allow it to provide support for the narrator's evaluation. Further, Irijah's "not listening" to Jeremiah adds irony in several ways, particularly as the text plays on the different meanings of שמע— "listen" vs. "give heed to/obey." On the one hand, if the people of Jerusalem were placed under siege because they "did not give heed to/obey" Jeremiah's words, here Jeremiah himself is placed in confinement because Irijah "did not listen" to his words. On the other hand, it appears that Irijah did, in fact, "listen to" Jeremiah's message advocating surrender, which is exactly why he accused the prophet of desertion and arrested him. Ironically, Jeremiah is persecuted and imprisoned expressly because Irijah and the officials have listened to him; but because they hold a conflicting perspective, they refuse to give heed to/obey his message.[65]

After being arrested, Jeremiah is the object of a series of verbs. This represents the beginning of Jeremiah's loss of freedom, his ability to act as an agent; instead, he is controlled by others. In a sense, the remainder of the story revolves around the officials' reducing Jeremiah's physical agency, his personal freedom, because they fear his ideological and political agency, a notion that is underscored by the verbal nature of the text. Jeremiah is "brought" to the officials, who were "enraged" at him and "beat" him and "put" him into confinement. This string of verbs recalls Jeremiah's oracles in vv. 6–10 which employed an onslaught of verbs to describe Jerusalem's fate.[66] If the Babylonians would not "go away" from Jerusalem (v. 9) but would instead destroy the city, then the officials will not let Jeremiah "go out" from the city and will wreak havoc on him personally. If Jeremiah says that the Babylonians will turn back and destroy, Irijah and the officials turn Jeremiah back and punish him. Specifically, the repetition of the verb נכה carries some ironic connotations. If the people successfully struck down (נכה) the Babylonians, the city nonetheless would not escape destruction (v. 10). Now the officials strike down (נכה) Jeremiah (v. 15), apparently attempting to silence his word; however, as the following narrative illustrates, Jeremiah's word cannot be muted. Striking down the Babylonians and Jeremiah will not lead to salvation for Jerusalem.

The four uses of בֵּית in vv. 15b–16—בֵּית הָאֵסוּר ("jail"), בֵּית יְהוֹנָתָן ("house of Jonathan"), בֵּית הַכֶּלֶא ("prison"), בֵּית הַבּוֹר ("cistern-house")—depict the irony of Jeremiah's situation and his limited freedom. The narrative here is playing on symbolic spaces—homes and prisons. The prophet had claimed that he was not deserting, implying that he would return home from Benjamin. The officials, however, ensure that he returns "home"—ironically to a prison that had formerly

---

65. There is nothing for Irijah to "obey" in this scene because the prophet, as in the last episode, gives no instructions, but rather only makes assertions.

66. Bar-Efrat points out how the rapid accumulation of verbs (or nouns) is used to express significance (*Narrative Art in the Bible*, 216–17).

been a house (of Jonathan). Just as the people of Jerusalem found their own homes turned into prisons during the siege, so Jeremiah finds himself confined in a prison that was once a home. Here the different meanings of the verb ישׁב develop this house/prison concept: one "dwells" in a house but "remains" in a prison. For Jeremiah and the people, it is one in the same: both "dwell" (ישׁב) in their "home" for many days, which is tantamount to "remaining" (ישׁב) in prison. Further, much as the people who resided in Jerusalem needed desperately to be freed from their home/prison (the city) to avoid death, so Jeremiah, as will be seen, needed to be released from his home/prison to escape death (37:20).

Finally, there is some important verbal repetition that links this episode with the previous one and which highlights the prophet's reduced freedom. The opening part of v. 16 reads, "Jeremiah came (בא) to the cistern-house (בית הבור)."[67] Although many commentators, following the Greek, render "Jeremiah was put," the text seems to be playing on v. 4 which says that Jeremiah "came and went (בא and יצא) among the people (בתוך העם)." In vv. 12–16 the prophet had attempted to יצא בתוך העם, but he was arrested and forced to come (בוא) to the "house of the pit." Not only is Jeremiah denied the freedom to go out (יצא), he is also impelled to come (בוא) to prison. The prophet could no longer יצא or בוא among the people.

Intertextuality
This episode is related to other texts in the book of Jeremiah through the mention of different names. Jeremiah is arrested by Irijah who is identified as the son of Shelemiah, who is the son of Hananiah. A clue to understanding the behavior of the characters in this episode can be found in Irijah's patronymic; providing such information for a sentry is unusual, and thus attention is called to it.[68] One is reminded that it was a certain prophet named Hananiah who earlier had opposed Jeremiah's message regarding the length of the exile (ch. 28). Jeremiah had condemned Hananiah for encouraging the people trust in a lie (שׁקר) and had uttered an oracle against him predicting his death (28:15–16), which was fulfilled (28:17). Here one must entertain the possibility—the text is not conclusive—that the Hananiah who was killed by Jeremiah's curse is the grandfather of Irijah who apprehends Jeremiah. The possibility that this is the same Hananiah is strengthened when one considers Shelemiah, Irijah's father. In v. 3, a certain Shelemiah was the father of Jehucal who, along with Zephaniah, comprised the delegation that Zedekiah sent to Jeremiah. This Jehucal is one of the officials who later suggests killing Jeremiah (38:1) and subsequently throws him into a pit (38:6). It is

---

67. Later (38:6) the officials throw Jeremiah into a בור ("pit").

68. Family names and relations are important in the book. For instance, scholars have long documented the consistent support of the prophet by the Shaphan family. See Andrew Dearman, "My Servants the Scribes: Composition and Context in Jeremiah 36," *JBL* 109 (1990): 403–21 (408–14); Jurgen Kugler, "The Prophetic Discourse and Political Praxis of Jeremiah: Observations on Jer 26 and 36," in *God of the Lowly: Socio-Historical Interpretations of the Bible* (ed. E. W. Schottroff and W. Stegemann; Maryknoll, N.Y.: Orbis Books, 1984), 47–56 (50–53); Robert Wilson, *Prophecy and Society in Ancient Israel* (Philadelphia: Fortress, 1980), 241–42.

possible, then, that Jehucal and Irijah were brothers, both sons of Shelemiah and grandsons of Hananiah. One then can understand why it is Irijah who arrests Jeremiah, for he (on this reading) is part of a family—his grandfather Hananiah, his father Shelemiah, and his brother Jehucal—who have consistently opposed Jeremiah and his message (unlike the Shaphan family who supported the prophet). In this vein, Irijah's actions could also be interpreted as an attempt to exact revenge on Jeremiah for the death of his grandfather.

Even if it is deemed that Hananiah the prophet was not Hananiah the grandfather of Irijah, the very mention of the name Hananiah in this context rehearses the previous story.[69] Jeremiah had declared Hananiah's message "false" (שֶׁקֶר); here he declares Irijah's accusation "false" (שֶׁקֶר). This can serve to highlight the difference between the conclusions to the two stories. In ch. 37 Jeremiah's charge of "falsehood" is powerless and he is arrested, beaten, and imprisoned, rather than vindicated by the death of his opponent as in ch. 28.

Furthermore, the echo of ch. 28 recalls the argument over the length of exile—Hananiah promising a quick return, while Jeremiah did not. The report in 37:12 that Jeremiah was going to Benjamin echoes ch. 32 in which Yahweh instructed Jeremiah to purchase some land in Benjamin as a sign of the future restoration of the people.[70] This motif fits the context in ch. 37 quite well since the Babylonians have withdrawn from the city and some were evidently interpreting this as an indication of imminent salvation (vv. 7–10). The association of 37:11–16 with ch. 32 joins, in turn, with ch. 28 in which Jeremiah argues with Hananiah about when restoration would occur. That is, Jeremiah's traveling to Benjamin in ch. 37 recalls Jeremiah's purchase of land in Benjamin as a sign of salvation (ch. 32), which links with the question of when salvation would arrive (ch. 28)—a relevant question by virtue of the mention of Hananiah and שֶׁקֶר. This intertextual constellation becomes more interesting in light of the mystery concerning Jeremiah's full intentions and motivations for going to Benjamin. In light of his silence and these intertexts, readers may wonder if Jeremiah himself thinks that the Babylonian withdrawal is the harbinger of salvation and the renewal of the land which was promised in ch. 32. Perhaps Jeremiah does not reveal his motive lest Irijah and the officials draw that conclusion? As on other occasions there are no definite answers, but it is expedient to raise the questions in order to illustrate the narrative's sophistication. In this instance, the intertextual relations within the book combine with issues of point of view to create a multivalent episode.

---

69. Commentators do not trace out these (possible) family dynamics. Seitz (*Theology in Conflict*, 256) does remark in a footnote, "Irijah is the grandson of Hananiah," and although Seitz does not make it clear, one might assume he means the Hananiah of ch. 28 since he takes the time to point it out. Else Holt also writes in a footnote: "The significance of family names in the book of Jeremiah should not be underestimated" ("The Potent Word of God," 164). She does not discuss any of the names, however.

70. If one understands Jeremiah to be going to Benjamin in order "to receive his portion of the inheritance"—a possible translation but not one endorsed here—then the connection to ch. 32 is even stronger.

Third Episode: 37:17–21

(17) King Zedekiah sent for and received him; and the king asked him in his house in secret and said, "Is there a word from Yahweh?" Jeremiah said, "There is." And he said, "Into the hand of the king of Babylon you will be given." (18) Then Jeremiah said to King Zedekiah, "What wrong have I done against you or your servants or this people that you all have put me in prison? (19) Where[71] are your prophets who prophesied to you all saying, 'The king of Babylon will not come against you all or against this land'? (20) Now please hear me, my lord the king. May my supplication be well received by you. Do not return me to the house of the secretary Jonathan or I will die there." (21) King Zedekiah commanded that they commit Jeremiah to the court of the guard[72] and that they give to him a ration of bread daily from the street of the bakers[73] until all the bread in the city was gone. So Jeremiah remained in the court of the guard.

In contrast to the first two episodes, there is not a specific temporal relationship between episodes two and three, although a general one is implied in that the third episode occurs after Jeremiah is imprisoned. At an unspecified time, Zedekiah summoned Jeremiah for an interview with him; this is the first direct contact between king and prophet in the text. This episode, like the first two, also consists of two scenes—the actual interview at the palace (vv. 17–20) and Jeremiah's being escorted to the court of the guard by unnamed figures (v. 21). Thus the two scenes are distinguished both by characters and setting. Similar to the first episode, the king is portrayed as receptive enough to consult Jeremiah. The reader, again, is invited to weigh the apparent tension between the narrator's evaluation and the king's actions, especially since the specific use of שׁמע (v. 20) directly recalls 37:2.[74]

Setting

The meeting between Zedekiah and Jeremiah takes place in the king's house, but the narrative also states that Zedekiah questioned Jeremiah "in secret" (בסתר).[75]

---

71. Reading ואיה ("where"), instead of ואיו ("where is he").

72. The precise location of the חצר המטרה ("court of the guard") is debated. Jer 32:2 places the חצר המטרה in the בית מלך יהודה ("house of the king of Judah"); accordingly, most scholars surmise that the court of the guard was in the palace. McKane, however, suggests that it was a "court associated with the prison in which Jeremiah had been held and so was located in the proximity of Jonathan's house" (*Jeremiah XXVI–LII*, 931). In support of this, the Greek renders εἰς οἰκίαν τῆς φυλακῆς. While it is clear that the court of the guard is an improvement in the prophet's conditions, it is equally evident that he remained confined. Not only does מטרה ("guard") come from the verb נטר, meaning to "keep watch" or "guard," but also elsewhere Jeremiah was "confined" (כלוא, 32:2) and "restrained" (עצור, 33:1; 39:15) in the court of the guard.

73. The significance and location of the "street of the bakers" is not known. The primary question is whether it suggests that Jeremiah received inferior (i.e. left over) bread. The Greek takes חוץ to mean "outside" (ἔξωθεν οὗ πέσσουσιν, "from outside where they bake"). Accordingly, some have proposed that Jeremiah was supplied with a lower quality bread that was sold outside the shops in the street.

74. Willis, "'They Did Not Listen to the Voice of the Lord,'" 76–78, discusses שׁמע as a "significant verbal theme" in the story. He also observes the significance of שׁב, יצא, and יד.

75. The text first refers to the prophet with two pronominal suffixes; his name is not mentioned until after Zedekiah has posed his question. Thus, the episode itself begins in secret, withholding the identity of the one whom Zedekiah summoned.

This is a significant detail, although often misunderstood, for understanding the story, particularly as it concerns Zedekiah's characterization. The word בסתר is puzzling, for the text provides no reason for the secrecy, and it plays no role in the episode as it does in 38:14–28. There is, however, a crucial distinction: the contents of the conversation between Zedekiah and Jeremiah are kept secret, not the interview itself. It was a closed-door meeting, not a meeting that no one else knew about. As the text indicates, the "asking" was "in secret," not the "sending for" and "receiving" which would be much harder to achieve clandestinely. Not recognizing this distinction, many commentators assume that the meeting itself was intended to be a secret, and they assert that the secrecy is motivated by Zedekiah's fear of the officials.[76] Nothing in the text, however, warrants this. Zedekiah's behavior demonstrates that he is not concerned about the officials, for he exercises his authority to call Jeremiah from imprisonment at Jonathan's house (where the officials had confined him) and to assign him to a new location at the "court of the guard." This change in Jeremiah's location confirms that the meeting itself was not intended to be a secret; moving the prophet from one place to another would inevitably have drawn the attention of the officials and others. In fact, the secrecy of the meeting may illustrate the king's power over the officials —the power of information management. This discussion is reserved for the sixth episode where there is more furtive contact between the king and the prophet.

Point of View
Zedekiah's perspective is presented first in this episode by way of direct discourse, as he asks Jeremiah, "Is there a word from Yahweh?" Zedekiah continues to remain open to the prophetic word. At the close of this scene, it appears that the king has even begun to accept it. If nothing else, he has in some sense listened to Jeremiah, as he does not require him to return to Jonathan's prison.

Jeremiah response to the king's inquiry is terse: "There is." The narrator then supplies another ויאמר before Jeremiah continues. As Bar-Efrat explains, when the phrase "he said" is repeated even though the same character continues speaking, the narrator is indicating a pause in order to allow for a reply or reaction.[77] Zedekiah does not respond. Perhaps the prophet paused to see if the king really wanted to know the contents of the word. When there was no response, Jeremiah continued, asserting that Zedekiah would be handed over to the king of Babylon. Here Jeremiah does not use the oracle formula, "thus says Yahweh" as he had done previously in response to Zedekiah's delegation (vv. 7, 9). It is thus unclear whether Jeremiah is presenting his own point of view or if he is speaking on behalf of Yahweh. The lack of the messenger formula here is notable because in the first episode the use of the formula seemed incongruent since Zedekiah had

76. Holladay, for instance, says, "Zedekiah consults Jrm directly, but secretly, doubtless out of fear of his courtiers (*Jeremiah 2*, 288). Thompson claims, "The consultation was in secret because of the king's fear of his officials" (*Jeremiah*, 634).

77. Bar-Efrat, *Narrative Art in the Bible*, 43. Cf. also Alter (*The World of Biblical Literature*, 127) who claims that in such a situation, the reader is "invited to wonder why there is no intervening response from the other party."

asked for prayer, but here it would seem apposite since the king had solicited a word from the deity. The uncertainty as to whose view Jeremiah is presenting is similar to the ambiguity in the first episode due also to Jeremiah's unusual speech patterns.

After Jeremiah speaks, there is again a pause in the narrative; one anticipates a reply from the king. But there is no response; his perspective is still not expressed. The king's silence is underscored by yet another ויאמר before Jeremiah continued. Thus, much as in the first episode, the king's point of view remains unknown. What, the reader wonders, did he think of the prophet's word? The prophet then launches into a monologue about his imprisonment and beseeches the king not to send him back to Jonathan's prison (vv. 18–20). Here the point of view is Jeremiah's, not Yahweh's. The prophet is tendering his own perspective on matters and addressing his own plight. The sustained concentration on Jeremiah's point of view is key because the conversation began with the king petitioning a word from Yahweh, but the majority of the scene centers on Jeremiah's analysis of his personal matters; the deity's view of the city and king appears to be inconsequential.

Included in Jeremiah's speech is a quotation of the optimistic prophets (v. 19). Instead of Jeremiah conveying Yahweh's view to the king, the prophet verbalizes the view of the prophets who proclaimed a different message. Again, viewpoints are refracted through the words of others. In this way, Jeremiah juxtaposes his word (you will be handed over to the king of Babylon) with that of other prophets (the king of Babylon will not come against you all and against this land) in order to strengthen his case.[78] Like Jeremiah's earlier quoted direct speech (v. 9), this quotation is unverifiable because the original speech is lacking. In other passages, the optimistic prophets argued more generally that "it will go well with you" and that "no calamity will come upon you" (23:17) and that the king and people "will not serve the king of Babylon" (27:9). Therefore, how accurately Jeremiah is articulating the viewpoints of his opponents is nebulous. Burke O. Long has observed that in prophetic conflict these quotations can be laced with irony, sarcasm, and exaggeration, which does not convey the nuances of the opponents' view; instead a flattened and one-dimensional view is often presented.[79] One wonders if this is the case here. Although Jeremiah's quotation appears credible, some ambiguity remains because there is no reported speech of the optimistic prophets that is equivalent to Jeremiah's quotation of them.

Jeremiah addresses Zedekiah as "my lord the king," uses the particle נא twice, and asks that the king hear his prayer (תחנתי). The way that a character engages another can often indicate point of view.[80] Here Jeremiah's speech reveals that he

---

78. Savran (*Telling and Retelling*, 21) maintains that quoted direct speech is designed "to have a calculated effect on the audience" and that "frequently the quotation is a prelude to a request or a demand by the speaker, often introduced by the adverbial particle *'attâ* to mark the passage from past to present." This is precisely the case in this scene—quoted speech followed by עתה and then a request.

79. Burke O. Long, "Social Dimensions of Prophetic Conflict," *Semeia* 21 (1981): 31–53.

80. Berlin explains that it is important to understand how different characters usually address one another (*Poetics and Interpretation*, 59).

perceives the king as a superior and accordingly adopts a respectful and subservient position in relation to him. Ebed-melech, a servant of the king, will later address the king in the same way (38:9). Remarkably, in only one other conversation between a prophet and king in the Hebrew Bible does a prophet address the king as "lord."[81] This occurs in Nathan's conversation with David regarding the king's successor (1 Kgs 1:24, 27). One recalls that there too the prophet clearly held a personal vested interest in who was named king (1:26; see Chapter 5). In view of this, it can tentatively be concluded that prophets do not typically address/view kings as superiors, but in cases when personal well-being is at stake, a prophet—perhaps because he is not acting in the role of a prophet—may adopt a subordinate position as part of his attempt to persuade the ruler to act on his behalf.

A similar shift in naming unfolds when Jeremiah refers to the officials as "your servants." Here Jeremiah adopts the perspective of the king. To the ordinary citizen, the men who imprisoned Jeremiah are powerful "officials" (v. 15). To the king, however, these men are "your servants"—subordinates who must obey his orders. In this way, Jeremiah reminds the king of his authority over his officials. In the following question (v. 19), however, Jeremiah assumes the view of the king for a different rhetorical effect. He refers to "your prophets" whose words have not been fulfilled. These are prophets whom Jeremiah considers false; but rather than identifying them as such, he elects to call them "your prophets." By naming them in this way Jeremiah employs differing points of view to suggest to Zedekiah that the "false prophets" are in fact his prophets, which is to take a more aggressive, riskier line of argumentation. This approach also differentiates "your prophets" from Jeremiah himself who thereby claims (implicitly) that he is not one of the king's prophets—which is somewhat ironic given that, of course, Jeremiah is the one whom Zedekiah has chosen to consult.

In Zedekiah's response in v. 21—narrated in indirect discourse—the king instructs unnamed people to commit (פָקַד)[82] Jeremiah to the court of the guard and to furnish the prophet with bread until the supply in the city was depleted. Here the king appears resigned to the fact that the bread in the city will run out; one consequently wonders if he has completely abandoned any hopes for salvation. The king, in fact, may be subtly articulating Jeremiah's point of view; he appears to have accepted the prophetic word.

The Dialogue
The nature of the dialogue in this scene can be elucidated by attention to its judicial context. In his study of legal procedures in the Hebrew Bible, Pietro Bovati observes that "it is fairly clear that between the crime (real or alleged) and the trial the *arrest* of the accused takes place (the verbs *lqh* and *tps*); this seems

---

81. Cf. Uspensky, *Poetics of Composition*, 25–26.

82. Irijah was identified as the פקדת בעל. If earlier he is the one who controls Jeremiah's movement, in this scene Zedekiah is the one who has the authority to appoint (פָקַד) the prophet to a given location.

to happen when the crime committed is such as (possibly) to deserve capital punishment."[83] He then cites Jer 26 and 27 as examples of this. He also notes that arrest and imprisonment were a "preventative measure in anticipation of a formal judgment."[84] Interpreted in this light, after his arrest by Irijah and the officials, Jeremiah is awaiting a formal trial in which he will be tried for treason for attempting to desert to the enemy. In this forensic context, Zedekiah's inquiry concerning the word of Yahweh is unexpected for both reader and prophet. Why is the king questioning a suspected traitor about a word from the deity? This suggests that the king does not see Jeremiah as a defector but rather as a prophet who can deliver a message from Yahweh. Perhaps Zedekiah is employing the forensic context to his benefit, hoping that Jeremiah will speak a positive word about the future of the king and city in order to prove that he is not guilty of treachery. Perhaps the king determined that Jeremiah's attempt to go to Benjamin indicated a shift in the prophet's views. Whatever the case, this would certainly be the time for the king to anticipate a hopeful message since the prophet's personal circumstances necessitated assistance from the king. In this light, the negativity of Jeremiah's message is underscored: he apprises Zedekiah that he will become a prisoner of the Babylonians despite the fact that at that moment he himself is a prisoner. Not only, then, has Zedekiah petitioned Jeremiah who has been charged with treachery, but he also, remarkably, ameliorates Jeremiah's conditions by removing him from Jonathan's prison even though the prophet seems to confirm the charge against himself, at least from a certain perspective, by yielding an unconditional word of defeat for Zedekiah.[85]

The judicial context also explains Jeremiah's directing the conversation to legal matters: he deemed his meeting with the king as an opportunity for an appeal. In one sense, Jeremiah is not speaking as a prophet, per se, in this scene, but rather as a defendant who is pleading his case. The king, however, addresses him as a prophet ("Is there a word from Yahweh?"). Not only does Jeremiah not answer that inquiry in prophetic form ("Thus says Yahweh"), but he also quickly abandons that role in favor of the role of a petitioner. Thus, there exists some tension between the role Jeremiah takes and the role the king wishes him to take. Notably, neither the narrator nor the king identifies Jeremiah as a prophet in this scene.

Certain aspects of Jeremiah's speech illustrate its forensic nature. Jeremiah first claims that he has not wronged (חטא) anyone—חטא functioning as a legal term[86]—and then his "protestation of innocence becomes an accusation."[87] According to Bovati, the declaration of blamelessness "should not be considered

83. Pietro Bovati, *Re-Establishing Justice: Legal Terms, Concepts and Procedures in the Hebrew Bible* (trans M. J. Smith; JSOTSup 105; Sheffield: JSOT Press, 1994), 226.

84. Bovati, *Re-Establishing Justice*, 227.

85. Jeremiah was held in prison "for many days" (v. 15). This could imply that the officials were not eager to bring Jeremiah to trial before the king because they were not confident of a conviction. Maybe the officials were suspicious of Zedekiah's sympathetic stance toward Jeremiah.

86. Bovati, *Re-Establishing Justice*, 66.

87. Bovati, *Re-Establishing Justice*, 114.

apart from the overall juridical controversy." Specifically, the ‫כי‬ clause (v. 18) both "carries forward the declaration of innocence, especially in the interrogative form" and it "introduces a criticism of whoever is doing the accusing, and lays the accuser under accusation."[88] Jeremiah asserts his innocence and simultaneously levels his own accusation against the king and officials. However, in the process of declaring that he has been wrongly accused, Jeremiah, ironically, wrongly accuses the king of imprisoning him, for it appears that the officials were solely responsible for his incarceration. In addition, Bovati comments that a protestation of innocence, which is transformed into an accusation, "is not a statement of absolute innocence but the appropriate response to a particular accusation, which often takes the form of a mortal threat."[89] In Jeremiah's case, he is likely protesting the charge that he was deserting the city, a specific allegation, but he indeed may have not been able to claim his "absolute innocence" regarding his views (cf. episode four, below).

Jeremiah's question about the "false" prophets (v. 19) appears to be a variation on the expected form of legal argumentation. As Bovati points out, "a declaration of innocence often brings about an explicit comparison between the different behaviour of the two disputants."[90] Jeremiah's question in v. 19 deviates from the norm by comparing his behavior to the other prophets, not to the king. That is, if in v. 18 Jeremiah puts the accuser under accusation, he then shifts his argumentation to contrast his behavior with the prophets, not the parties that he just accused (king, servants, and people). Zedekiah's position then changes from the accused (v. 18) to the judge (v. 19) who must decide between the two kinds of accused prophets. The implication of Jeremiah's argument is that it is the false prophets who deserve to be imprisoned.

Furthermore, the word ‫תחנתי‬ ("my supplication") also functions as a legal term, but it is somewhat ambiguous as it can be utilized both in the request for a pardon in which there is confession of guilt and in a complaint or appeal. Bovati explains that there is a fundamental distinction between these two: a supplication/pardon "is the act of asking something that goes beyond a right, or with an altogether precise awareness of not being able to claim anything," while a complaint or appeal "is the procedure of someone speaking in the name of the law . . . addressing a judge . . . with the authority to decide in favour of the one who is (in the) right."[91] Jeremiah, it seems, is employing the term in a complaint/appeal, but connotations of its other use may reverberate here, especially since from one perspective his crime is obvious (i.e. speaking against the city).

While it is helpful to consider the forensic nature of this encounter between king and prophet, there are other features of their dialogue worth exploring. The king initiates the conversation with a short, four-word question, "Is there a word

---

88. In addition to the present text, Bovati cites Gen 20:9; 31:36; 40:15; 1 Sam 20:1; 1 Kgs 18:9; Jer 2:5 (Bovati, *Re-Establishing Justice*, 114–15).

89. Bovati, *Re-Establishing Justice*, 114.

90. Bovati, *Re-Establishing Justice*, 115. He cites as examples Judg 11:27; 1 Sam 24:12; Job 33:9–11; 34:5–6, etc.

91. Bovati, *Re-Establishing Justice*, 312.

from Yahweh?" First, the form of the king's inquiry—using ‏הֲיֵשׁ‎—implies that he anticipated an affirmative answer (yes, there is a word), but this is different from expecting the message itself to be positive, as many commentators mistakenly assume.[92] Secondly, Jeremiah's response plays on the king's question, for at first the prophet only answers the literal question by saying, "there is" (‏יֵשׁ‎)—that is, there is a word from Yahweh. After a pause, he then responds to the obvious intended sense of the question (what is the word from Yahweh?): "Into the hand of the king of Babylon you will be given" (v. 17).

The brevity and form of Jeremiah's response connects it to his answer to Irijah in the previous episode. The text, it seems, summons the reader to see Jeremiah's two speeches in light of one another because both are five words in length, and the answer to Zedekiah grammatically and verbally reverses the prophet's rejoinder to Irijah. To Irijah, Jeremiah had said, "False, I am not deserting to the Babylonians." To the king, Jeremiah declared, "Yes, into the hand of the king of Babylon you will be given." In both instances, Jeremiah's reticence is noteworthy; he grants no explanation to Irijah regarding his intentions for leaving, nor does he offer instructions to the king or discuss why he will be delivered to the Babylonians.

If Zedekiah would be given into the hand of the Babylonians, Jeremiah does not want to be given back into the hands of the officials. Indeed, this is a remarkable scenario in which the prophet proclaims a word of judgment and still expects the king to treat him favorably. If Zedekiah regards Jeremiah as a prophet who can deliver the word of Yahweh, and not as a treacherous criminal, Jeremiah views the king as someone who can accept the word of Yahweh. That is, both figures appeal to something noble in each other's character. Zedekiah treats Jeremiah as a "true" prophet and Jeremiah trusts the king to help him, the messenger, in spite of the message of defeat that he carries.

Jeremiah's speech consists of two rhetorical questions—in contrast to Zedekiah's genuine question that opened the dialogue—and a concluding request.[93] The use of a rhetorical question in one's defense is, as Bovati shows, not uncommon. Further, prophets frequently employ rhetorical questions in their conversations with kings.[94] Thus, Jeremiah's questions to the king are expected on two levels. Rhetorically, a question functions differently from an assertion. By posing an inquiry, rather than explicitly stating his position, Jeremiah draws the king into the conversation and challenges him to contemplate the matter for himself.[95] In

92. Cf. Brueggemann, *Jeremiah*, 359; Bracke, *Jeremiah 30–52*, 66; Holladay, *Jeremiah 2*, 288.

93. Some commentators argue that vv. 18–19 are secondary insertions. See, for example, Seitz, *Theology in Conflict*, 259, who argues that these verses are the work of an exilic redactor who desires to portray the king, rather than the officials, as Jeremiah's primary opponent.

94. Cf. 1 Sam 15:13–14; 28:15–16; 2 Sam 7:5–7; 12:9; 1 Kgs 1:24, 27; 14:6; 20:13; 21:19; 2 Kgs 1:3; 3:13; 5:8; 6:22.

95. Cf. Conroy (*Absalom, Absalom!*, 139) concerning the rhetorical force of questions: "The person addressed is summoned to take up a position, either by giving a genuine answer or by having the expressive and emotional force of the speaker's words impressed more vividly upon him." Conroy further points out that "rhetorical questions . . . stimulate the reader's emotional response more than

the case of the first question, an answer is easily ascertained from the narrative: he had been imprisoned because he was suspected by Irijah and the officials of being a traitor and deserting to the Babylonians. Moreover, in the next episode (38:1–6), the officials pose another potential answer: his counsel to surrender was discouraging the people and soldiers who remained in the city. Thus, there were several possible and plausible responses to the prophet's question, answers that the prophet, king, and reader know.[96] In light of the judicial context, then, this is somewhat ironic, for a rhetorical question offered in one's defense should clearly have a negative implied answer: you have done nothing wrong. But that is not the case here.

Matters, however, are not that simple, for point of view must be factored in. The possible responses to Jeremiah only answer the question "why" he was imprisoned. Jeremiah had not asked "why," but "what wrong" he had done. Jeremiah may have been fully cognizant of "why" he was incarcerated, but from his standpoint he had not wronged anyone, but simply related the painful truth. Jeremiah's question is rhetorically effective because it compels the king to (re)consider the view that Jeremiah was being disloyal or had in any way acted against the king and people. That is, it invokes the king to assess the situation from Jeremiah's perspective. This invitation to the king works in conjunction with the second rhetorical question (v. 19), although it functions somewhat differently because the answer to it is not as clear—at least to the reader. Jeremiah may be suggesting that his word had been essentially correct (i.e. the Babylonian siege had resumed; cf. vv. 7–10), while the optimistic prophets had been proven wrong, and, therefore, had deceived the king—a motif that connects to v. 9 ("do not deceive yourselves") and to subsequent episodes. Thus he objected to being imprisoned while the "false" prophets were free. It is possible, however, that Jeremiah's question implies not that the "false prophets" were free, but that they were nowhere to be found—that they were the ones who had "slipped off" (v. 12) somewhere in an act of desertion or disloyalty.[97] Either way, Jeremiah's question is again aimed at engaging the king.

Although he is speaking only to the king, the prophet addresses both questions to the king, his servants, and the people, asking why "you"—in the plural—have put me in prison.[98] The narrative does not indicate that the king had any part in imprisoning Jeremiah; the king, in fact, had already removed Jeremiah out of

mere affirmations would do." See also Walter Brueggemann, "Jeremiah's Use of Rhetorical Questions," *JBL* 92 (1973): 358–74.

96. Similarly, Carroll remarks, "The question may be naïve in the light of Jeremiah's constant preaching of sedition" (*Jeremiah: A Commentary*, 677). Thus, Carroll interprets this episode independently of its present context.

97. In this case, Jeremiah would not be contrasting their freedom with his incarceration, but his availability and fidelity to the king with the absence and infidelity of the "false prophets" (cf. 38:22). This would make for some irony since Jeremiah had been imprisoned for suspected treason.

98. The phrase "that you (pl.) have put me in prison" connects with v. 4, "they (pl.) had not put him in prison." The third-person plural "they" in v. 4, typically translated as a passive ("he had not been put in prison"), becomes interesting in light of the issue raised here: who exactly were the ones who put Jeremiah in prison?

prison to have an appointment with him. Nonetheless, it appears that Jeremiah held the king ultimately responsible for his imprisonment. By implicating the king, he also acknowledges that the king has the authority to remove him from Jonathan's prison. In this way, Jeremiah simultaneously indicts and empowers Zedekiah.[99]

To this point Jeremiah's argument is leading toward the claim that he should not be imprisoned or confined in any way. His two rhetorical questions functioned as two rationales to support this thesis. He, first, had done no wrong (v. 18), and, secondly, he was a true prophet who had not abandoned the king and/or whose words had been fulfilled (v. 19); therefore he should not be incarcerated. Jeremiah, however, consistent with his indirect approach, does not conclude with a forceful request for the king to grant him full freedom. Rather, his final appeal is a cautious withdrawal that takes his argument in a different direction. Jeremiah makes this shift by revealing that his life is threatened in Jonathan's prison ("or I will die there"). Now the prophet is asking to be saved from death, not to be released from prison. Neither the narrator nor Jeremiah has indicated that death was imminent in Jonathan's prison, so here Jeremiah uncovers important new information for the king and reader.

This rhetorical strategy is circumspect for two reasons. First, Jeremiah does not indicate what specific action he would like the king to take—he only asks not to be sent back to Jonathan's prison. Thus, he offers the king several options, and thereby avoids an "all or nothing" scenario. This subtly leaves the power in Zedekiah's hands. Secondly, by setting up his argument as if he is going to ask for a lot (full freedom), but then ultimately only asking for a little (not to be sent back to Jonathan's prison), Jeremiah increases his chances of receiving at least minimal relief. By keeping various options open, the prophet may recognize that both he and the king have limited choices, so it was best for as many of them as possible to remain available. It may also reflect the notion that the king did not have a completely free hand; the officials were not entirely "his servants." In short, Jeremiah's speech is open-ended. This serves to engage the king (and the reader) in conversation with the prophet.

The Plot: The Second Scene
The prophet's rhetoric in which he assumed the position of a subordinate and submitted no forceful requests seems to work, for the king asserts his authority—he is now acting independently of the officials as they previously acted without appeal to him—and orders that Jeremiah be moved to the court of the guard. One may wonder, however, to what extent Zedekiah has complied with Jeremiah's request. Has Zedekiah "listened" to Jeremiah? In one sense, the king did accede to Jeremiah because he did not return him to Jonathan's prison. In another sense, Zedekiah did not grant his request of complete freedom for which he had argued

99. On another level, Jeremiah's use of the plural may reduce the confrontational nature of his discussion with Zedekiah because it indicates that the king was not the only one responsible; the use of the plural also heightens the troubles that Zedekiah could expect to face if he sided with Jeremiah (i.e. there were others who opposed the prophet).

(vv. 18–19) prior to the climax of the speech. Thus, it might be concluded that Zedekiah's decision appeased the literal meaning of Jeremiah's request, but not the spirit or overall sense of it. Zedekiah could have sent Jeremiah anywhere except back to Jonathan's house and he would have technically been honoring Jeremiah's petition. This reminds one of the beginning of the conversation when Jeremiah responded, initially at least, only to the literal sense of the king's question ("Is there a word from Yahweh?"—Yes). In short, since the prophet only asked that the king refrain from an action, Zedekiah's response, contrary to most interpreters, is not an unambiguous assent to Jeremiah's supplication. The precise nature, therefore, of Zedekiah's relationship with the prophet and his stance regarding the prophet's ideological perspective also remain uncertain.

Contextual Analysis

The narrative plays on the word בית and the notion of freedom. The previous episode concluded with the word בית used four times to described the prophet's confinement (vv. 15–16); v. 17 reports that the king called Jeremiah to "his house" (ביתה). Both houses are in reality prisons. Jeremiah is incarcerated in Jonathan's house and the king is trapped in his own house because of the siege. To be in a house is to be in prison. Both the king and prophet are depicted as prisoners who are seeking a word from each other in order to acquire freedom from their respective prison-houses.[100] Ironically, Jeremiah declares that Zedekiah would be taken captive by the Babylonians and Zedekiah commands that Jeremiah be held at the court of the guard. By the word of each other, both king and prophet are to be freed from their houses, but only to be moved to another prison. Further connecting the plights of Jeremiah and Zedekiah is the fact that both have been imprisoned for the same reason: they have been disloyal, Zedekiah to the Babylonians and Jeremiah to the city (depending, of course, on one's point of view). Thus, Nebuchadrezzar is to Zedekiah as Zedekiah is to Jeremiah. The fates of Zedekiah and Jeremiah are intertwined and infused with elements of tragic irony.

Jeremiah was imprisoned because Irijah had "not listened" (שׁמע) to his defense (v. 14), so here Jeremiah explicitly requests that the king "listen" (שׁמע) to his case.[101] This again recalls the narrator's evaluation of Zedekiah (37:2)—an evaluation which seems somewhat at odds with the king's behavior in this scene. The connection between this episode and the introductory statement in v. 2 is further established by Jeremiah having alluded to v. 2 when he accused the same triad (king, servants, and people) of wrongfully imprisoning him (v. 18).[102]

---

100. The use of נתן also connects Jeremiah's and Zedekiah's imprisoned condition, for the officials had "put" (נתן) Jeremiah into prison, and now Jeremiah declares that Zedekiah will be "put" (passive of נתן) into the hand of the Babylonians.

101. Cf. Samuel Meier, *Speaking of Speaking: Marking Direct Discourse in the Hebrew Bible* (Leiden: Brill, 1992), 113: "the summons to hear appears in mid-discourse in order to focus attention on a key issue or specific advice. . . . The imperative 'listen!' draws attention to the speech already in progress, underscoring the particular course of action the listener is to heed."

102. In v. 2 it is "the people of the land"; in v. 18 it is "this people."

According to Jeremiah's speech, however, this triad was not the one who refused to listen to the words of Yahweh spoken through him, but rather was the one who acted against him by putting him in prison. Similarly, in v. 20 when Jeremiah implores the king to "listen to" him, he desires personal assistance, not obedience to the words of Yahweh. In this episode the use of שׁמע has little to do with obeying the words of Yahweh spoken by Jeremiah; instead it involves treating the prophet well and securing his personal safety. As Jeremiah himself says to Zedekiah, "listen to *my plea*." That it is Jeremiah's message and not the deity's is underscored by the fact that it reverses the standard prophetic message. Traditionally prophets called for the king to "listen" and to "repent/turn" (שׁוב). Here Jeremiah solicits the king to "listen" and "not return" (שׁוב) Jeremiah to prison. In brief, the various contexts in which שׁמע occurs serve to question the narrator's summary thesis concerning Zedekiah's character; the repetition of שׁמע also complicates the manner in which Jeremiah embodies his various roles and the king's response to those roles.

Intertextuality
The implicit reasoning behind Jeremiah's rhetorical question in v. 19 regarding the "false" prophets revisits the narratives of prophetic conflict in chs. 27–29. There, in his confrontation with Hananiah, Jeremiah had decreed: "As for the prophet who prophesies peace, when the word of that prophet comes to pass, then it will be known that Yahweh has truly sent that prophet" (28:9). Here, Jeremiah evokes the Deuteronomistic distinction between true and false prophets (Deut 18:20–22). However, as many have observed, this is not a particularly useful criterion for the one seeking to distinguish among prophets. Jeremiah's rhetorical question in v. 19 calls attention to the precariousness of Zedekiah's position. He could not conceivably know whether or not the optimistic prophets were from Yahweh until it was too late. Jeremiah's argument, of course, is that history is his ally, proving him correct both in his word of destruction against Hananiah and in his warning of Babylonian aggression. It is ironic that in the context of pleading with the king to spare his life, Jeremiah echoes a story in which his word had culminated in the death of an optimistic opponent. In this vein, Jeremiah's question about the whereabouts of the optimistic prophets is cruelly ironic (v. 19).

Jeremiah's suffering in Jonathan's prison recalls promises of divine protection in Jer 1—a chapter which, as others have shown, reverberates throughout the book. One of the basic assumptions in Jeremiah's argument is that a true prophet of Yahweh ought not to be imprisoned. However, because prophets of Yahweh often proclaimed judgment (28:8) and because they could expect to be mistreated by others as Yahweh had warned (1:19), Jeremiah could have pointed to his imprisonment as evidence of his authenticity, rather than as an injustice. Uriah, for instance, had articulated the same message as Jeremiah and he was killed by King Jehoiakim and the officials (26:20–23). Yahweh, however, had promised that he would deliver Jeremiah from his opponents (1:19). While Jeremiah's ill treatment and subsequent imprisonment by the officials represent the foretold opposition, the promised divine protection is conspicuously absent and the prophet must seek help from Zedekiah. Indeed, Jeremiah appeals to Zedekiah, his "lord" (אדני), rather than the Lord (יהוה), to save him. Perhaps Jeremiah was basing his hope for assistance on the fact that he had already once been freed in a judicial context, despite delivering a critical message (Jer 26).

This theme, in turn, links with other contexts beyond the book of Jeremiah in which prophets are threatened with or experience physical abuse and are in need of rescue.[103] These connections further reinforce the notion that it is King Zedekiah, rather than Yahweh, who protects the prophet. There are three such instances in the DH in which prophets are explicitly threatened with death.[104] In each case in the DH it is the royal power that threatens the prophet; by contrast Zedekiah rescues Jeremiah. First, 1 Kgs 18:4 reports that Jezebel was eliminating prophets of Yahweh; secondly, in 1 Kgs 19 Jezebel promises to kill Elijah in retaliation for his slaughtering the prophets of Baal. In the latter story, Elijah flees and is fed by an angel of Yahweh (1 Kgs 19:5–8). In the present episode, not only does the royal power not threaten the prophet, but he, not Yahweh, is the one who rescues and feeds Jeremiah. While this reflects well on Zedekiah, it also highlights the deity's absence.

The third text is 2 Kgs 6:31 where the king of Israel, employing almost the exact phrasing as Jezebel, threatens to kill Elisha because of the famine that is plaguing the city. When the king confronts the prophet, Elisha promises that the siege and famine will terminate the very next day, which it does. Again it is the king who threatens to kill the prophet, which contrasts with Zedekiah's intervening in Jeremiah's plight. Further, unlike Zedekiah's reaction to a message of defeat, the unnamed king of Israel appears to be placated only by a salvation oracle from Elisha. The fact that Elisha's oracle of salvation emerges at a time when the city is under siege makes it analogous to the Jeremianic narratives, as well as to the Isaiah–Hezekiah stories. Isaiah promised that the Assyrians would "hear" a rumor and return to their land (2 Kgs 19:7); in Elisha's case Yahweh caused the Arameans to "hear" the sound of a massive army so that they fled in terror, fulfilling Elisha's word (2 Kgs 7:6).[105] For Jeremiah, however, although the Babylonians have "heard" a report of the Egyptian advance, they will return and destroy the city. In fact, during the Babylonian siege, it is Jeremiah himself who pursues personal salvation rather than extending a promise of deliverance to the king, a notion that is underscored by comparison to these other prophet–king narratives.[106]

---

103. See Robert Culley, *Themes and Variations* (Atlanta: Scholars Press, 1992), 63–67, for the "rescue sequence" in biblical narrative. He does not mention any of the texts discussed here.

104. In addition to the three discussed here, physical danger may be implied in 1 Kgs 17 (after Elijah announces a famine to Ahab) and 2 Kgs 1 (after Elijah predicted death for Ahaziah). In 2 Kgs 6:8–23 the king of Aram attempts to seize Elisha for miraculously learning of his battle plans.

105. The Aramean flight is discovered by four lepers who decided to desert to the enemy since they had nothing to lose. If they remained, they were sure to die because of the famine. One imagines that Jeremiah would advise Zedekiah to employ the same logic. In the case of the lepers, in fact, surrendering led to the salvation of the whole city.

106. Jeremiah's plea to be saved from death is unique among prophetic narratives, although there are other situations in which prophets voice concern for themselves.

The general structure and context of this episode is analogous to the prophet–king encounter in 1 Kgs 22. There Ahab elicits counsel from Micaiah regarding a military campaign against Aram. First, in both stories, the king summons the prophet seeking a word from Yahweh. This seemingly small detail is, in fact, quite essential for linking the two stories because 1 Kgs 22 is the only other text in which a king calls a prophet to his presence for a personal, face-to-face meeting.[107] Secondly, both Ahab and Zedekiah are caught in the middle of conflicting prophetic ideologies—Ahab has the 400 optimistic prophets on one side and Micaiah on the other side, while Zedekiah has both the officials and the court prophets representing one position and Jeremiah another. Accordingly, the theme of "true" versus "false" prophecy is central in both stories. Jeremiah's raising the topic of the optimistic prophets (v. 19) could be seen as a taunt; if so, this would not be unlike Micaiah who first mocks the message of the optimistic prophets (1 Kgs 22:15). In this vein, it should be noted that Ahab had been reluctant to consult Micaiah because of his history of delivering messages of disaster (1 Kgs 22:8); only after Jehoshaphat insisted did Ahab do so. Zedekiah, by contrast, willingly solicits a prophet who has repeatedly conveyed messages of defeat, most recently in Jer 37:3–10. Thus, it may be ironic that Jeremiah refers to the optimistic prophets since, unlike Ahab, Zedekiah's voluntarily consulting a "negative" prophet reflects well on him.[108]

Many commentators are puzzled by Zedekiah's consulting Jeremiah a second time. While some comment approvingly on Zedekiah's respect for the prophet's personal well-being (37:21), they interpret Zedekiah's question to Jeremiah as a pointless effort to receive a new word from Yahweh. John Bracke, for instance, "can hardly imagine what might have led King Zedekiah to seek Jeremiah's counsel," and suggests that it was "desperation."[109] Brueggemann describes the exchange as a "desperate, pleading one" by the king who is "an empty-handed suppliant."[110] When seen in connection with 1 Kgs 22, however, Zedekiah's seeking Jeremiah can be understood as a noble maneuver.

Thirdly, both 1 Kgs 22 and Jer 37:17–21 feature a contrast between public confrontation and private conversation which has implications for the prophet's safety. Micaiah confronted the court prophets directly and his public word of defeat jeopardized his physical safety (22:24). Jeremiah, by contrast, discloses his word to the king in a private conversation. The intertext with 1 Kgs 22 sheds light on the possible reason for the secrecy between Jeremiah and Zedekiah: the king was concerned for Jeremiah's safety and the privacy facilitated Zedekiah's ability to manage the flow of information, which was critical for Jeremiah's well-being.

---

107. Ordinarily the prophet approaches the king without any request. There are a few instances when the king initiates contact (1 Kgs 14; 2 Kgs 6; 19), but it is never for a personal consultation.

108. If Jehoshaphat asks where a prophet of Yahweh may be found (1 Kgs 22:7), Jeremiah asks rhetorically where the "false" prophets were to be found.

109. Bracke, *Jeremiah 30–52*, 66.

110. Brueggemann, *To Build, to Plant*, 143. Jeremiah is the "suppliant" in this scene, not Zedekiah.

Fourth, in both stories the prophet momentarily withholds the word. Micaiah mimics the message of the court prophets (22:15) and Jeremiah replies simply "There is." Fifth, both Jeremiah and Micaiah deliver a message of defeat which pertains specifically to the king. Micaiah's vision of Israel scattered on the mountain like sheep that have no shepherd suggests that if Ahab goes to battle, he will be killed, which is what ensues. Jeremiah explicitly informs Zedekiah that he will be handed over to the king of Babylon. The connection between these two stories is strengthened by the fact that these are the only two prophet–king encounters in which the prophet predicts military defeat for the king.[111] This makes it all the more striking that the scene in Jer 37 is the only one in which a king assists a prophet.

Sixth, the reaction of the two kings to the prophetic word can be compared. Ahab responds, "See, I told you he would not prophesy anything good about me," and then ignores Micaiah's counsel not to go to battle (22:18, 29). Zedekiah, differently, makes no specific response, but his instructions to feed the prophet until the bread in the city expired imply that perhaps he has acquiesced to the prophetic word.[112]

Finally, the two stories have uniquely similar conclusions: the king orders that the prophet be imprisoned and given bread (Jer 37:21; 1 Kgs 22:26–27). The two scenarios are different, however, for Jeremiah asks not to be "returned" to the place from which he was summoned; thus his being appointed to the court of the guard is an improvement in circumstances. Likewise his receiving bread is an act of beneficence on Zedekiah's part. Ahab, by contrast, commanded that Micaiah be "returned" to the place from which he came (Amon the governor of the city) and that he be imprisoned there; thus Micaiah loses freedom and his "reduced rations of bread and water" is punishment from the king. Although both prophets are detained and fed bread, Zedekiah, unlike Ahab, ameliorates the prophet's condition. The conclusions to the two episodes also paint differing images of the prophets. Micaiah utters the final words in the story as he says to Ahab, "If you return in peace, Yahweh has not spoken through me. Listen, you peoples, all of you!" Jeremiah, by contrast, is led off in silence; he makes no public declaration to confirm that he has spoken the word of Yahweh and does not beckon for the king and people to "listen." Rather, Jeremiah's intent was that the king "listen" to his own personal word regarding his own fate.

---

111.   Cf. 1 Kgs 20:13; 2 Kgs 3:17–18; 7:1; 19:6–7, in which prophets promise military victory or salvation from the enemy.

112.   One difference is that Jeremiah has not given any specific instructions to Zedekiah, whereas Micaiah has advised Ahab to take certain action, namely, to withdraw from attacking. Neither Micaiah nor Jeremiah employs the messenger formula when giving his word.

Chapter 3

OF PROPHETS, KINGS, AND DESTRUCTION: PART 2

Fourth Episode: 38:1–6

(1) Now Shephatiah son of Mattan, Gedaliah son of Pashhur, Jucal son of Shelemiah, and Pashhur son of Malchiah[1] heard the words that Jeremiah was speaking to all the people, saying: (2) Thus says Yahweh: Whoever remains in this city will die by the sword, by famine, and by pestilence; but whoever surrenders to the Chaldeans will live; he will have his life as a prize of war, and will live. (3) Thus says Yahweh: This city will surely be given into the hand of the army of the king of Babylon, and he will capture it. (4) Then the officials said to the king, "This man should be put to death, for he is weakening the hands of the soldiers who are left in this city and the hands of all the people by speaking these words to them. For this man is not seeking peace for this people, but evil. (5) King Zedekiah said, "Here, he is in your hands; the king is not able[2] to do anything against you."[3] (6) So they took Jeremiah and threw him into the pit of Malchiah, the king's son, which was in the court of the guard; and they lowered Jeremiah with ropes. Now there was no water in the pit, but only mud, and Jeremiah sank in the mud.[4]

There is no indication of when the events in this episode occurred in relation to the previous episode, nor is any specific setting recorded. Because it is unclear how Jeremiah could have spoken to the people of the city while confined in the court of the guard, some critics have identified 38:1 as the start of the second cycle of imprisonment–release–interview.[5] That is, 38:1 represents the location where the structure of the narrative becomes circular rather than linear. This feature, as Callaway has pointed out, tends to loosen the story from its particular historical setting in the final days of Jerusalem and allows the "stories to bob

---

1. The Greek does not list "Pashhur son of Malchiah."

2. Because of the peculiar יוּכַל here (*BHS* suggests reading יָכֹל) the word is exactly the same as the name of one of the officials listed in v. 1, יוּכַל (Jucal). Given that the story is partly about agency, perhaps this is significant—Jucal and the officials were able to do what they wanted with Jeremiah because Zedekiah said he was not able (יוּכַל) to stop them.

3. For "the king is not able to do anything against you" the Greek reads ὅτι οὐκ ἠδύνατο ὁ βασιλεὺς πρὸς αὐτούς ("for the king was not able to overcome them").

4. The division of 38:1–13 into two episodes is based on v. 6, which reports that Jeremiah sank into the mud. This concluding note indicating Jeremiah's location is parallel to the end of the second scene in episodes two (37:16), three (37:21), five (38:13), six (38:28), eight (39:14), and ten (40:6).

5. Cf. Clements, *Jeremiah*, 220. Ernest Nicholson, *The Book of Jeremiah Chapters 26–52* (Cambridge: Cambridge University Press, 1975), 118; Bright, *Jeremiah*, 232–33; McKane, *Jeremiah XXVI–LII*, 968–71. Others, however, argue that chs. 37 and 38 refer to two different occasions. Cf. Holladay, *Jeremiah 2*, 282–83. Still others reserve judgment, admitting both possibilities, such as F. B. Huey, *Jeremiah, Lamentations* (NAC 16; Nashville: Broadman, 1993), 332.

freely against each other." As a result, the story of Jeremiah "echoes themes of other times and places" and "limns its ancient tropes."[6] This apparent disjointed chronology encourages an intertextual hermeneutic. The narrative's lack of chronological indicators and the tension at 38:1, however, does not altogether eliminate the linear structure. Historical knowledge of Jeremiah's conditions at the court of the guard is not sufficient to arrive at such a decision. The prophet may have still had ample opportunity for contact with the people, the army, and the officials even though he did not have complete freedom.[7] It seems likely that, if nothing else, Jeremiah would have been under the surveillance of guards with whom he could have spoken—advising his "captive" audience to surrender. Furthermore, in ch. 32 Jeremiah speaks while in the court of the guard. There is nothing in the story, then, that compels the reader to assume that a second cycle has begun, that the linear structure of the story has ended. Indeed, the debate among scholars over the linear or circular structure is evidence of its ambiguity. Both structures, then, exist in tension with each other.

Point of View

The narrator in this episode juxtaposes multiple and contrasting points of view, which again creates an entertaining scene. First, the narrator quotes Jeremiah's speech addressed to the people (vv. 2–3), but it is quoted via the "hearing" (שמע) of the officials. This is to be differentiated from direct speech ("Jeremiah said") and from another character quoting direct speech (as in 37:19). Furthermore, since the quotation is of prophetic speech prefaced with the messenger formula, it is actually the narrator quoting Jeremiah's speech which is quoting God's speech. Unlike 37:6–10, in which there was some ambiguity concerning whose perspective was being voiced, Yahweh's or the prophet's, and 37:17, where the prophet did not explicitly speak in the name of Yahweh, here there is no immediate reason to doubt that Jeremiah is presenting the words of the deity. The reader can trust that this is Yahweh's view in part because it is the narrator, and not another character, quoting the prophet, and because the prophet himself had uttered a very similar message in the name of Yahweh in 21:8–9. However, to use Savran's language, it is technically unverifiable as there is no independent report of Yahweh's perspective.

Verses 2–3 contain the content of Jeremiah's/Yahweh's message, uttered in the form of two oracles.[8] Here the prophet explains that if the people surrender to the Babylonians, they would live, but if not, they would die (v. 2).[9] However,

---

6. Callaway, "Black Fire on White Fire," 178.

7. Holt ("The Potent Word of God," 164) says that Jeremiah's prisons are "public places, belonging to the ruling party."

8. Jeremiah seems to speak in sets of two: he offered two oracles in response to Zedekiah's delegation (37:7–10), asked the king two rhetorical questions (37:18–19), and now announces his message in two oracles.

9. The three-fold way in which death will come for those who remain in the city (sword, famine, and pestilence) is balanced by three references to "life" for the one who surrenders ("he will live," "he will have his life as a prize of war," and "will live").

regardless of whether or not one surrendered, Jeremiah's second oracle declares that the city would be conquered by the Babylonians (v. 3).[10] Here Jeremiah's/ Yahweh's point of view regarding Jerusalem is not different from the one expressed in the oracles in 37:7–10—it would be given over to the Babylonians unconditionally. What has changed is the audience; here Jeremiah is addressing the soldiers and people, not the king.[11] Accordingly, the people have an opportunity to save their lives by surrendering, but the oracle says nothing specifically about the king's fate, which, like the city's, was unconditional capture (37:17).

The officials then expound their point of view to the king in direct speech. How they address the king and how they refer to Jeremiah are symbolic of their perspective, or at least the rhetorical stance they choose to adopt in this setting. Unlike Jeremiah (37:20), the officials offer no reverent address to Zedekiah. They do not portray themselves as "servants" of the king; nor, unlike the prophet, do the officials employ an indirect rhetorical approach. Their strategy is to assert boldly their proposition ("this man should be put to death").

Further, the officials do not identify Jeremiah by name, but refer their accusations against "this man," which serves to distance and objectify Jeremiah and evidences their opinion of him.[12] They then submit two reasons to support their position that Jeremiah should die. The first emanates from an external, objective perspective: "he is weakening the hands of the soldiers who are left in this city and the hands of all the people." The second accusation addresses Jeremiah's own internal perspective: "this man is not seeking peace for this people, but evil." Here the officials attribute motivation to Jeremiah's actions—he is a traitor who does not have the city's best interest at heart. Jeremiah's speech is first quoted by the narrator, through the "hearing" of the officials (38:1), and then his internal ideas are presented by the officials. If previously Jeremiah, in his dialogues with the king, had voiced other people's words (37:19) and expressed their motivations (37:7), here the prophet has his words and internal dispositions refracted through the voice of others during their interview with the king. As in the previous cases, this technique creates ambiguities and invites readers to generate their own perspectives.

Although it is clear that the officials maintain an ideological perspective different from Jeremiah, their speech in this scene does not specifically reject the content of Jeremiah's message. Instead, they charge that its propagation and influence is deleterious for the people, as is the prophet's supposed ill will toward the city.[13] The narrative offers no reason to doubt the officials' first allegation:

10. The passive voice here in the second oracle—"this city will surely be given into the hand of the army of the king of Babylon"—places the emphasis on Yahweh as the agent rather than on the Babylonians (contrast 37:6–10).

11. Cf. v. 1: "to all the people," and v. 4: "to the men of battle" and "to the people."

12. Their allegations against Jeremiah play on the prophet's own words, for he had prophesied that those who stay in "this city" will die (ימות), and now the officials say that "this man" should die (יומת, hophal).

13. If one assumes that the city is under siege at this time, this might explain why the officials simply do not attack the actual content of Jeremiah's message, for destruction did indeed loom nearby.

Jeremiah's message was weakening morale in Jerusalem. This calculation will be punctuated with additional support later in the story (38:19). The more difficult question is whether the second charge—that Jeremiah was not seeking שָׁלוֹם ("peace") for "this people" but רעה ("evil")—is accurate. From the officials' standpoint, timing was crucial; the national crisis demanded patriotism, and Jeremiah's defeatist attitude, understandably, needed to be contained. From Jeremiah's vantage point, he was pursuing good, not evil, by advising people how they could preserve their lives. In fact, Jeremiah's message in vv. 2–3 purports a distinction between "this city," for which he foretold defeat and "this people," whose welfare he was seeking. Moreover, from Jeremiah's point of view (presumably) it was the officials who were unconcerned about the שָׁלוֹם of the people.

The officials' disclosure of Jeremiah's words to the king can be understood in terms of loyalty to the king. Specifically, their responsibility is to apprise the king of any slanderous or malicious speech. Here Lasine is instructive. He points out that the vassal treaties of Esarhaddon focus primarily on uncontrolled speech. Any "improper, unsuitable or unseemly word" hostile to the king must be reported by the hearer. The same holds true for those who utter "malicious whispers" or who "spread rumors." Those who enter the treaty are not only required to report those who do not speak well of the king, but also they themselves must not say any slanderous or evil words against the king and may only "speak good of the king."[14] In this light, the officials, as loyal courtiers, are constrained to report Jeremiah's actions to the king. Not to do so would be remiss and potentially fatal.[15] J. J. M. Roberts offers further insight regarding the perspective of the officials. He writes:

> The royal suppression, persecution, and execution of what the biblical tradition regards as the genuine prophets of Yahweh must be seen as a rational act. Within the ancient Near Eastern context, if one believed that a Jeremiah had truly been sent with a genuine and reliable oracle from Yahweh, it would, of course, be folly to oppose him, much less persecute him. If, on the other hand, one rejected his claims and believed him to be a

---

14. Lasine, *Knowing Kings*, 57–58, 62–63.

15. Here Lasine's analyses (*Knowing Kings*, 39–50) of the story of Saul, David, and Doeg in 1 Sam 21–22 are helpful. David comes to Nob and secures holy bread and Goliath's sword and asks Ahimelech to inquire of Yahweh for him. Doeg is present at Nob. Later, Saul accuses his courtiers of conspiracy for failing to inform him ("open his ear") about Jonathan colluding with David. Doeg then informs the king that he has seen David come to Ahimelech at Nob. After questioning Ahimelech, Saul orders that all the priests of Nob be killed because they did not inform him of David's activities. When his servants refuse to follow Saul's commands, Doeg kills the priests and the people of Nob. When David discovers this, he assumes responsibility for the deaths of those in Nob because he knew that Doeg would apprise Saul. This scenario demonstrates the importance of loyalty and relaying information to the king. Lasine explains that, *contra* most commentators, Saul's behavior in this scene is quite understandable: he executed people who did not fulfill their responsibility to inform the king. In short, it is incumbent upon the officials to report Jeremiah's message to the people and its effects. On an intertextual aside, the word דאג appears in v. 19 as Zedekiah expresses his "worry" about the Judeans who had deserted. Does this word recall the story of דאג (Doeg), since it too is about loyalty to and betrayal of the king?

paid agent of the Babylonian enemy, then the execution of Jeremiah that is demanded by
the royal officials was a perfectly reasonable, legal, and moral course of action. Everything hinged on which belief about the particular prophet were true, but how one
resolved that quandary was never self-evident to the contemporaries of the prophets.[16]

Without the advantage of hindsight, the officials' point of view can be read
sympathetically.

What is strikingly absent from this scene is any word from Jeremiah, any
indication of his perspective. Although the narrative does not explicitly state that
Jeremiah was present during the conversation between the officials and Zedekiah,
there are several indications to the affirmative. First, the officials refer to Jeremiah
as "this man," which would seem more appropriate if he were present. Second,
and similarly, Zedekiah responds, "Here (הנה); he is in your hands," which suggests that the prophet is already on the scene.[17] Third, the story reports that the
officials took Jeremiah and put him into the pit; they did not first have to locate
him (contrast Ebed-melech in the next episode). Although most commentators
fail to speculate on Jeremiah's presence or absence (which is mandatory for a full
understanding of this episode), it seems best to imagine that Jeremiah was present for the interview between the officials and the king, but remained silent. This
is, on the one hand, reminiscent of Jeremiah's reticence in his confrontation with
Irijah, although there he at least denied the allegations. On the other hand, one
wonders why Jeremiah remained silent, for he had not hesitated to speak up and
defend himself to the king in the previous episode. Indeed, the prophet's passivity
in this episode is not only physical, as the officials put him into the pit, but also
verbal. If Jeremiah had been a powerful agent of discouragement, now he has, or
expresses, no agency whatsoever.

In Zedekiah's response to the officials, he refers to himself in the third person,
which is notable given the narrative's use of naming as a method of signaling
point of view. Because Zedekiah does not say "I (first-person) can do nothing
against you," it is possible that he is making a distinction between himself and
his office.[18] More significantly, Zedekiah does not address the veracity of the
officials' allegations; thereby he conceals his opinion of the prophet's internal
motives. Readers, then, are left to wonder if the king agrees with the officials that
the prophet deserved death. Furthermore, the king's claim of being powerless
against the officials is a peculiar one; it provides the reader with multiple interpretive options regarding both Zedekiah's perspective and the reality (in the story
world) of the situation. Did Zedekiah perceive that he was powerless against the

16. J. J. M. Roberts, "Prophets and Kings: A New Look at the Royal Persecution of Prophets
against its Near Eastern Background," in *A God So Near* (ed. B. A. Strawn and N. R. Bowen; Winona
Lake, Ind.: Eisenbrauns, 2003), 341–54 (353–54).

17. The word הנה in direct discourse encourages the hearer to focus on a particular person or
event; it also used similarly in 37:7 (cf. Berlin, *Poetics and Interpretation*, 91).

18. Perhaps the implication is that the "king" could in fact not deny the charges of treason that the
officials had brought against the prophet and thus was "unable" to stop them. But Zedekiah himself,
apart from his role as king, was able to act against the officials, namely, by appointing Ebed-melech
to rescue Jeremiah from the pit.

officials, or does he simply adopt this view for one reason or another?[19] Does Zedekiah mistakenly perceive that he cannot stop the officials, or was he correct when he described himself as powerless? Power is disseminated in subtle ways, and the king's statement calls one to reflect on this power distribution. The king's statement, however, must be interpreted in the context of his actions. His removing Jeremiah from Jonathan's prison suggests that he possessed at least some degree of power over the officials, although his not freeing the prophet entirely may indicate certain limitations.[20] Further, the very fact that the officials approach the king regarding Jeremiah implies that the king was not, in fact, powerless. Indeed, while Zedekiah does not seem to have the power normally ascribed to kings, the "actual" distribution of power—as is reflected in the events of the story—is more complex than Zedekiah's claim that he has none.

Contextual Analysis

The *leitwort* שמע emerges again in this episode; in fact, it is the very first word. As has been discussed, this word points to the narrator's statement in 37:2. It also forms thematic connections with previous uses (37:14, 20) and plays on its various meanings. The officials do "hear" the words of Jeremiah but they do not "obey" by surrendering. However, if the soldiers and people were being discouraged by the prophet's message, then here is suggestive evidence that, *contra* 37:2, the people were not only "hearing" the words but were also "obeying" them, or at least the words were having an effect on the people. Later, it will be corroborated that some people had heeded Jeremiah's message and deserted to the Babylonians (38:19). Thus, ironically, the success of Jeremiah's message elicits still more problems and complications.

This episode also plays on the word דבר. Zedekiah says to the officials that there is nothing יוכל אתכם דבר. The use of דבר is noteworthy given that it is precisely the power of the king's "word" in 37:20 and 38:10 that overcomes the officials' actions. The officials heard Jeremiah's "words" (v. 1) and objected to the influence that those "words" (v. 4) were imposing on the people, and the king claims that his "word" is incapable of influencing the officials. The king, therefore, was overcome by the words of the officials and surrendered Jeremiah into the their hands, rather than being persuaded by Jeremiah's word and surrendering

19. Most commentators take Zedekiah at his word and conclude that he feared the officials and was unable to deter them. Carroll, however, rightly argues that Zedekiah "clearly has sufficient power to modify the actions of the princes (37.17; 38.10, 14)." On this reading Zedekiah's reply to the officials is not truthful—he is assuming a view that he knows is not correct. Carroll does not consider this, however, and surmises, oddly, that "even the king cannot release a traitor like Jeremiah and permit him to undermine further the attempt to repulse the Babylonians" (*Jeremiah: A Commentary*, 680). The question here is not one of release, but of death. That is, it was not imperative for Zedekiah to release Jeremiah; he could have determined that the prophet should remain confined in the court of the guard, but not killed, as the officials proposed.

20. Because the image of the king as powerless and passive and willing to allow harm to the prophet stands in some tension with the depiction of the king in the previous episode, Seitz (*Theology in Conflict*, 258) and others attribute these episodes to two different sources. Attention to matters of point of view, however, exposes the narrative's artful complexity.

the city into the hands of the Babylonians. Further, the trio "sword, famine, and pestilence" is common in the book of Jeremiah,[21] but in its context here, "pestilence" (דֶבֶר) takes on ironic tones. "Pestilence" (דֶבֶר) echoes "word" (דָבָר), and although Jeremiah proclaims death by "pestilence," the officials fear he is inducing death by his "word." Indeed, the power of דבר is particularly salient in this scene.[22]

There are several other word-plays in this episode that also connect to earlier scenes. First, the officials claim that Jeremiah is not "seeking" (דרש) the well-being of Jerusalem.[23] The word דרש is also the technical term for "inquiring" of Yahweh, but here the officials employ the terms in a different sense. Prophets are expected to "inquire" of Yahweh, not to "seek" evil for the people.[24] Second, the phrase "weakening of the hands," with the word יד appearing twice in v. 4, is framed by references to "hand" in vv. 3, 5.[25] Because Jeremiah had said that the city would be given into the "hand" of the Babylonians (v. 3), a view which in turn weakened the "hands" of those remaining, the prophet himself is given into the "hands" of the officials. Their "hand" overpowers the prophet, just as the "hands" of the Babylonians will overcome the weak "hands" in Jerusalem.[26] These metaphoric references to "hand" underscore that one issue is that the officials presumably do not believe that Yahweh has spoken "by the hand of Jeremiah" (37:2). In other words, is Jeremiah an agent of Yahweh or the enemy? Indeed, this scene represents a contest of power, which is one of the main connotations of יד.

Third, the mention in v. 4 of the "men of battle (אנשי המלחמה) who are left (נשאר)" in the city connects to 37:10. There Jeremiah declared that if the Judeans were to defeat the army of the Babylonians, even the injured "men" (אנשים) who "were left" (נשאר) from the Babylonian army would arise and defeat the city. The prophet was discouraging the "remnant" of Jerusalem's army by proclaiming that even a "remnant" of the Babylonian army would destroy them.[27] Finally, when

---

21. It occurs fourteen other times in Jeremiah: 14:12; 21:7, 9; 24:10; 27:8, 13; 29:17, 18; 32:24, 36; 34:17; 42:17, 22; 44:13.

22. One might regard the movement of the "word" in this episode as a reversal of the movement, or desired movement, of the word in the first episode (37:3–10). There the word traveled from king, to delegation, to prophet, to Yahweh—although the prophet did not offer prayer as requested. Here in 38:1–6, the word moves from Yahweh, to Jeremiah, to the officials, to the king. If earlier the king sent two delegates to ask Jeremiah to offer a prayer to Yahweh on behalf of king and people, here four officials confront the king in regard to the words that Jeremiah was speaking to the people on behalf of Yahweh. Thus, the king receives a word from the officials rather than sending one with them, and the people receive a word from Yahweh, rather than having one offered on their behalf.

23. Ironically perhaps, Jeremiah's earlier instruction to the exiles in Babylon is to seek the peace (דרש שלום) of Babylon (29:7).

24. Ahab agrees to call Micaiah so that he can "inquire" of Yahweh, but says that he hates Micaiah because he always prophesies "evil" concerning him (1 Kgs 22:8 = 2 Chr 18:7).

25. This phrase is also found in the Lachish letters.

26. In 23:14, Jeremiah accused the prophets of Jerusalem of "strengthening the hands of evil doers."

27. One may speculate about what had happened to the rest of Jerusalem's army. Had they been killed in battle, or had they already deserted, as 38:19 suggests (see below)?

Jeremiah announces that "whoever יֹשֵׁב in this city will die by the sword, by famine and by pestilence," it is likely that יֹשֵׁב would initially be interpreted as "dwell" until it was placed in contrast to יֹצֵא ("surrender"), when it would then be understood as "stay/remain." This echoes earlier word-plays on יֹשֵׁב regarding prisons and houses; one cannot "dwell" in the city for in reality it is a prison in which one will die if one "stays/remains."

The Plot: The Second Scene

The second scene includes no direct or indirect speech, only the officials' actions against Jeremiah. The lack of speech links it to the second scene in the second episode (37:15–16), which is the only other such scene among the twelve in chs. 37–38; fittingly, there too the focus is on the physical abuse of the prophet. Much as the previous episode ended somewhat surprisingly as Jeremiah was moved to the court of the guard rather than being totally freed (or sent back to Jonathan's prison), this episode's culmination is also somewhat unexpected. One anticipates that the officials will kill Jeremiah as they had proposed, but instead they throw him into a pit. If Zedekiah could not give Jeremiah his freedom (37:21), the officials could not execute him as they had asserted.[28] Most interpreters (rightly or wrongly) construe the king's actions in this episode as weak and indecisive ("he is in your hands"), but few observe that the officials' action is equally ambivalent and irresolute. Both the king and the officials move Jeremiah to places that carry different levels of freedom and comfort; but neither acts clearly and decisively. The story beckons readers to compare the actions of the king and the officials: as the king sent for (שׁלח) and took (לקח) Jeremiah from prison (37:17; 38:14), so the officials took (לקח) and sent (שׁלח) him down by ropes (38:6). If in the previous episode the king had sent for Jeremiah to come up from the "house of the pit" (בֵּית הַבּוֹר, 37:16), here the officials again send him down into the "pit" (הַבּוֹר, 38:6). If before the officials turned a house into prison, here they turn a cistern, another necessary human commodity, into a place of con–finement, and perhaps death. Spaces, again, are symbolic.

The ambiguity of the officials' actions, which mirrors that of the king, is represented by the construction of v. 6, the first half of which reads: "So they took Jeremiah and threw him (שׁלך) into the pit." The violence of the officials and the place where they put him—a "pit" is sometimes a symbol for the place of the dead (Ps 28:1; Isa 28:18)—make it appear initially that they have attempted to put the prophet to death.[29] The mood, however, shifts abruptly in the middle of the verse: "And they let Jeremiah down (שׁלח) by ropes and there was no water in the cistern, but only mud, and Jeremiah sank in the mud." The similarity in the verbs forms—שׁלך and שׁלח—draws attention to the two different images of the

---

28. Carroll comments (*Jeremiah: A Commentary*, 681) that the officials "are more interested in preventing him from damaging the war effort than in killing him." Further, he writes, "To have killed him outright would have been the ruination of a good story!"

29. The cross-section of most domestic cisterns was shaped like a bottle, with a small opening in the top, often covered by a stone (Holladay, *Jeremiah 2*, 289). If this were the shape of Malchiah's cistern, it would be impossible for Jeremiah to climb out.

officials' treatment of the prophet.[30] Further, the reader learns that the cistern was only muddy, not full of water, so now it looks as though the officials were not attempting to kill Jeremiah by drowning him, as might initially have been thought.

Moreover, the pit was located in the court of the guard and was thus presumably visible and accessible. The officials therefore acted very publicly, not secretively, and so friends and supporters of Jeremiah would be aware of his predicament. This plot development is ironic in several ways. One of the primary themes in this episode is the officials' objection to Jeremiah's openly spreading a message of destruction for the city. Yet, it was their public action against Jeremiah that led to his rescue, at least in part. Another reason for his deliverance was the lack of water in the cistern, presumably a result of the siege.[31] If people perish because of the lack of water—that is, famine—during the siege, Jeremiah lives because its absence. There may also be some symbolism in the officials' actions: they attempt to destroy the prophet in one of the places that represented their destruction (the dry cistern)—a destruction that was brought about in part by Jeremiah's message. If Jeremiah, as the officials claimed, was not (אֵין) seeking the good of the city (v. 4), and since the king was not (אֵין) able to hinder the officials (v. 5), Jeremiah was thrown into a cistern; but because there was no (אֵין) water, the prophet was able to survive.

In addition, Jeremiah's fate at the hands of the officials parallels that of the city's fate at the hands of the Babylonians. Just as Jeremiah was left in the cistern to suffer a slow death by starvation (38:9) and neglect, so too the city was slowly being starved to death by the siege. Jeremiah was being punished for treason against the city (in the officials' view); the city was being punished for unfaithfulness to the Babylonians (and, in Jeremiah's view, to Yahweh as well). Similarly, the nature of the punishment—not immediate death—allowed both Jeremiah and the city an opportunity to be saved.

The officials' confident and direct rhetorical approach to the king (v. 4) contrasts with their ambivalent actions at the end. If their strategy was only to silence the prophet, placing him in a muddy cistern in the middle of the court of the

30. Because the two verbs give two incompatible versions of how Jeremiah entered the pit, some see the second verb as a gloss to soften the harsh treatment depicted in the first one. Alter, discussing composite artistry, offers an alternative solution that is applicable in the present case: "The contradiction between [the two accounts] . . . is so evident that it seems naïve . . . to conclude that the ancient Hebrew writer was so inept or unperceptive that the conflict between the two versions could have somewhat escaped him. . . . In linear logic, the same action could not have occurred twice in two different ways; but in the narrative logic with which the writer worked, it made sense to incorporate both versions available to him because together they brought forth mutually complementary implications of the narrated event, thus enabling him to give a complete imaginative account of it" (*Art of Biblical Narrative*, 138).

31. It is possible that the cistern was simply out of use and was not dry because of harsh conditions in the city; however, the fact that it had mud in it suggests that it had recently contained water. The word טיט denotes wet mud (Holladay, *Jeremiah 2*, 289). The officials would not have thrown Jeremiah into the cistern if it held water, for this would have ruined one of their few precious resources.

guard was hardly a good way to insure this. For both the king and the officials, Jeremiah was a prophet whose message had to be addressed, but the political, military, and theological turmoil that undoubtedly characterized the last days in Jerusalem prevented them from taking strong positions and acting resolutely. Indeed, the king's and officials' behavior toward Jeremiah demonstrates their lack of sureness and conviction. There were no obvious answers, after all, as to how to handle a prophet who spoke in the name of Yahweh and yet proclaimed destruction on Jerusalem and advocated surrender.

One other factor points to the complexities of the plot. The pit into which Jeremiah was placed is identified as belonging to "Malchiah, the king's son." As has been observed above, the naming of minor characters punctuates their role in the story and invites the reader to explore their relations with other characters. Here "son" may be taken literally or it may designate a member of the royal family,[32] but either way those within Zedekiah's family appear to be in opposition to Jeremiah. Furthermore, it is quite possible that the Malchiah in v. 6 is the same Malchiah as in v. 1, who is the father of Pashhur, one of the officials accusing Jeremiah. If this is the case, then there were at least two members of the royal family who were adversaries of the prophet (Pashhur and his father Malchiah). This attention to the minor characters may lead to an insight regarding Zedekiah's actions in this scene. If his own son (Malchiah) and grandson (Pashhur) were among those accusing the prophet, Zedekiah may have felt more compelled to yield a guilty verdict (see below on the judicial context) and hand over Jeremiah to them.

Although Jeremiah is not put to death, his safety and security is jeopardized as he is left sinking in the mud, which contrasts with the less ominous conclusion to the previous episode where he "remained at the court of the guard" (37:21). If the prophet perceived that the conditions in Jonathan's prison were life-threatening (37:20), his predicament in the "pit" was indubitably even worse.[33] Indeed, Jeremiah's being thrown into the cistern represents a low point for him literally and figuratively. As Jeremiah reaches his nadir, the drama in the plot reaches its peak: what will happen to Jeremiah now?[34]

Intertextuality

Much like the intertextual web that was woven around Irijah's patronymic in 37:13, here too a series of related texts, images, and motifs are interconnected by the list of the officials' names and the names of their fathers in v. 1. The first two men, Shephatiah and Gedaliah[35] appear only here in the book. However, the other

---

32. Cf. Holladay, *Jeremiah 2*, 289. No commentator discusses the significance of Malchiah.

33. Here one may be reminded that Yahweh had told Jeremiah that his trials would intensify: "If you have raced with foot-runners and they have wearied you, how will you compete with horses? And if in a safe land you fall down, how will you fare in the thickets of the Jordan" (12:5).

34. This dramatic climax is also the scene immediately prior to the center unit of the loose chiastic structure for this whole section (37:1–40:6; see above); the plot and structure coincide.

35. This is not the same Gedaliah who is appointed governor after the fall of Jerusalem, for the two men have different fathers; cf. 39:7.

two men, Jucal and Pashhur, have been seen previously. Pashhur son of Malchiah (as he is identified in both places) was sent by Zedekiah, along with Zephaniah, to speak with Jeremiah in ch. 21. J(eh)ucal[36] son of Shelemiah (as he is identified in both places) was also sent with Zephaniah to approach the prophet in the first episode (37:3). In this way, the narrative incorporates the points of view of two of the men who comprised the king's delegations: both Jehucal and Pashhur oppose the prophet and advocate hostile actions against him. Both men accompanied Zephaniah who appears elsewhere in the book as the priest who supported and protected Jeremiah in his quarrels with the "false" prophets (29:24–32). Hence, each of the two delegations in 21:1–10 and 37:3–10 were composed of one friend and one foe of Jeremiah, which makes Zedekiah's decision to send specifically these men quite curious.[37] The composition of each delegation epitomizes a key theme in the story, namely, conflict surrounding Jeremiah and his perspective.

Additional connections are associated with the other Pashhur mentioned in this list, specifically Pashhur the father of Gedaliah.[38] In 20:1–6, a certain priest named Pashhur, son of Immer, arrested, beat, and restrained Jeremiah in stocks for a day (20:1–6).[39] Jeremiah retaliated with an oracle against Pashhur and his family, predicting that they would all be taken captive and would die in Babylon. It is quite possible that the Pashhur of ch. 20 is the same Pashhur in 38:1.[40] If so, then here is another scenario of a family (Pashhur and his son Gedaliah) continuing their opposition to Jeremiah. In this case, the officials' actions would also be somewhat ironic, for Gedaliah's participation in the attempt to kill the prophet by throwing him into a cistern would mean an ignominious death for the prophet in his own land—a reversal of the curse spoken against Pashhur his father (20:6). This would be reminiscent of Irijah's efforts to exact revenge on Jeremiah by arresting him and handing him over to the officials (37:14) in retribution for Jeremiah's earlier cursing (to death) his grandfather Hananiah.

This fourth episode also recalls ch. 21, as did the first episode. Jeremiah's message in 38:2 is nearly a word for word quote of his message to Zedekiah's emissaries and the people in 21:9–10. In that text, Jeremiah, speaking in the divine first-person, offered a rationale for advising the people to surrender: "For I have set my face against this city for evil (רעה) and not for good, says

---

36. The form of the name is slightly different. In 37:3 it is יהוכל; in 38:1 it is יוכל. But it is almost certain that the same person is indicated because the father is identified as Shelemiah in both places. Many commentators, in fact, render the name Jehucal in 38:1 to agree with the same form in 37:3. Recall also that J(eh)ucal appears to be the brother of Irijah (both are identified as the son of Shelemiah) who arrested Jeremiah in 37:13 (see above).

37. It is not clear if Pashhur and Jehucal opposed the prophet prior to serving as an emissary or only subsequently adopted that view.

38. It is possible, but seems unlikely that Pashhur, father of Gedaliah, and Pashhur, son of Malchiah, are the same person (38:1).

39. This Pashhur is different from the Pashhur of 21:1 who is the son of Malchiah.

40. Carroll mentions, but does not pursue, this possibility (*Jeremiah: A Commentary*, 678). Even if it were deemed that these are not the same person, the very possibility of this suffices to make the intertextual link.

Yahweh."[41] This explanation is vital for a consideration of the officials' charge that Jeremiah was "seeking evil" for "this people."[42] The connection with ch. 21 enables one to see a crucial difference in the theological perspectives of Jeremiah and the officials. If, as in the officials' point of view, Yahweh would always defend and save Jerusalem, then Jeremiah had to be speaking false words, he had to be the one seeking evil for the city. But, according to Jeremiah's view, or Yahweh's view voiced through Jeremiah, Yahweh was the one who willed evil for the city. This juxtaposition of competing theologies summons the reader into the conversation. The reader, it would seem, is likely to be at least sympathetic of the officials' position; for one can understand how they would suppose that Jeremiah, rather than Yahweh, was the one who had set his face for evil against the city (and was thus a false prophet). The officials, of course, were standing in a long tradition of "Zion theology" that asserted Yahweh's eternal fidelity to the Davidic king and Jerusalem. If Jeremiah were a true prophet of Yahweh, then the allegation that the officials level against Jeremiah should be aimed at Yahweh, for the deity was the traitor who deserved death.[43] Indeed, a sharp difference exists between the officials' and Jeremiah's understanding of Yahweh's relation to Jerusalem, a difference which lies at the heart of the conflict.

Contributing to the intertextual constellation surrounding 38:1–4 is the Rabshakeh's encounter with Jerusalem in 2 Kgs 18:19–37. Jeremiah and the Rabshakeh both deliver the same message: surrender (יצא) and live (see above). Also, in both cases a primary concern was the effect that the message of surrender would have on the people who heard it (2 Kgs 18:26).[44] Much like Hezekiah's officials heard the words of the Rabshakeh and apprised the king (2 Kgs 18:37), here in 38:1–4 Zedekiah's officials hear Jeremiah's proclamation and approach the king. This connection between 38:1–4 and the account of Hezekiah and the Rabshakeh highlights the subversive nature of Jeremiah's word as it undermined the Zion tradition. Accordingly, it is easy to comprehend how challenging it would be for the characters in the story to adopt the prophet's point of view. In effect, he was not only taking the enemy's position by repeating the message of the Assyrians, but he was also advocating a view that had turned out to be completely wrong the last time Jerusalem had faced such a crisis. The

---

41. This oracle of conditional salvation (21:8) follows a covenantal formula found in Deut 30:15, 19: "I am setting before you the way of life and the way of death." Speaking in the divine first person and using a covenantal formula adds significant authority to the proclamation to surrender.

42. Jeremiah 21:10 says that Yahweh has determined evil and not "good" (טוב) for the city, whereas in 38:4 Jeremiah is said to seek evil and not the "welfare" (שלום). This difference would seem to reflect more poorly on Yahweh than Jeremiah, for in the prophet's case it could be argued that he was still seeking the "good" for the city, but was proclaiming that somehow it involved punishment—i.e. not שלום—by defeat at the hands of the Babylonians. Hope and life are more easily found in someone who does not seek שלום than in someone who does not seek טוב.

43. To say "if Jeremiah *were* a true prophet" is to adopt the officials' perspective—"were" as the subjunctive indicating a condition contrary to reality.

44. Also linking the two texts is the phrase "this city, which occurs three times in 38:1–4 and in 2 Kgs 18:30; 19:32, 33, 34; 20:6.

Hezekiah–Isaiah paradigm enables the reader—regardless of temporal location—to appreciate the difficulty of Zedekiah's situation.

The episode in 38:1–6 is a judicial procedure with Jeremiah being tried for treason or sedition.[45] This recalls Jeremiah's trial after preaching his so-called Temple Sermon in ch. 26, a text which also alludes to the time of Hezekiah and his interaction with prophets. Thus it represents an additional node in the network of resonances. Jeremiah 26 has been identified as the most detailed account of a court procedure in the Hebrew Bible.[46] Accordingly, one can detect all the formal elements of a trial in this scene: a pre-trial accusation (v. 9); summons to trial in a public location (v. 10); a formal accusation (v. 11); defense by the accused (vv. 12–15); counter-argument and counter-witnesses (vv. 16–19); and sentence (v. 20). In ch. 38, the officials initiate the process by formally taking their accusation to trial before Zedekiah, thereby acknowledging his jurisdiction as judge. They identify the malefactor, charge him with sedition, and demand the death sentence. Similarly, in ch. 26 the priests and prophets approach the officials and the people and charged that Jeremiah be put to death because he had spoken against Jerusalem (26:11). Notably, however, in ch. 26 the officials function as the judge, not the prosecutors, and the proceedings transpires in public "before all the people" (26:10–11). The trial in ch. 38, by contrast, appears to lack the necessary public setting, although this is not entirely clear. If the trial is private, it creates a sense of irony because the officials' accusation pertained to the prophet's public words and actions. The private trial would also correspond nicely to the two private conversations between the prophet and king in the third (37:17) and sixth episodes (38:16).

In his defense in ch. 26 Jeremiah first reiterates his message encouraging the people to repent and avert disaster, and he then declares, "As for me, here I am in your hands. Do with me what is good and right in your eyes. Only surely know that if you put me to death, you will bring innocent blood on yourselves and on this city and its inhabitants, for truly Yahweh has sent me to you to speak all these words into your ears" (26:14–15). Here Jeremiah asserts that he is a true prophet of Yahweh, and consequently should not be put to death. This reminds one that in ch. 38 the dispute between Jeremiah and the officials is based fundamentally on Jeremiah's legitimacy as a true prophet. In striking contrast to ch. 26, there is no mention of this defense stage of a proper trial in ch. 38. Instead, the narrative moves directly to the judge's pronouncement, "Here, he is in your hands," which functions as a guilty verdict and sentence.[47] Zedekiah, however,

---

45. Clements (*Jeremiah*, 220) recognizes that "the treasonable nature of Jeremiah's encouragement to the population to desert to the Babylonian lines (v. 2) is quite unmistakable."

46. Bovati, *Re-Establishing Justice*, 228. See also Hans J. Boecker, *Law and Administration of Justice in the Old Testament and Ancient East* (Minneapolis: Augsburg, 1980), 44; and William McKane, "Jeremiah and the Wise," in *Wisdom in Ancient Israel: Essays in Honour of J. A. Emerton* (ed. J. Day, R. P. Gordon, and H. G. M. Williamson; Cambridge: Cambridge University Press, 1995), 142–51. For a literary analysis of the trial scene in ch. 26, see Herbert C. Brichto, *Toward a Grammar of Biblical Poetics* (New York: Oxford University Press, 1992), 226–30.

47. For a discussion of this phrase, see Bovati, *Re-Establishing Justice*, 381–83.

seems to compromise his impartiality as the judge with his statement, "The king is able to do nothing against you."[48] If this, in fact, is accurate, then Zedekiah is powerless to serve in a judicial capacity.

At any rate, Jeremiah's trial in 38:4–5 is defective due to the lack of a defense. It is only defective, however, if Jeremiah was not granted the opportunity to defend himself; in this scenario, he has been denied basic rights and the trial is a sham.[49] Alternatively, one may imagine that Jeremiah chooses not to construct a defense, for he has proven reticent in crucial situations—understating his views and motives (37:14). As was noted, Jeremiah's silence in this scene is remarkable, especially since it is likely that he was in fact present at the trial. As Bovati delineates, in a judicial context silence by one party connotes that the other party is correct and has won the trial. Silence is equivalent to saying there are no more arguments and therefore one's adversary is right. In short, "keeping silent rather than speaking up to defend oneself is an admission of guilt."[50] Perhaps Jeremiah would assent to his guilt from the officials' perspective, in which case his silence would signal an understanding of their views.[51] Either way, a recognition of the forensic context complicates Jeremiah's portrayal.

After Jeremiah's defense in ch. 26 the officials and the people switch from the role of judge to that of defense attorney—dual role playing in trials in the Bible is not uncommon[52]—and they submit a counter-argument in Jeremiah's behalf: Jeremiah did not deserve to die, for he had spoken in the name of Yahweh (26:16). Indeed, the officials (!) affirm that Jeremiah is a true prophet of Yahweh. Then "elders of the land" also offer a counter-argument in support of Jeremiah by pointing out that Micah had promulgated a message of defeat for Jerusalem, yet Hezekiah had not put him to death. Instead, the king had "entreated the favor of Yahweh" who changed his mind and did not destroy the city (26:17–19).[53] Remarkably, then, in analogous texts to ch. 38 Jeremiah is compared both to Micah and the Rabshakeh. This is the question confronting all the characters in the story and the reader: Is Jeremiah a Micah or a Rabshakeh?

In ch. 38, of course, there are no counter-arguments or witnesses in Jeremiah's behalf. One indeed may wonder about the absence of the "elders of the land"—had they relinquished their support of Jeremiah? If they had been present, would it have influenced Zedekiah's decision? Further, the city was saved in Hezekiah's day because he turned to Yahweh, as the elders recollected. Jeremiah's message

48.   See Bovati, *Re-Establishing Justice*, 188, where he discusses impartiality. See also Moshe Weinfeld, *Social Justice in Ancient Israel and the Ancient Near East* (Jerusalem: Magnes, 1995), 45–56, on justice as the specific responsibility of the king.

49.   Bovati (*Re-Establishing Justice*, 337–38) explains that not allowing the accused to speak is a denial of their rights and equality before the law.

50.   Bovati, *Re-Establishing Justice*, 340–42.

51.   Jeremiah's reticence is reminiscent of Jesus at his trial in the Gospels, which fits with the Christian tradition of seeing parallels between the two figures.

52.   Bovati, *Re-Establishing Justice*, 236.

53.   Here the elders quote the direct speech of Micah, much as the narrator had quoted Jeremiah's direct speech (vv. 2–3). The notion of God changing his mind lends additional support to Zedekiah's decision not to capitulate. Maybe God would again reverse his thinking.

in 38:3, however, does not permit this possibility. The utter hopelessness and futility of any action on Zedekiah's or the people's part is underscored by comparison to Hezekiah's plight in which hope for salvation still existed (cf. also Jeremiah's message to Jehoiakim in 26:13).

In ch. 26 Jeremiah is "not given into the hands of the people to be put to death," unlike Zedekiah who declared, "Here; he is in your hands." Perhaps Jeremiah's defense in ch. 26 sheds light on the officials' ambivalent treatment of Jeremiah in 38:6: they did not want his blood on their hands (26:15). Furthermore, ch. 26 reports the fate of the prophet Uriah, who was is in fact killed with the sword by King Jehoiakim (26:20–23). Uriah's fate provides an obvious contrast to Jeremiah's fate not only in ch. 26, where Jeremiah is exonerated, but also to his fate in 38:1–6 where he is relegated to the pit (not killed).[54] Indeed, Jeremiah, unlike Jerusalem, still has a chance to survive.[55]

In sum, the comparison to Jeremiah's trial in ch. 26 serves to illuminate the distinctive features of 38:1–6. It also enlightens the previous two episodes by revealing the missing elements in Jeremiah's "trial" before the officials (37:15–16) and how his plea not to be sent back to prison (37:18–20) functions as a formal (and successful) appeal. Ebed-melech's actions in the next scene can also be interpreted as legal intercession on behalf of the indicted prophet.

Turning to another intertextual matter altogether, Jeremiah's being thrown into the pit is reminiscent of Joseph and Daniel.[56] Closer examination of these three stories uncovers some interesting parallels not previously noted. The stories of Daniel are set during the Babylonian exile and may possibly have been circulating concurrently with the stories of Jeremiah (although they are typically dated later). It has also been argued that the Joseph stories are an exilic or post-exilic wisdom tale.[57] It is therefore possible—though not requisite for the observations made here—that the stories of Jeremiah, Daniel, and Joseph were formed at roughly the same time.

The stories of Daniel and Joseph contain structural similarities which they also share with the stories of Jeremiah in 37:1–40:6.[58] All three narratives have the following general pattern:

---

54. The image of Jeremiah in a pit may also echo Pss 69 and 88 and other similar Psalms of lament. Psalm 88 may be particularly significant because it twice mentions being put in the pit (בור) and it is one of the few lament Psalms that does not conclude with an assurance of deliverance. The laments of the "falsely accused" may tie in as well.

55. One may recall that in ch. 36 the officials "threw" (שלך) the scroll into the fire, thus destroying the word of Yahweh, whereas the officials only "throw" (שלך) Jeremiah into a pit, allowing the personified word of Yahweh to survive.

56. Callaway ("Black Fire on White Fire," 178) cites *Midrash Lamentations Rabbah*, on Lam 3:52, as linking the three characters because all spoke the truth and were thrown into a pit to die.

57. Donald Redford, *A Study of the Biblical Story of Joseph (Gen 37–50)* (Leiden: Brill, 1970).

58. For analyses of the Joseph and Daniel stories, see John Collins, *The Apocalyptic Vision of the Book of Daniel* (Missoula, Mont.: Scholars Press, 1977), 49–54; and George W. Nickelsburg, *Resurrection, Immortality, and Eternal Life in Intertestamental Judaism* (Cambridge, Mass.: Harvard University Press, 1972), 48–58. The plot structure presented here is adapted from these studies. As Nickelsburg shows, it can also be found in Esther, Dan 3, Susanna, and the Story of Ahiqar.

1. The protagonists are in a comfortable condition: Joseph is his father's favorite son (Gen 37:3). Daniel is one of the three chief ministers and the king intends to appoint him over the whole kingdom (Dan 6:1–3). Jeremiah is free to come and go and the king seeks his intercession with Yahweh on behalf of the king and people (37:3–4).

2. Conflict arises as a result of some sort of scheming against the heroes: Joseph's brothers are jealous of him and plot to kill him (Gen 37:12–23). The other governors are apparently jealous of Daniel and convince Darius to decree a law that people could not pray to anyone except him, for they knew that Daniel would faithfully pray to his deity (Dan 6:4–15). Irijah arrests Jeremiah for attempted desertion of Jerusalem, although the prophet denied the allegation (37:13).

3. The protagonists are confined in a life-threatening location. Joseph's brothers throw him into a pit (Gen 37:24). Daniel is put into the lions' den (Dan 6:16). Jeremiah is beaten and held in Jonathan's prison (37:15–16).

4. The protagonists are released with some assistance from others: Reuben and Judah advise against killing Joseph (Reuben wants to rescue him), and so Joseph is sold to merchants (Gen 37:29–36). Daniel is miraculously preserved and removed from the den by the king who was intent on saving him (Dan 6:19–23). Jeremiah is summoned by the king who decides not to send him back to the life-threatening prison (37:21).

5. Conflict arises a second time (for Joseph and Jeremiah[59]) due to further plotting against the protagonists: Potiphar's wife accuses Joseph of attempted rape (Gen 39:1–19). The officials accuse Jeremiah of weakening morale in Jerusalem and seeking evil for the people (38:4).

6. The protagonists are again confined: Joseph is put in prison (Gen 38:20). Jeremiah is thrown into a cistern (38:6).

7. The protagonists are released with assistance from others and the king. The butler remembers Joseph's ability to interpret dreams and Pharaoh summons him from prison (Gen 41:9–13). Ebed-melech hears of the officials' actions and receives the king's authority to remove the prophet from the pit (38:7–13).

8. The protagonists meet with the king and foretell what will happen: Joseph interprets Pharaoh's dreams about the coming prosperity and famine (Gen 41:14–36). Jeremiah counsels Zedekiah (38:14–28) regarding the imminent destruction.

9. The opponents are punished: Those who had accused Daniel are thrown into the lions' den (Dan 6:24). Those who did not surrender to the Babylonians are killed or taken into exile (39:1–9).

---

59. Both the Joseph and Jeremiah stories have a "double-V-shaped" plot. However, Jeremiah is first put into prison and then the pit, whereas Joseph is first put into the pit and then prison.

10.   The protagonists are vindicated and honored: Joseph is exalted to a position of honor in the kingdom and all must bow to him (Gen 41:37–45). Daniel "prospered" during the reigns of Darius and Cyrus (Dan 6:28). Jeremiah is cared for by the Babylonians and given food and a gift (39:11–14; 40:4–6).

11.   The foreign ruler proclaims Yahweh: the Pharaoh recognizes that the spirit of God is in Joseph and that God has revealed to him the dream (Gen 41:38–39). Darius decreed that all should fear and tremble before Yahweh (Dan 6:25–27). Nebuzaradan states that Yahweh had brought about the disaster (40:1–3).

In addition to this similar structure, other common themes and verbal connections can be identified. For instance, Jeremiah's question to Zedekiah, "What wrong have I done to you?" (37:18), parallels Daniel's statement to Darius, "Before you, king, I have done no wrong" (Dan 6:22), and Joseph's assertion to the butler, "I have done nothing that they should put me into the pit (בור)" (Gen 40:15). Further, the Joseph narrative describes the pit into which he is thrown: "The pit (בור) was empty; there was no water in it" (37:24). This mirrors the description of Jeremiah's pit: "There was no water in the pit (בור), but only mud" (38:6). The Midianite traders "drew out (משׁך) and lifted up (עלה) Joseph from the pit (בור)" (Gen 37:28), while Ebed-melech's men drew out (משׁך) Jeremiah with ropes and lifted him up (עלה) from the pit (בור).[60]

Of more significance are the broader comparisons that can be drawn among the three narratives, comparisons which complicate Jeremiah's portrayal. First is the nature of the accusations. Joseph and Daniel are incarcerated because of conspiracies against them. Joseph is wrongly thrown into the pit by his brothers and then later falsely accused of rape by Potiphar's wife. The charge against Daniel, praying to someone other than Darius, is technically true, but the whole scenario has been contrived by Daniel's peers who are jealous of his success. Daniel was not guilty of treason. The issue in the Joseph and Daniel stories is one of loyalty: Joseph had been faithful to his master Potiphar, and Daniel had been loyal to his superior Darius. By contrast, the officials' charge against Jeremiah—that his message was weakening morale in the city—is not portrayed as a conspiracy motivated by selfish ambition; furthermore, it is accurate. Jeremiah's intentions behind the message might be ambiguous, but at least from one perspective he is disloyal to his city and people. Notably, Jeremiah does not dispute the charge.

Second is the notion of divine intervention. God does not play a direct role in the story of Joseph, but as many commentators have observed, an important theme is Joseph's repeated assertion of divine providence. When Joseph reveals

---

60.   One may also observe that the Joseph story has been investigated according to the various house locations: Jacob's house, Potiphar's house, the house of prison, the house of Pharaoh, and the house of Joseph (Mary Mills, *Biblical Morality: Moral Perspectives in Old Testament Narrative* [Burlington, Vt.: Ashgate, 2001], 127–33). This is not unlike the events in Jer 37–38, which feature Jonathan's house-prison, the king's house, and Yahweh's house.

himself to his brothers, he claims three times that God had been orchestrating the events in his life (Gen 45:5–8) and at the end of the story Joseph again says that "God intended it for good" (50:20). Likewise Daniel professes that God shut the mouths of the lions (6:22). If Joseph and Daniel affirm that God was watching over them in their respective pits, Jeremiah says nothing about divine rescue. The deity is absent, not mentioned at all. In fact, in the scene in which Ebed-melech rescues Jeremiah, the prophet is conspicuously silent.

Third are the related motifs of food and salvation. Joseph preserves food to survive the famine in Egypt. By contrast, Jeremiah prophesies first that those in Jerusalem and then those in the Egyptian community would die by famine (44:27). If Joseph saves his people, his family, from the famine by bringing them to Egypt, Jeremiah dies (or at least disappears) with a God-forsaken community in Egypt for whom death by famine is prophesied. If this food theme is extended to Daniel and the reading of Daniel to ch. 1, it is revealed that Daniel requests permission not to eat the king's food. Jeremiah, by contrast, is given food by the Babylonians after the fall of Jerusalem (40:6). Jeremiah is "rewarded" with food from the foreign king, while Daniel is blessed for abstaining from the foreign king's food.

Fourthly, Joseph and Daniel (and Esther) are "Jews in the court of a foreign king" and accordingly they are vindicated/rewarded by a foreign monarch.[61] Jeremiah is a prophet in the court of a Judean king, yet he too is vindicated by a foreign king. Joseph and Daniel also submit to a large extent to their respective rulers. In this sense, they are collaborators as they hold high places in their governments. Given Jeremiah's connections with Joseph and Daniel, he too may be depicted as a collaborator with the Babylonians. Like Joseph and Daniel, Jeremiah is in a sense also a "Jew in the court of a foreign king," for, after all, Nebuchadrezzar is the real king and Zedekiah is only the "king" appointed by Nebuchadrezzar. Accordingly, Jeremiah is vindicated/rewarded by the foreign ruler. If Joseph (and Esther) successfully utilizes his position as a Jew in the court of the foreign king to save the people of Israel, Jeremiah, by contrast, is a failure and witnesses the destruction of his people at the hands of the foreign king. One could, indeed, brand Jeremiah as an anti-Joseph and anti-Daniel figure.[62]

---

61. See Lawrence Wills, *The Jew in the Court of the Foreign King: Ancient Jewish Court Legends* (Minneapolis: Fortress, 1990).

62. The books of Jeremiah and Daniel are connected by Daniel citing Jeremiah's word that the time of desolation will last seventy years (Jer 25:11, 12; 29:10), at the end of which Daniel prays for renewal (Dan 9). Here the connection between Joseph, Jeremiah, and Daniel takes on another dimension. Joseph was pulled out from his pit and taken to Egypt which eventually resulted in the exodus led by Moses. Jeremiah is rescued from his pit, but ends up going down to Egypt, symbolizing a reverse exodus (see below). Daniel, also saved from his pit, is the one who at the end of the seventy years calls Yahweh to restore Jerusalem—to bring about a second exodus. Daniel's prayer, in fact, specifically mentions the exodus from Egypt (Dan 9:15) in hopes of rousing Yahweh to restore his people.

Fifth Episode: 38:7–13

(7) Ebed-melech the Cushite, a eunuch[63] who was in the king's house, heard that they put Jeremiah in the pit. The king was sitting at the Benjamin gate. (8) So Ebed-melech went out from the king's house and spoke to the king saying, (9) "My lord king, these men have acted wickedly in all that they did to the prophet Jeremiah[64]; they threw him into the pit that he may die[65] of hunger, for there is no bread left in the city."[66] (10) Then the king commanded Ebed-melech the Cushite saying, "Take with you from here thirty[67] men and lift up the prophet Jeremiah from the pit before he dies. (11) So Ebed-melech took the men with him and went to the house of the king, under the store-room,[68] and he took from there worn out clothes and tattered rags and he sent them down to Jeremiah in the pit on ropes. (12) Ebed-melech the Cushite said to Jeremiah, "Put the worn out clothes and rags under your armpits beneath the ropes." Jeremiah did so. (13) Then they drew out Jeremiah with ropes and they lifted him up from the pit. And Jeremiah remained in the court of the guard.

Like the people in the city, Jeremiah finds himself trapped and in danger of death if he does not find a means to escape. There is again no temporal marker, so the reader is uncertain how long Jeremiah has been in the pit before Ebed-melech approaches the king concerning the officials' actions (scene one) and then rescues the prophet (scene two). Ebed-melech is the one character who appears in both scenes; thus he is the focus of this episode. Ebed-melech is identified as a Cushite three times (vv. 7, 10, 12), which underscores his foreigner status, as does the fact that he is the only named character (other than Jeremiah and Zedekiah) whose patronymic is not given.[69] He is also referred to ambiguously as a סריס, which could indicate either a eunuch or an official. Indeed, Ebed-melech's outsider status and the lack of clarity regarding his position are representative of the mystery that surrounds him, a character who plays such a crucial role in the narrative.[70] Is he a personal servant of the king? Is he an avid supporter of Jeremiah? Is he simply sent by other more powerful people who are proponents of the

---

63. The Greek does not represent the phrase איש סריס.

64. For the phrase "these men . . . the prophet Jeremiah," the Greek reads ἐπονηρεύσω ἃ ἐποίησας τοῦ ἀποκτεῖναι τὸν ἄνθρωπον τοῦτον ("you have done wrong in what you did, to kill this man"). It is noteworthy that even in the Greek, Ebed-melech leaves open the possibility that Jeremiah is already dead (see next note).

65. Most repoint the MT וְיָמׇת ("and he has died") to וְיָמֻת ("that he may die") or they attach to וְיָמֻת the sense ("and he will inevitably die"). Cf. McKane, *Jeremiah XXVI–LII*, 953.

66. It is possible to render the כי clause as a comment by the narrator, rather than as part of Ebed-melech's speech.

67. Most commentators (cf. also *BHS*) render "three" instead of "thirty," reasoning that "thirty men seems an excessive number for pulling Jeremiah out of a cistern (Holladay, *Jeremiah 2*, 954). But as McKane notes, "there is virtually no textual evidence to support (this) emendation" (*Jeremiah XXVI–LII*, 954).

68. The Greek reads τὴν ὑπόγαιον.

69. His is also one of the few names that does not have the theophoric element "Yahweh" in it (Mattan and Pashhur are the other two).

70. It is possible too that he is not even named if one takes עבד־מלך as "servant of the king" rather than a personal name.

prophet?[71] Ebed-melech's identity and portrayal are only one of a number of complex elements in this episode.

Setting

Zedekiah's location at the Benjamin gate functions as a symbolic space in the narrative, for earlier it was where Irijah arrested Jeremiah for attempted desertion of the city (37:13). Irijah and Ebed-melech mirror one another: Irijah detained the prophet at the gate and escorted him to a group of men (the officials) who imprisoned him. Ebed-melech met the king at the gate and then headed a group of men to rescue Jeremiah.

It is well known that in ancient Israel public affairs and trials were held at the gate; specifically, it is where the king would sit (יָשַׁב) in a judiciary role.[72] According to Bovati, the city gate was an appropriate location because "it was an area given over to public events" and "the comings and goings of the population made judgment open to intervention by any passer-by."[73] However, under the current circumstances—the Babylonian siege—there would be no normal "comings and goings" by the people. There may be, therefore, some irony in Zedekiah's holding court at the gate.[74] Additional irony may arise from the fact that a gate is also the location where one would "go out" (יָצָא, "surrender") to the enemy, as Jeremiah advised the people to do. Zedekiah, however, sits/remains (יָשַׁב) in the gate/city.[75]

Bovati also observes that "a trial 'at the gates' is the direct opposite of a secret procedure . . . or of private vendettas or summary executions."[76] Although the public nature of the setting may be somewhat compromised due to the inability of people to enter and exit freely, Zedekiah's position at the city gate generates a contrast with the previous trial scene which lacked the public setting and the subsequent scene in which Zedekiah and Jeremiah engage in a private meeting.[77] In light of the forensic context, one can interpret Ebed-melech's actions as intercession, seeking mercy on the prophet's behalf. Indeed, his "going out" (יָצָא) is a verb "which indicates the juridical initiative."[78]

The nature of Ebed-melech's intercession can be understood by contrasting it to a formal appeal which seeks justice, not mercy. Bovati explains that in

---

71. Cf. Brueggemann, *To Build, to Plant*, 148.

72. Bovati, *Re-Establishing Justice*, 230–31. The setting in 38:1–6 is never named, so perhaps the officials too had approached the king and charged Jeremiah at the Benjamin gate.

73. Bovati, *Re-Establishing Justice*, 230. Here Bovati cites E. A. Speiser, "'Coming' and 'Going' at the City Gate," *BASOR* 144 (1952): 20–23; and G. Evans, "'Coming' and 'Going' at the City Gate—A Discussion of Professor Speiser's Paper," *BASOR* 150 (1958): 28–33.

74. It also seems ironic that Zedekiah compromised his judicial authority with the phrase "I am not able to do anything against you," and then in the very next scene serves in a judicial capacity.

75. When the city is captured, the Babylonian officials sit (יָשַׁב) in the middle gate (39:3).

76. Bovati, *Re-Establishing Justice*, 230.

77. The public nature of the trial in 38:7–13 may also be suggested by Zedekiah's command to Ebed-melech to take "from here" (מִזֶּה) a group of men to rescue the prophet (i.e. others were present).

78. See Bovati, *Re-Establishing Justice*, 313.

the appeal process, "the *accused* weakling . . . denounces the lying . . . against him . . . [and] becomes the *accuser* of the accusers (and demands the condemnation of those who . . . had plotted the condemnation of the innocent)."[79] In the present scene, it is Ebed-melech, not Jeremiah himself, who approaches the king (unlike the third episode, 37:17–21). More notably, Ebed-melech does not denounce the "lying" of the accusers or demand their condemnation. He neither refutes the claims made by the accusers, nor maintains that Jeremiah has been wrongly charged. This concurs with the notion that Jeremiah's silence implicitly admitted his guilt. In this sense, the king truly, as he protested, was powerless to do anything but declare Jeremiah guilty. The paradox, however, from Ebed-melech's perspective is that while the accusation may have been correct, it did not warrant punishing the prophet, for he spoke the truth: Yahweh had willed evil/harm for the city, so the prudent course of action was surrender. Thus, Ebed-melech's intercession seeks mercy for the prophet.

Contextual Analysis

As in the previous episode, this one opens with the word וֹשמע, a structural feature which draws attention to its importance. The narrator's introduction had specifically said that the servants of the king did not heed the words of Yahweh spoken through Jeremiah. Yet here it is a "servant of the king" whose actions support Jeremiah. If in 38:1 the four officials "heard" the words of Jeremiah and approached the king, here Ebed-melech "heard" what the officials had done and he approaches the king. Like the officials, Ebed-melech "hears" and proceeds to the king, but paradoxically it was the officials, not Ebed-melech, who "heard"— but did not obey—the words of Jeremiah. If Ebed-melech listens to and obeys anyone in this episode, it is Zedekiah (vv. 10–11). This adds another element to the "listen/hear" vs. "obey" subtleties and nuances of שמע.

Several other words and phrases in this episode link it with earlier ones, thereby developing various themes. First, the narrative reports that the king was sitting (ישׁב) at the Benjamin gate when Ebed-melech went out (ויצא) from the king's house to speak with the king. The words ישׁב and ויצא recall Jeremiah's message in 38:2 that those who dwell (ישׁב) in the city would die, but those who go out (ויצא) would live. Here the same words are used with different meanings, and yet the different connotations echo one another. The king was "sitting" by the gate, for he had decided to "remain" in the city, while Ebed-melech performs the action that Jeremiah had urged the king to take, namely, "he went out (ויצא) from the house of the king."[80]

Second, Ebed-melech instructs Jeremiah to place the rags "under your armpits," literally, "under the joints of your hands (ידיך)." This creates a nice connection with the previous story where the officials had declared that Jeremiah was "weakening the hands (ידי)" of those remaining in Jerusalem (v. 4). Now in this episode it is the prophet's hands that are weak and in need of support. Jeremiah

---

79. Bovati, *Re-Establishing Justice*, 307–8.
80. This is the only time in chs. 37–38 that ישׁב means "to sit" rather than "to dwell" or "remain."

did receive the support, literally and figuratively, that he needed, whereas support was precisely what the prophet refuses to offer the people in the city (at least in the officials' view). Third, the prophet could survive due to the lack of water (אין־מים) in the pit, but because there was no bread (אין לחם) his life was in danger (according to Ebed-melech). Lack of water meant life; lack of bread meant death. Fourth, the officials had "sent" (שלח) Jeremiah down by ropes (v. 6); here Ebed-melech sends (שלח) the ropes down to Jeremiah. In this context, חבלים ("ropes") may play on its other meanings—"sorrow/pain" or "company/band." All three meanings seem appropriate here as the prophet's pain is relieved by a company of men who throw him a rope.[81] Finally, Ebed-melech is identified three times as a Cushite, which may mean that he was an "Egyptian." If so, then ironically Judah was hoping for aid from Egypt (37:7), which they did not receive, whereas Jeremiah (the person who declared that foreign help was useless) is the one who actually does acquire life-saving assistance from an Egyptian. As Alter observes, "strategically introduced specification"—in this case, the specification of a Cushite—has a great deal of "thematic functionality."[82]

Point of View

As in previous episodes, the narrator skillfully interweaves various points of view to create a complex scene. First, the circumstantial clause at the end of v. 7, "and the king was sitting (יושב, participle) at the Benjamin gate," shifts from the point of view of the narrator to Ebed-melech's perspective.[83] The narrator reports that Ebed-melech heard that the officials had "put" (נתן) Jeremiah into the pit. However, when speaking to the king, Ebed-melech claims that the officials "threw" (שלך) the prophet into the pit, thus subtly calling attention to his interpretation of events. The narrator's report of the officials' actions—saying that they "threw" Jeremiah and "let him down by ropes" (v. 6)—was ambiguous and left room for various perspectives on the event; here Ebed-melech voices his view. The reader, then, is alerted to the idea that Ebed-melech is presenting his perspective on the situation, which is important for the reader to recognize since it is through Ebed-melech's view that other aspects of the officials' actions are rendered and evaluated.

Ebed-melech respectfully addresses Zedekiah as "my lord king," adopting a humble position in relation to the king in the same manner as Jeremiah (37:20)—although it is notable that he approaches the king, as did the officials, without summons, unlike Jeremiah who is called to his interviews. Ebed-melech also names Jeremiah as a "prophet," which elevates Jeremiah's standing; neither the narrator nor anyone else, incidentally, has referred to Jeremiah as a prophet since the second episode (37:13). However, when Ebed-melech speaks directly to

81. Further, סחבות ("rags") is derived from the verb סחב, which means "to drag," which has obvious connotations here.

82. Alter, *World of Biblical Literature*, 105–6.

83. Cf. Berlin, *Poetics and Interpretation*, 63, for a discussion of how circumstantial clauses indicate a shift in point of view from the narrator to a specific character. She cites as examples 2 Sam 4:7; 13:8; Esth 7:8.

Jeremiah in the second scene (38:12), he does not employ any appellation of respect, and, in fact, does not even acknowledge Jeremiah by name.

Ebed-melech takes a clear stance regarding the officials, referring to them only as "these men" and accusing them of acting wickedly (רעע). He now objectifies and depersonalizes the officials, resembling their behavior toward Jeremiah when they charged "this man" with seeking evil (רעה) for the people. Both allegations incorporate the notion of wickedness/evil, but Ebed-melech's charge evaluates the official's external actions, while the officials target Jeremiah's internal attitude.[84] Ebed-melech calls additional attention to the officials' behavior with the phrase "in all they did to Jeremiah the prophet." Perhaps here he is intimating that the officials have committed acts against the prophet other than relegate him to the pit. If so, the reader is unaware of these actions. Alternatively, maybe it is a rhetorical strategy to remind the king that the officials had generally been hostile toward Jeremiah, as displayed by their earlier physical abuse (37:15). This ambiguity is illustrative of the dilemma in interpreting Ebed-melech's speech: how does one distinguish his rhetorical strategy from what he "really" thinks or knows (i.e. his "real" point of view)? This question becomes considerably more perplexing in light of text-critical and translational issues.

Most commentators repoint וַיָּמָת ("and he has died") to וְיָמָת ("that he may die"), but one could interpret the Masoretic pointing as part of Ebed-melech's strategy designed to stress the urgency of the situation; he informs Zedekiah that the prophet is dead, or at the point of death, in hopes of grabbing the king's attention. Support for this rendering may be found in Ebed-melech's last phrase, "for there is no bread left in the city." Here it seems likely that Ebed-melech is exaggerating the conditions in the city, manipulating the facts, in order to bolster his own agenda. Another conceivable interpretation, if one follows the MT reading, is that Ebed-melech is simply misinformed about both of these matters. He mistakenly thinks that Jeremiah is dead and that famine has overtaken the city.[85] After all, Ebed-melech had only "heard" what had happened to Jeremiah. On this reading, Ebed-melech knows less than the reader. If Ebed-melech thought Jeremiah was deceased, his objective for approaching the king would presumably be to point out the wickedness of the officials' actions and to call for their punishment, not to save Jeremiah (since that would be impossible). In short, if one follows the MT, there are several interpretive options regarding Ebed-melech's portrayal: he is aware of the situation but adopts a more drastic perspective for rhetorical purposes, or he is genuinely ignorant of the circumstances. Here point

---

84. It may be somewhat ironic that in Ebed-melech's view the officials have acted wickedly, for Zedekiah had authorized them to kill Jeremiah so their decision to put him in the cistern was quite mild in comparison to the alternative.

85. Since the narrator has not specifically stated that Jeremiah was still alive and that there was still food in the city, the first-time reader might not realize that Ebed-melech is incorrect until the story unfolds. This reading would also serve to heighten the drama—the first-time reader concludes that the officials have already killed Jeremiah as they proposed. Concerning the sustenance in the city, the story never mentions lack of food as a problem, and it is related in other places that the bread was not depleted before the end of the siege (cf. 52:6–7).

of view is closely associated with questions of knowledge—what does Ebed-melech know and how does he present it?

If one reads, as is common, the repointed MT, *"that he may die* under the presence of the famine,"[86] then Ebed-melech is attributing motivation to the officials' actions. Neither the narrator nor the officials explicated why they cast Jeremiah into the pit—hence the ambiguity of the action (noted above). Here Ebed-melech purports to know the reason: they sought to kill Jeremiah through starvation. In this way, the officials' point of view is voiced by Ebed-melech. As in other instances in which one character's perspective is refracted through the voice of another, here too uncertainty exists. In the previous scene it was the officials who assessed Jeremiah's motives (seeking evil for the city), and now Ebed-melech offers a perspective on their intentions. Just as readers may doubt the officials' assessment of Jeremiah, they may also question if Ebed-melech's attributed motivation is accurate.[87] Again, readers are drawn into the story as they are challenged to develop their own perspective both on the events and the motivations of the characters embroiled in this conflict.

Finally, concerning Ebed-melech's perspective, it is possible that, as a loyal courtier who had "heard" (שָׁמַע) of the officials actions against Jeremiah, he is compelled to inform the king, just as the officials were obligated to apprise the king when they "heard" (שָׁמַע) Jeremiah's seditious words (v. 4).[88] Based on Lasine's insights into the nature of knowledge, power, and loyalty, both Ebed-melech and the officials serve as faithful informants to the king. Lasine observes that "the courtiers must all shell, armor, wall, and mask themselves against one another in order to survive. The king must try to do so as well, but his exposed position in the center makes it difficult."[89] Zedekiah, it appears, is surrounded by loyal courtiers whose ideological views threaten to overtake him. Again, Lasine is instructive: "the very fact of the leader's being surrounded by servants suggests that he could become totally dominated, even as he is lauded for being totally dominant."[90] On one level this is precisely what is happening in episodes four and five: both the officials and Ebed-melech bring information to the king; by so doing they are endeavoring to mask one another in an effort to survive. Both groups implicitly "laud" the king by relating to him as the all powerful judge; yet the king's "exposed position at the center" makes it precarious for him to maneuver and threatens total dominance by his courtiers.

As for Zedekiah's perspective, he names Jeremiah as a prophet, as did Ebed-melech. The king did not expressly agree with the officials' charges against Jeremiah, and here he does not explicitly concur with Ebed-melech's evaluation

---

86. The phrase is awkward, but it seems apparent that hunger or starvation is the intended sense.

87. The possibility that Ebed-melech is misinformed about the status of bread in the city (rather than saying there was no bread for rhetorical effect) may add to the doubtfulness of Ebed-melech's perspective here.

88. It is not clear whether or not Zedekiah knew of Jeremiah's fate. Either way, Ebed-melech would still be required to inform the king.

89. Lasine, *Knowing Kings*, 7.

90. Lasine, *Knowing Kings*, 3.

of the officials' behavior. Zedekiah had delegated power to the officials by declaring that "he is in your hands" (v. 5); now he bestows authority to Ebed-melech by commanding him to take men "into his hands" and rescue Jeremiah. In both scenes the king leaves Jeremiah in the "hands" of others, appearing to be dominated by his loyal informants. While saving the prophet is a significant measure, the reader may be mystified as to why Zedekiah expresses no concern for providing additional assistance to Jeremiah.[91] As has been witnessed before, the king acts in an irresolute fashion. In the previous episode the officials voiced their perspective by bringing a charge against Jeremiah, with no alternative view presented (i.e. Jeremiah's); here Ebed-melech expresses his viewpoint and no alternative position is stated (i.e. that of the officials). With only one perspective presented in each case, Zedekiah acquiesces. Indeed, in all three instances in which the king expresses a thought about Jeremiah's fate—37:20, 38:5, and 38:10—there is a certain ambiguity in his response. In short, the reader may be able to decipher Zedekiah's view of Jeremiah's rescue; little else, however, about the king's perspective is revealed by his words or actions.[92]

Rhetoric
Two aspects of Ebed-melech's speech need to be mentioned. First, similar to Jeremiah in the third episode (37:17–21), Ebed-melech employs a rhetorically indirect approach when conversing with Zedekiah. His strategy is not to make an assertion and then support it with rationales (as the officials had done, 38:4), but rather to leave the situation open-ended, placing all the authority in the king's hands. Although Ebed-melech initiates the meeting with the king and declares that the officials acted wickedly, he offers no plan of action for punishing the officials or saving Jeremiah. Ebed-melech does not recommend that Jeremiah be pulled from the pit. This was the king's initiative (much as it was the king's idea, not Jeremiah's, to put Jeremiah in the court of the guard, 37:21). Thus, Ebed-melech's intercession in Jeremiah's behalf—not unlike Jeremiah's own appeal (37:20)—is somewhat cautious, placing the onus of any decision solely on Zedekiah. As a result of this approach, Ebed-melech's motivations remain unclear.[93]

Secondly, while Ebed-melech may be understood as an effective rhetorician—subtly persuading the king to rescue the prophet, if that was his objective—it must be noted that it is difficult to follow his argument, mainly because of the last phrase, "for there is no bread left in the city." If earlier Zedekiah had promised to feed Jeremiah until all the food in the city was consumed (37:21), here

91. Note that the command is not where to place Jeremiah, but from where he is to be removed. This contrasts with 37:21 where Zedekiah commanded (צוה) that Jeremiah was to be placed in the court of the guard and that he be given bread daily.

92. If Zedekiah was aware of Jeremiah's circumstances, then the very fact that Ebed-melech must come to the prophet's aid exposes something of the king's views.

93. While some commentators point out that the motivation for Ebed-melech's actions remains nebulous (cf. Carroll), it is not recognized just how opaque even his words are. He expresses no explicit desire to help Jeremiah or to punish the officials. Ebed-melech does not make a "powerful plea on behalf of the beleaguered prophet," as Brueggemann asserts (*To Build, to Plant*, 149).

Ebed-melech informs him of the prophet's lack of food, but the logic evidences little sense. If there were no food in the city, the prophet would be in danger of starving, regardless if he was in the cistern or not.[94] Also, if there were no bread in Jerusalem, it is odd to argue as Ebed-melech does that the officials would try to starve Jeremiah by confining him in a pit. Likewise, removing Jeremiah from the pit would not stave off his hunger.[95] This כִּי clause referring to the lack of bread is all the more unusual given the forensic context in which one anticipates Ebed-melech to employ a כִּי clause to declare that the officials have wrongly accused Jeremiah (i.e. they have acted wickedly because Jeremiah is innocent).[96] This peculiar line of argumentation must be taken into account when considering Ebed-melech's portrayal. Perhaps, for instance, he is to be seen as a simple, energetic courtier who could not be expected to speak logically and coherently.[97] Maybe Ebed-melech's assertion is an exaggeration—there was only a shortage of bread and a prisoner would be the first one to be denied food. Whatever the case, the nature of this speech elicits as many questions about his portrayal as it answers.

The Plot: The Second Scene

Zedekiah commands Ebed-melech to gather thirty men and go rescue the prophet. Perhaps thirty men were needed for protection since they may have encountered opposition from the officials. If the king were powerless against the officials, perhaps thirty men would be more formidable. This scenario may imply that Zedekiah was committed to extricating the prophet regardless of the commotion that it might cause. The king's drastic and resolute action in this scene stands somewhat in contrast with other elements of his depiction.

After Ebed-melech meets with Zedekiah, he returns to the king's house to acquire provisions for the rescue operation. Here the narrator focuses the reader's attention on Ebed-melech by supplying the details of his actions, which slows down the narrative. Ebed-melech creatively fulfills his duties; he acts on his own initiative and takes center stage as he determines the manner in which the prophet will be extricated. He is now the one who is free to come (בּוֹא, v. 11) and go (יָצָא, v. 8), while Jeremiah is stuck in the pit. When he reaches the pit, Ebed-melech instructs the prophet to put the rags between his flesh and the ropes, presumably to reduce Jeremiah's pain. Apparently Jeremiah has "sunk in the mud" in the

---

94.   Thus some regard the phrase as a mistaken gloss (Bright, *Jeremiah*, 237) or an addition from 37:21 (*BHS*).

95.   Cf. Carroll, *Jeremiah: A Commentary*, 682.

96.   This phrase represents, in Riffaterre's terms, an "ungrammaticality."

97.   This would be similar to Bar-Efrat's analysis of 2 Sam 18:29 where Ahimaz offers an awkward and disjointed response to David's question regarding Absalom's condition—that is, the nature of Ahimaz's speech reflects his emotion (*Narrative Art in the Bible*, 64–69). This image of Ebed-melech, however, may be hard to square with his reasoned and practical action in the actual rescue of Jeremiah. However, perhaps even taking the time to be sure that the prophet was not hurt by the ropes is illogical, for a little discomfort or a minor injury would seem trivial if the situation were as dire as he painted it.

cistern (v. 6) which necessitates a degree of force to free him. By detailing Ebed-melech's rescue, the narrator gives the reader a sense of Jeremiah's conditions in the pit without actually describing them; one becomes aware of the additional discomfort the prophet would experience if he were hoisted up by the ropes alone. The narrator, then, focuses the reader's attention both on Ebed-melech's concern and Jeremiah's suffering. It is an oddly intimate moment between the two.

The narrative reports that in response to Ebed-melech's commands, "Jeremiah did so."[98] This is the only scene in the ten episodes in which only one party speaks, in which there is no dialogue; this, too, highlights the narrator's focus on Ebed-melech's words and actions. Here a servant of the king enjoins (imperative) the prophet, and he complies. Rather than Jeremiah counseling the king and others on how to save their lives, he is now the one instructed on how to save his own life. If the prophet's vocal message had landed him in the cistern; now he silently obeys the words of a servant of the king in order to live.

After the narrator's extended focus on Ebed-melech and the vivid details of the dramatic rescue, the abbreviated conclusion indicating that Jeremiah "remained in the court of the guard" seems anticlimactic. Jeremiah inauspiciously resumes the place that he was before being thrown into the pit. Given the events that have just occurred, the reader now knows that the court of the guard is not a safe haven for the prophet—arrest and mistreatment by the officials remain possibilities. The king's previous concession to transfer Jeremiah from Jonathan's prison to the court of the guard proved to be of little value for Jeremiah, if it did not place him in greater danger. Despite the meticulous care taken by Ebed-melech to rescue Jeremiah, the prophet's return to the court of the guard strikes an ominous chord. It may also be ironic since it is not even a "return," for the cistern was located in the court of the guard (v. 6). Whether one reads the story in a linear or circular fashion, Jeremiah's rescue from the cistern is hardly evidence of a "charmed existence."[99] Although not the central theme in this scene, the prophet suffers at the hands of the officials. The focus, moreover, on Ebed-melech is all the more interesting considering the ambiguity surrounding his identity, perspective, objectives, and motivations.

Intertextuality

The account of Jeremiah's rescue from the pit is reminiscent of other texts in which a prophet is saved or delivered from those intending to harm him. There are two other such instances within the book of Jeremiah. In ch. 26, which has

---

98. This phrase "and X did so" is often used in response to a command by Yahweh or to a human figure in a position of authority. Cf. Gen 42:20; 45:21 (Joseph's brothers in response to Joseph and the Pharaoh); Exod 7:10, 20; 8:17; 14:4 (Moses and Aaron in response to Yahweh); Exod 16:17; Num 5:4 (children of Israel in response to Yahweh); Exod 17:6; Num 17:11 (Moses in response to Yahweh); Num 8:3 (Aaron in response to Yahweh); Josh 4:8; 10:23 (children of Israel in response to Joshua); Josh 5:15 (Joshua in response to the captain of the army of Yahweh); Judg 6:20 (Gideon in response to the angel of Yahweh); 2 Sam 5:25 (David in response to Yahweh); 1 Kgs 14:4 (Jeroboam's wife in response to Jeroboam); Ezek 12:7 (Ezekiel in response to Yahweh).

99. Carroll (*Jeremiah: A Commentary*, 680) twice uses this phrase to describe Jeremiah's rescue.

already been echoed, the narrative reports that "the hand of Ahikam son of Shaphan was with Jeremiah, so that he was not given into the hands of the people to be put to death."[100] Similarly, in ch. 36, after Jehoiakim heard Jeremiah's scroll, the king ordered that the prophet and Baruch be arrested. Their capture, however, is foiled because "Yahweh hid Jeremiah." In contrast to these two references, in the present episode it is not Yahweh or the Shaphan family who comes to Jeremiah's aid. Rather it is an unknown foreigner. On the one hand, this might stimulate thought as to why Yahweh or others who previously had supported and protected Jeremiah did not assist him this time. On the other hand, it may suggest that the circle of Jeremiah's allies was increasing, with Ebed-melech representing a third party to intervene. Still, Yahweh had vowed to protect Jeremiah from the officials (1:18–19), yet it is Ebed-melech who, without any reference to or mention of Yahweh, saves Jeremiah.[101] As Brueggemann observes, "The rescue of the prophet is no act of direct divine intrusion, but a determined, detailed human act."[102] Of course, human agency does not preclude divine agency. In fact, the text here may be inviting the reader to contemplate the issue of agency, for although it is Ebed-melech who rescues the prophet, Zedekiah is the power (the agent) behind the operation. This is a unique scenario in Hebrew Bible narrative; there are no other instances in which the words or actions of an Israelite or Judean king save the life of a prophet (excluding the third episode). Ebed-melech performs the rescue, but the agent behind him is the king. Does the agency stop there, or is Yahweh the agent behind the king?

This episode also echoes stories in the DH, namely, Elijah's encounter with Obadiah in 1 Kgs 18.[103] First, the names Obadiah ("servant of Yahweh") and Ebed-melech ("servant of the king") are similar. Both stories are set during a time of hardship, and both figures play a similar role as an overseer of the king's house. After introducing Obadiah, the narrative relates that he "feared Yahweh greatly" and as evidence states that "when Jezebel was killing prophets of Yahweh, Obadiah took one hundred prophets and hid them fifty to a cave, and provided them with bread and water" (1 Kgs 18:3). The actions of Obadiah and

---

100.   Migsch notes structural and stylistic connections between chs. 26 and 38; for example, he points to the verbal similarities between 38:7 and 26:10 and between 38:1 and 26:7 (*Gottes Wort*, 222–24).

101.   Jon Berquist ("Prophetic Legitimation in Jeremiah," *VT* 39 [1989]: 129–39 [132, 137, 138]) shows how "prophetic legitimation" in the book of Jeremiah is closely connected to the prophet's relationship with Yahweh which manifests itself in the promise that Jeremiah "will confront and overcome opposition," that "Yahweh will support Jeremiah's message and rescue him from his enemies" and that "Jeremiah will be vindicated." The stories in Jer 37–40, at the very least, complicate Jeremiah's legitimation since his divine support and rescue and his vindication are dubious.

102.   Brueggemann, *To Build, to Plant*, 149. Brueggemann makes this statement in passing and does not consider its implications. He does see Yahweh's hand at work behind the episodes (hence his use of the word "direct"). Although this is by no means evident from the text, one should observe that on this reading Yahweh is employing quite unlikely agents—the king and a foreigner to save Jeremiah, and the Babylonians to execute judgment on the people.

103.   Carroll (*Jeremiah: A Commentary*, 682) mentions Obadiah in comparison with Ebed-melech but does not pursue it.

Ebed-melech are thematically linked. Obadiah gathered the prophets and hid them underground in order to save them; Ebed-melech lifted up the prophet from his underground confinement to rescue him. Obadiah fed the prophets bread and water to sustain them; Ebed-melech was concerned that Jeremiah would not survive without necessary provisions (i.e. the bread of 37:21). Obadiah—one man—saved a large group of prophets (one hundred); Ebed-melech assembled a large group of men (thirty) to save one man. Obadiah's rescue of the prophets is prompted by his fear of Yahweh, which is stated explicitly (1 Kgs 18:3). In contrast, Ebed-melech is etched as enigmatic figure, his motivations and objectives mysterious. Later in the story, however (39:15–18; see below), the reader discovers that Ebed-melech trusted in Yahweh, so one might make the assumption that, like Obadiah, this is what motivated him to rescue the prophet. These connections with the story of Obadiah foster insight into the portrayal of Ebed-melech, or at least fodder for further reflection.

One other story can enter the conversation at his point—the account of Moses' birth. As has been well documented, Moses and Jeremiah relate to one another in a variety of ways, so it may be appropriate to perceive an additional link here. Moses had been hidden in a basket in the Nile in order to save him from Pharaoh's edict to kill all the Israelite baby boys; he is soon rescued from the Nile by Pharaoh's daughter. As the prophet Moses was "drawn out" (מֹשֶׁה) from the water by a foreigner and saved from impending death, so the prophet Jeremiah is drawn out (מֹשֶׁךְ) from his watery grave by a foreigner.

Sixth Episode: 38:14–28

(14) King Zedekiah sent for and received the prophet Jeremiah at the third entrance of Yahweh's house. The king said to Jeremiah, "I am asking a word from you. Do not hide anything from me." (15) Jeremiah said to Zedekiah, "If I tell you, you will put me to death, will you not? And if I counsel you, you will not listen to me." (16) Then King Zedekiah swore an oath in secret[104] to Jeremiah saying, "As Yahweh lives, who made for us this life, I will not put you to death or give you into the hand of those men who are seeking your life."

(17) Jeremiah said to Zedekiah, "Thus says Yahweh, the God of hosts, the God of Israel: If you will only surrender to the officials of the king of Babylon, then your life will be spared, and this city will not be burned with fire, and you and your house will live. (18) But if you do not surrender to the officials of the king of Babylon, then this city will be handed over to the Babylonians, and they will burn it with fire, and you yourself will not escape from their hand." (19) King Zedekiah said to Jeremiah, "I am worried about the Judeans who have deserted to the Chaldeans, for they might give me into their hands and they would abuse me." (20) Then Jeremiah said, "They will not hand you over. Listen to the voice of Yahweh that I am speaking to you and it will go well with you and you will save your life. (21) But if you refuse to surrender, this is the word which Yahweh has shown to me: See, all the women remaining in the house of the king of Judah are being led out to the officials of the king of Babylon, and they are saying, 'They seduced you and have overcome you—your trusted friends. Your feet were sunk

---

104. The word בסתר is not represented by the Greek.

in the mud[105] and they turned away from you.' (23) They are leading out all your women and your children to the Babylonians, and you yourself will not escape from their hand, for you will be seized by the hand of the king Babylon, and you will burn[106] this city with fire."

(24) Then Zedekiah said to Jeremiah, "Do not let anyone know of these words or you will die. (25) If the officials should hear that I have spoken with you, and they should come and say to you, 'Tell us what you said to the king; do not hide anything from us and we will not put you to death. What did the king say to you?' (26) Then you will say to them, 'I was presenting my plea to the king not to send me back to the house of Jonathan to die there.'" (27) All the officials came to Jeremiah and they asked him, and he told them according to all these words which the king had commanded him. So they stopped asking him because the matter had not been heard. (28) And Jeremiah remained in the court of the guard until the day that Jerusalem was captured.[107]

In this final episode before the fall of Jerusalem, Zedekiah consults Jeremiah for a third time—the second time directly. There is again no temporal marker indicating a relationship between this episode and the previous one, but neither is there anything that prevents one from reading in a linear mode. This episode clearly features thematic parallels with the previous private encounter between the king and the prophet (37:17–21), yet it is much lengthier and more complex. Unlike the dialogues in all the other episodes, both parties speak several different times. This conversation reveals some important new information and contains a number of ironic elements. The well-crafted features in these two scenes paint a complex image of king and prophet as they struggle to negotiate the complicated and tragic circumstances in Jerusalem on the eve of the city's fall.

Setting
The meeting between the king and the prophet occurs at the third entrance of Yahweh's house. This location is unknown and it is unclear why it would be an appropriate place for a clandestine meeting, especially compared to the king's house where their previous encounter took place.[108] Perhaps the king could no longer expect privacy in his palace, or he may have reckoned the temple to be an unsuspecting place. In a sense, the location of the meeting and its significance is kept "secret" from the reader, at least modern readers. Unlike the third episode in which the meeting itself was not secret, but only the contents, here the exact meaning of the king swearing his oath "in secret" is vague. The nature of the secrecy is held in abeyance until the second scene, and even then some ambiguity remains: does the conversation itself need to be kept secret, as v. 24 seems to suggest, or only its contents, as v. 25 implies? Either way, the secret nature of the meeting is concealed from the reader until the close of the episode.

---

105.   Some suggest repointing the passive hophal הָטְבְּעוּ to a hiphil הִטְבִּיעוּ, making "your feet" the object instead of the subject (cf. McKane, *Jeremiah XXVI–LII*, 960).

106.   Following the Greek, *BHS* suggests repointing תִּשְׂרֹף to תִּשָּׂרֵף ("this city will be burned").

107.   This rendering omits the second part of v. 28, "and it happened when Jerusalem was captured." The Greek does not represent this phrase; many transpose it to 39:3.

108.   Bright suggests that it may have been the king's private entrance, leading directly from the palace (*Jeremiah*, 231).

Point of View
Zedekiah again voluntarily summons the prophet for a personal meeting. He apparently remains open to the prophetic word.[109] An important question is whose view Zedekiah is seeking and whose view Jeremiah is presenting—Jeremiah's view or Yahweh's (cf. above for similar issues in the first and third episodes). In their previous interview, Zedekiah had sought a word from the deity: "Is there a word (דבר) from Yahweh?" (37:17). In this second interview, by contrast, Zedekiah is soliciting Jeremiah's counsel ("I am asking a word from you"). The prophet responds accordingly, as is demonstrated by his response, "If I tell you (נגד). . . . And if I counsel you (יעץ), you will not listen to me." Neither נגד nor יעץ is a verb associated with giving an oracle, that is, speaking for the deity; and in fact, יעץ is specifically distinguished from rendering an oracle.[110] Thus, Jeremiah confirms that he will articulate his own view—his own advice—not Yahweh's. This is consistent with the fact that Jeremiah subsequently advises the king as to what specific action to take, rather than simply announcing the current or impending circumstances, as in an oracle (cf. 37:7–10, 17). It is also in accord with Jeremiah saying "you will not listen to me"—rather than "you will not listen to Yahweh." Jeremiah, then, is not playing the role of a prophet, but of a counselor—reminiscent of their earlier meeting in which he had played primarily the role of a petitioner (making a formal appeal), not a prophet.

After Zedekiah swears an oath promising to protect Jeremiah (see below), the prophet utters a long message prefaced with the messenger formula.[111] In view of Jeremiah's claim to offer advice, it is incongruous that now he delivers a word in the name of Yahweh. This is particularly striking because in their previous meeting when Zedekiah asked if there was a word from Yahweh, Jeremiah's response did not begin with the messenger formula. In the present scene the prophet mixes speech roles—that of prophet and counselor.[112] Furthermore, not only does Jeremiah render an unsolicited oracle, as he had in the first episode (37:7–10), but he also does not allow Zedekiah time to ask his question. The king's inquiry, an insight into his perspective, remains unknown, as has been the case in previous scenes. It is the prophet who again (cf. 37:3, 6–7) fails to listen to the king's

---

109.   All of the direct discourse relates to the characters' point of view; this section of the study will only examine the places where issues of point of view are especially prominent. The other features of the dialogue will be analyzed in the following section.

110.   The term יעץ appears frequently in the stories involving Ahithopel and Hushai (2 Sam 15–17) and in the account of the division of the kingdom where both Jeroboam and Rehoboam receive counsel (1 Kgs 12). In none of these instances does the counsel claim to be the word of Yahweh and in 2 Sam 16:23 the counsel of Ahithopel is said to be "as if one consulted the word of God." This distinguishes the two activities. Notably, in the stories in 1 Samuel and in Jeremiah the king is faced with conflicting counsel and must decide which to follow.

111.   Naming Yahweh as "God of hosts" conjures images of Yahweh as a warrior and the "God of Israel" reminds one of the covenant. Has the deity broken the covenant by leading an army against the city (cf. 21:3–7)?

112.   This presumes that one can distinguish between a prophet speaking for himself (giving counsel) and speaking for Yahweh (giving an oracle). The counsel may be based on the oracle(s), but they remain two separate speech genres.

point of view, rather than vice versa, which is of consequence in light of the narrator's introductory statement (37:2).

Zedekiah does not resist the prophet's oracle. Rather, his response implies that he accepts it or at least has considered its merits (see below). The king states, "I am worried (רָאֵג)[113] about the Judeans who have deserted to the Babylonians, for they might give me into their hands and they would abuse me." If Jeremiah and the reader presumed to know Zedekiah's one (unasked) question ("what is the word of Yahweh?"), then Jeremiah's oracle is not surprising. Now, however, Zedekiah's real concern emerges: "how will the Judeans who have already surrendered treat me if I now surrender?" Zedekiah begins to unravel the implications of following Jeremiah's advice. The king, as Brueggemann observes, is "enormously candid, now treating the prophet as his confidant and ally."[114] Although Zedekiah is "politically incapable of doing what he knows to be theologically correct,"[115] it is crucial to see that he does seem to understand what is "theologically correct"—at least in Jeremiah's view—even if the lateness of the hour and the messiness of his predicament make it nearly impossible to act upon that knowledge.

The importance of this expression of Zedekiah's view cannot be overestimated, especially since the narrative has presented his perspective sparingly. This is one of the rare cases in biblical narrative where the character knows more than the reader.[116] Zedekiah now reveals why he is hesitant to follow Jeremiah's/ Yahweh's advice and surrender: he is apprehensive that he will be mistreated by those Judeans who have already deserted to the Babylonians. Readers now have knowledge of Zedekiah's perspective; they know what he knows. Apparently, all along he has been stymied by this fear of the Judeans. If Zedekiah had earlier given Jeremiah into the "hands" of the officials, that is, other Judeans, now it is Zedekiah who fears being given into the "hands" of his countrymen. The king was reluctant to face the kind of abuse that Jeremiah himself had endured for advocating surrender.[117]

This revelation sheds light on Zedekiah's challenging situation. Not only must he take into consideration the competing views of the officials and Jeremiah, but he must also evaluate the perspectives of the Judeans who have deserted to the Babylonians. Zedekiah's statement anticipates their stance: they will be hostile to

---

113.   The word רָאֵג occurs only six other times in the Hebrew Bible (1 Sam 9:5; 10:2; Ps 38:18; Isa 57:11; Jer 17:8; 42:16). It occurs twice in the stories of Saul and his lost donkeys where Saul's father stops thinking about the donkeys and worries (רָאֵג) instead about Saul. Similarly in the present episode, Zedekiah has apparently stopped worrying about the Babylonians and how they might treat him and has turned his concerns to the Judean deserters.

114.   Brueggemann, *Jeremiah*, 367.

115.   Brueggemann, *Jeremiah*, 367. Brueggemann, however, does not press the implications of this observation.

116.   Most of the time the character knows less than the reader. The stories of Samson and Jonah are two other examples where the character has knowledge that the reader is lacking. Cf. Berlin, *Poetics and Interpretation*, 54–55; Sternberg, *The Poetics of Biblical Narrative*, 311–20.

117.   Likewise, Gedaliah will later have more to fear from those in Judea than he does from the Babylonian forces.

the king. Apparently his concern is that those Judeans would be upset with the king for resisting so long, for betraying them by not submitting to the Babylonians sooner in order to spare them and the city from the difficulties of the siege. If Jeremiah was abused for betraying the city, the king is now fearful of being abused by those who feel betrayed by him, namely those who have surrendered. Of course, regardless of what action Zedekiah took—surrender or not—he would inevitably alienate one group of people.

In addition to it being too late to surrender and avoid deleterious consequences, it is also too late to eschew the anger of his own people (at least according to his assessment). Ironically, if he surrenders, Zedekiah is afraid of retaliation from those who have surrendered, not from those who do not advocate surrendering. It is indeed remarkable that Zedekiah expresses no concern about the Judeans who did not support a policy of surrender, namely, the officials (perhaps because this group would not be in a powerful position after the fall). They and their perspective remain a factor in the equation, but they are not the primary ones about which Zedekiah is worried.

Finally, if one renders the verb actively ("they will hand me over") rather than passively and assumes that the subject is the Babylonians, then the viewpoint of the Babylonians becomes a fourth element in the equation (in addition to the ones expressed by the officials, Jeremiah, and those who deserted). Zedekiah anticipates that they would hand him over to the Judeans, even if he were to surrender. According to the familiar adages, Zedekiah is stuck between a rock and hard place; he is damned if he does and damned if he doesn't; he is in a no-win situation.

Jeremiah's reply to Zedekiah encourages the king to "listen to/obey the voice of Yahweh that I am speaking to you." This is a unique phrase within the Hebrew Bible and raises the question whether Jeremiah is claiming to speak for the deity (the voice of Yahweh) or for himself (that I am speaking to you). Is Jeremiah now counseling (יָעַץ) the king and accordingly importuning the king to listen to him (v. 15), or is he still speaking as a prophet as in vv. 17–18 and thus voicing the deity's view? A prophet, of course, can give counsel, but it is essential to know for whom he is speaking. The lack of the oracle formula in v. 20 contrasts noticeably with v. 17 which could imply that Jeremiah is speaking for himself (i.e. giving counsel). A similar ambiguity occurs in v. 21 with the phrase, "this is the word that Yahweh has shown to me." Again, Jeremiah makes reference to Yahweh without claiming to deliver the words/view of the deity. It may be a "vision" from Yahweh, but it is reported to the king in Jeremiah's words.

If vv. 17–18 are the words of Yahweh and vv. 20–23 are Jeremiah's, then the prophet takes a different rhetorical approach with the king; for unlike Yahweh's words which are equally divided between the results of surrendering and not surrendering, Jeremiah expounds at length on the negative consequences of failing to capitulate. Perhaps this depicts the prophet as less sympathetic than Yahweh, especially since the vision graphically outlines the fate of the king's wives and children.[118] Maybe Jeremiah is simply stressing the urgency of the situation.

---

118. Cf. Willis, "'They Did Not Listen to the Voice of the Lord,'" 72–73.

In short, as in the first episode, there is a blurring between the words and per-spective of Yahweh and Jeremiah, which accords with the observations about Jeremiah's various speech roles.

The הוה at the beginning of the vision (v. 21) serves to focus Zedekiah's attention on what follows. In the vision Jeremiah quotes the direct speech of the women. This is a different kind of quoted direct speech since it occurs in a vision; thus it is not verifiable or unverifiable.[119] Nonetheless, by this strategy Jeremiah expresses the view of the women as they "are being led out." To add to the complexity, the women's speech addresses the intentions of the king's "trusted friends," namely, that they have "seduced" (סות) him. Thus, the view of the king's friends is filtered through the perspective of the women, which is voiced by Jeremiah. This constructs a complex, multi-layered expression of points of view.

Zedekiah does not respond to Jeremiah's elaborate message; he does not reveal his point of view. Jeremiah has warned him, through the words of the women, that his trusted friends are leading him to disaster. Has Zedekiah interpreted this as a legitimate reason to doubt his officials? Is the king seriously contemplating Jeremiah's recommendation to surrender? Perhaps the king's silence insinuates that he has accepted the prophet's message. Again, neither the reader nor the other characters know the king's thoughts, which means that all the possibilities must remain open. Since the narrator does not provide Zedekiah's response, the reader must fill it in. This technique invites readers into the narrative—calling them to reflect on how they would react to Jeremiah's message. Interacting with the story in this fashion may lead some to see in themselves their own indecision upon hearing the prophet's word.

In the final segment of the conversation, Zedekiah quotes the hypothetical direct speech of others, namely, the officials (v. 25). If Jeremiah has a vision of what will occur and who will say what in the future, Zedekiah also has a premo-nition regarding future speech and actions. The king's speech represents yet another type of quoted direct speech. This juxtaposition of two similar yet differ-ent and unusual kinds of quoted direct speech enriches the narrative. Specifically, Zedekiah voices the perspective of the officials by anticipating what they will want to know. If at the beginning of this episode the king's perspective was muffled as he was not permitted to ask his question, here the king is allowed to pose a question, but it is only as he quotes the officials' inquiry ("What did the king say to you?", v. 25).

Zedekiah then instructs Jeremiah on what to say to the officials should they question him (v. 26). Just as Jeremiah answered before hearing Zedekiah's ques-tion, now the king provides Jeremiah with the answer to an unvoiced inquiry. Here Zedekiah effectively conveys to Jeremiah what perspective he is to adopt. The king anticipates and expresses both the point of view of the officials and of Jeremiah. Zedekiah, then, responds to the quoted direct speech in Jeremiah's

---

119.   Savran mentions but does not discuss this type of quoted direct speech (*Telling and Retelling*, 19–25).

vision with his own version of future quoted direct speech. According to the quoted direct speech of the women, Zedekiah would be deceived by his "trusted men"; now the king, through his own quoted direct speech, attempts to deceive his "trusted friends."

In the final scene (vv. 27–28), events play out as Zedekiah had foreseen. It is ironic that Zedekiah, whose view has been largely suppressed throughout the story, voices the final direct speech in this episode; his speech is a quotation of the future direct speech of Jeremiah (v. 26). Thus, in the last scene before the fall of the city, the prophet voices the words of the king (v. 27) as if it were his own perspective (see below).

Rhetoric

The themes of secrecy, knowledge, loyalty, and power are developed in multiple ways in this scene. While it becomes obvious at the end of their conversation that the king intends to keep matters private, his initial words express concern that Jeremiah will keep secrets from him ("Do not hide anything from me," v. 14). Jeremiah's response evinces fear that the king will kill him if he reveals all he knows. If the king does not trust Jeremiah to reveal a full answer, Jeremiah does not trust the king's response. The situation is tense as both characters are suspicious of one another's intentions or motivations. Jeremiah's fear that the king will kill him ostensibly arises from 38:1–6 where Zedekiah pronounced him guilty and handed him over to the officials to execute the death sentence.[120] However, Jeremiah's anxieties also contain a hint of irony because the reader and Zedekiah know that it was Zedekiah who preserved the prophet's life via Ebed-melech. Thus, on the one hand, given Jeremiah's sufferings, his apparent fear of death at the king's hands adds pathos to his portrayal. On the other hand, Jeremiah's hesitation to engage in conversation with Zedekiah depicts the prophet as "not excessively courageous,"[121] an element of his characterization that surfaces in the second scene as well.

Zedekiah's response plays on rhetorical expectations. The king swears an oath not to put the prophet to death (v. 16). As Lasine observes, "this is a variation of the normal loyalty oath, in which subjects swear to report all information to the king," with the threat of death if they do not comply.[122] So instead of the expected, "if you do not tell, you will die," here it is, "if you tell, you will not die." This reversal of the norm is accented in light of the fact that "diviners are obligated to inform the king or risk punishment."[123] That is, the king is entitled to

---

120. Seitz (*Theology in Conflict*, 262) and other redaction-oriented commentators see this reference as incompatible with other images of the king in this narrative and thus from a different source.

121. Brueggemann, *To Build, to Plant*, 151. Similarly, Calvin (*Commentaries on the Book* 4:403) maintains that by seeking protection first, Jeremiah "seems here to have acted not very discreetly; for when he ought of his own accord to have announced to the king the destruction of the city, he then made no good progress, since he now fails, as it were, in this hazardous act of this vocation, and dares not to expose himself to danger."

122. Lasine, *Knowing Kings*, 91.

123. Lasine, *Knowing Kings*, 44.

be apprised of everything—and Jeremiah would be obligated to tell. It is also a salient variation from the norm in two other ways: it is the king, not a subject of the king, who makes the oath[124]—pointing to a kind of role reversal—and it is made in private instead of in public in the presence of witnesses.[125]

Further, although Zedekiah did not want Jeremiah to hide anything from him, the king hides, keeps secret, his oath. While the oath itself promises to protect Jeremiah from those who seek his life (i.e. the officials), the king is reluctant for them even to be aware of the oath. The king insures that the oath remains a secret by instructing Jeremiah not to disclose their discussion to anyone; if he does, he will die (v. 24).[126] Thus, in order for the secret oath to be valid, it must be kept a secret.

The motifs of secrecy, trust, loyalty, and betrayal are further developed by the rhetoric at the close of the conversation. Here Zedekiah explains that he expects the officials to approach Jeremiah and command him not to "hide" (כחד) any-thing from them, agreeing not to put him to death if he complies, that is, if he is loyal to them by sharing information with them. The conversation began with the king issuing an imperative to Jeremiah ("Do not hide anything from me," v. 14) and now it ends with Zedekiah explaining to Jeremiah what to do if confronted by the officials ("you will say to them"). The second instruction, however, requires the very act that the first one had prohibited, namely, concealing the word. Here Jeremiah is to "hide" the word by dispensing misinformation to the officials ("I was asking not to be sent back to Jonathan's prison," v. 26). The officials are recipients of bad information, but as long as they are unaware of this, the prophet is safe. Although the officials have been skeptical of the prophet's motives and intentions, here strangely it seems, they accept his word at face value. Thus, the prophet is loyal to the king by not sharing information with the officials, whom he betrays by relaying fictitious data.

Zedekiah demands that nothing be "hidden" from him, but that everything be "hidden" from the officials. The king swore his oath in secret, and now he upholds that oath by keeping secret from the officials the contents of the interview. The prophet, on the one hand, feared death if he spoke openly with the king; now the prophet is threatened with death if he speaks openly with the officials. Likewise, if Jeremiah "made known" (נגד) to the king, he felt his life would be threatened (v. 15); if he did not "make known" (נגד) to the officials (v. 25), his life would be threatened by them. As Lasine observes, "with both the king and courtiers, sharing secret information is presented as a way for the informer to avoid being killed."[127] The prophet is caught in a tricky game of hiding and revealing, deceiving and truth-telling.

---

124. Cf. Lasine, *Knowing Kings*, 91.

125.   Cf. McKane, *Jeremiah XXVI–LII*, 956.

126. It is not entirely clear if Zedekiah is personally threatening Jeremiah with death, or if the king is stating that death will likely result if others know about the meeting; the latter seems to be the better option.

127. Lasine, *Knowing Kings*, 91.

One would generally expect the officials to control the king by concealing information from him, but in this case, the king withholds information from his officials in order to control them.[128] In this way, Jeremiah and Zedekiah create their own intimate community united by their secret. The king and prophet are faithful to each other, while the officials are left outside. As Lasine writes, "one can tell who is loyal to whom—who trusts whom—and who loves whom—by noting who shares information with whom."[129] The form of Zedekiah's oath may reflect this intimate bond between king and prophet. The phrase "who made for us this life" (אֲשֶׁר עָשָׂה־לָנוּ אֶת־הַנֶּפֶשׁ הַזֹּאת) deviates from the standard oath formula, and thus attention is called to it. Zedekiah's strategy here seems to be to build solidarity between the king and the prophet by use of the first-person plural ("us").[130] It may also suggest that Yahweh is somehow responsible for or involved in the very difficult circumstances that both he and Jeremiah face, which serves to unite them in their efforts.

The reader, too, of course, is an insider sharing the secret knowledge of what was spoken during the conversation; the officials are the only ones excluded. King and prophet, then, protect one another. As Carroll observes, "Jeremiah is protected by the king by protecting the king from the princes."[131] This raises another question, however: Why is it necessary to protect the king from the officials? Has he been persuaded by Jeremiah so that he now stands in opposition to his officials? Both Jeremiah and the reader are ignorant of Zedekiah's motivations for secrecy and of the benefit he himself will derive from Jeremiah's fabrication.[132] The king keeps some secrets all to himself.

In sum, if "secrecy lies at the very core of power,"[133] and if "it's the secrecy that grants the power, the content of the knowledge,"[134] then Zedekiah exhibits his power over the officials by withholding information from them. The king is engaged in the game of information management that monarchs continually play in order to survive, and in this instance, he is successful because the officials remain uninformed and thus controlled by the king. While most have commentated on Zedekiah as a "fearful, furtive king,"[135] who is so weak that he must keep secret the interview from his officials, Lasine calls attention to the power that lies behind such actions. Here the paradoxical nature of the king emerges—his simultaneous vulnerability, which his own speech highlights (v. 19), and his strength

128. Cf. Lasine, *Knowing Kings*, 91.

129. Lasine, *Knowing Kings*, 48.

130. McKane (*Jeremiah XXVI–LII*, 956–57) mentions the possibility that נֶפֶשׁ does not have its usual sense of "life," but rather has the nuance "who has fashioned for us the human feeling which we have." In swearing his oath to Jeremiah, Zedekiah expresses awareness of the emotional stress weighing on the prophet.

131. Carroll, *Jeremiah: A Commentary*, 689.

132. It is surprising how many commentators simply assume that Zedekiah is interested only in protecting himself, although he says nothing about his own security.

133. Elias Canetti, *Crowds and Power* (New York: Continuum, 1981), 290–92 (cited in Lasine, *Knowing Kings*, 42).

134. Lasine, *Knowing Kings*, 175.

135. McKane, *Jeremiah XXVI–LII*, 966.

and sagacity to manage the flow of information. Zedekiah, indeed, is both weak and powerful. Furthermore, the fact that Zedekiah colludes with Jeremiah and neutralizes the officials—rather than joining with the officials and leaving Jeremiah out of the loop—suggests that the king has accepted the prophet's word. Ultimately, he has "listened to" the prophetic word, but since surrendering at this time is not a viable option, the king is unable to "obey" it. It is remarkable that the king succumbs to Jeremiah's treasonous word and even employs his power of information management to protect him.[136]

Turning now to Jeremiah's rhetoric in vv. 17–18, it is requisite to consider exactly what Jeremiah is saying to Zedekiah. Here the prophet offers a long, conditional oracle outlining the results of surrendering and not surrendering to the "officials" (שׂרים) of Babylon—which plays on the notion of the king submitting to his own "officials." This oracle is unlike Jeremiah's unconditional message to the king in 37:8–10, and it serves to heighten the drama of the narrative since it holds forth the opportunity for the king to save the city from utter ruin. Scholars have long observed Jeremiah's oscillation between absolute and conditional messages. In this instance, however, one may wonder why Jeremiah chooses this particular time to deliver a conditional oracle. Diamond also observes this and writes:

> The contrast between alternatives offered the king in this episode and the earlier categorical predictions of disaster is surprising. Why does not the narrator have Jeremiah offer alternatives from the beginning? The prophet's bargaining with oracles in the context of personal threat with the clear motive of securing his own safety raises a troublesome possibility for the reader. The specter is raised of persecution subverting the integrity of oracular speech. Is the prophet trading away his authenticity, exploiting oracular powers for reasons of personal security?[137]

Diamond's observations and questions are right on target. He argues, however, that the narrator "shields the prophet from such a conclusion" because Zedekiah's guaranteeing the prophet's safety (v. 16) is "a sign of his readiness to hear the word," and thus "the prophet's prior oracles become revisable." This is a peculiar, and weak, argument. It is an excellent example of how arduously commentators work to protect Jeremiah's image. Quite simply, Zedekiah's voluntarily sending emissaries to consult Jeremiah in the first episode (37:3–10) and his voluntarily summoning Jeremiah from prison in the third episode (37:17–21) unequivocally demonstrate his "readiness to hear the word." Yet in those instances Jeremiah gave an unconditional message of destruction. Therefore, Jeremiah's conditional message cannot be attributed to Zedekiah's new-found "readiness to hear the word." If Diamond's reasons for dismissing the notion that

---

136. Others have examined the ambiguity of Zedekiah's portrayal from a redaction-critical perspective. See Hermann-Josef Stipp, "Zedekiah in the Book of Jeremiah: On the Formation of Biblical Character," *CBQ* 58 (1996): 627–48. He claims that the "inconsistent" depiction of Zedekiah is due to four different redactional layers which reflect the writers themselves and their communities more than the character of Zedekiah. Cf. also John Applegate, "The Fate of Zedekiah: Redactional Debate in the Book of Jeremiah," *VT* 48 (1998): 137–60.

137. Diamond, "Portraying Prophecy," 110.

Jeremiah "bargained with oracles" are insufficient, then the "troublesome possibility" concerning the prophet's image remains.[138] In fact, one commentator concludes that Jeremiah "clearly uses the bartering power he has by his access to the
divine word."[139]

What, then, is the divine word that Jeremiah presents? The contents of the
oracle in vv. 17–18 can de illustrated as follows:

> If you will only surrender to the officials of the king of Babylon,
>   (a) then your life will be spared,
>   (b) and this city will not be burned with fire,
>   (c) and you and your house will live.
> But if you do not surrender to the officials of the king of Babylon,
>   (a') then this city will be handed over to the Babylonians,
>   (b') and they will burn it with fire,
>   (c') and you yourself will not escape from their hand.

The content of the two protases (the "if" clauses) is almost perfectly parallel,[140]
but the contents of the three apodoses are not. The most obvious of these occurs
in the first clause of the apodoses. If the king surrenders, the king's life will be
spared (a); if he does not surrender, the city will be handed over to the Babylonians (a'). The first (a) addresses the fate of the king and the second (a') the fate of
the city. Further, the phrases "your life will be spared" (a) and "you and your
house will live" (c) are a tautology. Placing them in two different clauses, however, makes it appear that there are more benefits than are actually stated. If two
of the three results of surrendering are synonymous, two of the three results of
not surrendering are included in the very act of surrendering. The city being
given to the Babylonians (a') and Zedekiah not escaping from their hands (c') are
seemingly meaningless, for the act of surrendering entails giving the city (a') and
oneself (c') over to the enemy. Surrendering and not surrendering yield the same
results. This leaves the middle apodoses of the oracle (b and b') in which it is
clear that if the king surrendered, the city would not be burned; but if he did not,
it would be torched. This appears to be the only genuinely conditional element in
the oracle. Remarkably, it was one aspect of Jeremiah's warning that was not
fulfilled, as the city was not burned despite the fact that Zedekiah did not surrender (see below).[141]

---

138. If Jeremiah knew that Zedekiah had sanctioned his removal from the pit, then perhaps the
king had summoned Jeremiah hoping that he would return the favor with a positive oracle.

139. J. Gerald Janzen, "Withholding the Word," in *Traditions in Transformation: Turning Points
in Biblical Faith* (ed. B. Halpern and J. D. Levenson; Winona Lake, Ind.: Eisenbrauns, 1981), 97–114
(101).

140. The only difference is that Jeremiah uses an infinitive absolute, "if you surely/only surrender," in v. 17 and a simple verb, "if you do not surrender," in v. 18.

141. In v. 17, the first and third clauses have an active verb and both have the word חיה, while
the second clause has a passive construction. In v. 18, the first and third clauses have a niphal verb
and both have the word יד, while the second clause has an active construction. Both middle clauses
have the words שׂרף and אשׁ drawing attention to their parallelism. The first and third clauses of v. 17
are connected by the idea that surrendering brings life (חיה), while the first and third clause of v. 18
declare that not surrendering culminates in being handed over (יד) to the Babylonians.

Jeremiah assures the king that if he yields, he will at least survive and the city will not be burned.[142] One may conclude, therefore, that Zedekiah feared that even if he surrendered, he might be killed and the city burned. Zedekiah, however, does not expressly state this concern; it must be deduced from Jeremiah's words. This interpretation is substantiated by Zedekiah's response in v. 19 which says in essence, "Yes, I am afraid of dying if I surrender, but not at the hands of the Babylonians, but rather at the hands of the Judeans who have already surrendered."

Jeremiah does not offer Zedekiah and Jerusalem salvation from the Babylonians upon surrender; he promises only that the city would not be utterly destroyed by fire and that the king would live, which are not trivial assurances, to be sure.[143] In fact, Jeremiah has repeated the seditious oracle of 38:2–3, but this time directed it to the king, rather than to the people. Now the king too can save his own life, but the city will still be given to the Babylonians. The reader, then, may be sympathetic toward Zedekiah's hesitation to surrender, for at this point in the siege it is too late to capitulate. Presumably this notion is precisely what prompted Jeremiah to be cautious in his promises about the outcome of surrendering. As Carroll writes, "the king's surrender would hardly have made good his breach of trust against Nebuchadrezzar in the first place"[144] and accordingly, "it is doubtful that any action on the part of Zedekiah would divert the wrath of the Babylonians."[145] Therefore, Zedekiah's decision to wait and hope that Yahweh would intervene and save the city is reasonable and understandable. After all, Yahweh had intervened in similar circumstances during the time of Hezekiah, and, moreover, Jehoiachin had surrendered to the Babylonians some ten years earlier, and still the temple had been looted and thousands exiled to Babylon (2 Kgs 24:8–17). Undoubtedly, surrendering "is not a proper option open to him [Zedekiah]."[146] Thus, for Zedekiah, obedience to the prophetic oracle is not a feasible choice at this time, and the prophet certainly does not guarantee that it will bring salvation. Zedekiah's and Jerusalem's fate is all but sealed.[147]

142. He does not proclaim, however, that the king will die if he does not surrender.

143. Zedekiah had only promised that Jeremiah would not be killed; now the prophet too is equally reserved in his promises regarding Zedekiah's future. Both king and prophet are promised their lives and little else.

144. Carroll, *Jeremiah: A Commentary*, 685.

145. Keown, Smothers, and Scalise, *Jeremiah 26–52*, 225.

146. Carroll, *Jeremiah: A Commentary*, 686. It is surprising how few interpreters observe the futility of surrendering at this stage of the siege and, likewise, how many assume that Jeremiah still offers the king a good deal of hope. Even Carroll seems to be convinced by Jeremiah's rhetoric, for he claims that Jeremiah makes "unrealistic assurances," and, similarly, Keown, Smothers, and Scalise label the scenario depicted by Jeremiah as "a bit optimistic" (*Jeremiah 26–52*, 226). Jeremiah's rhetoric, however, is not unrealistic or overly optimistic. One may imagine that Jeremiah's desire was to make it appear as though his oracle extended such assurances to the king if he surrendered. One could argue that the oracle implies hope, but that is exactly the point: it is only implied and not stated. The structural nature of the oracle invites (or entices) one to conclude that the city would be rescued, but the prophet never issues such an assurance.

147. These observations explain some (not all!) of the tensions between Jeremiah's conditional and unconditional message to Zedekiah (i.e. even the conditional message offers little expectation).

If at the beginning of this conversation Jeremiah required assurance from the king before he spoke (v. 15), now the king requires assurance from Jeremiah before he can act. This he receives from the prophet in v. 20 as Jeremiah attempts to allay the king's fears by focusing on the actions of the Babylonians, rather than those of the Judeans. The prophet does not declare, "The Judeans will not abuse you." Rather, he assures the king that the Babylonians will not relinquish him into the hands of the Judeans.[148] It is unclear whether Jeremiah "knows" this or if the statement is meant mainly to motivate Zedekiah to surrender. If the prophet does "know" what actions the Babylonians will take, one may wonder if he has collaborated with them, as his treatment after the fall may suggest. In any case, if the king promised Jeremiah that he would not commit (נתן) him to the Judeans (i.e. the officials, v. 16), now Jeremiah promises the king that the Babylonians would not hand him over (נתן) to the Judeans.

While this assurance is conceivably realistic, Jeremiah's rhetoric takes a bold turn when he apprises the king that it would go well (יטב) with him if he surrendered. Here the prophet does border on offering some sort of "unrealistic assurance." In light of the discussion above, this could be interpreted, on the one hand, as a compromise on Jeremiah's part—he yields and offers true salvation.[149] On the other hand, his words are nondescript and pertain to the king specifically, which the three second-person singular suffixes in v. 20 highlight. Unlike the oracles in vv. 17–18, there is no explicit mention of the fate of the city, which is appropriate since the king had expressed fear over his own personal safety if he were to surrender. The possibility of reading Jeremiah's words as a compromise of his stance injects a sense of irony insofar as Jeremiah may be exercising his "bartering power" to secure his own safety by means of promising Zedekiah personal well-being.

Jeremiah's focus on the fate of the king continues in vv. 22–23. Unlike the much shorter two results of surrendering (it going well for the king and his surviving) the consequences of not surrendering are spelled out at length. They are recounted in the form of a "vision" (דבר) of the royal women being led off to Babylon, lamenting and taunting the king as they go. The women declare that the king's "trusted friends" have "seduced" and "overcome" him and have "turned away" from him as he is stuck in the mud. The women's words cleverly redirect the king's fear from the Judeans who had deserted (v. 19) to the "trusted friends" —whoever that might designate—who represent the greatest threat.[150]

---

148. Zedekiah, ironically perhaps, will later suffer abuse at the hands of the Babylonians, not the Judeans.

149. One can raise an objection to Brueggemann's assertion that although "the prophet gives considerable attention to his own well-being and safety . . . he does not do so . . . in a way that compromises anything of his subversive political opinion" (*Jeremiah*, 361). The notion that it would "go well" with the king does seem to discredit Jeremiah's hard-line, unconditional message of defeat (37:8–10; 38:3).

150. Could Jeremiah ironically be among the "trusted friends" since, after all, he is the one in whom the king is confiding?

The introduction of female characters and the words of the women serve as effective rhetorical tools. In a world where honor, which is by definition "public," is an extremely valuable commodity, the king would be publicly shamed by the words of the women, the possibility of which would be a powerful incentive to avoid such a circumstance. Humiliation by the women would compound the loss of honor that he would suffer at the hands of the Babylonians. It would "rub salt into Zedekiah's wounds."[151] In addition, the words of the women's song are significant. Women typically became possessions of the conquering king (cf. 2 Sam 16:21–22) and would likely be subject to abuse. Their assertion that Zedekiah has been "seduced" and "overcome" have connotations of sexual violence. The women's song functions as both a lament and a taunt—a lament for their own terrible fate and a taunt of Zedekiah, insinuating that he has been abused by his "men of peace." Both the king and the women will lose their honor through sexual violence—literal for the women, metaphorical for Zedekiah.

Jeremiah returns to his own voice in v. 23 in which he outlines further the consequences of not surrendering. These consequences, however, seem to be included in the act of surrendering—a feature that was also observed concerning the oracle in vv. 17–18. Specifically in this instance, Zedekiah's surrendering would involve three of the four results of not surrendering: (1) his wives and children will be led out to the Babylonians,[152] (2) he himself will not escape, and (3) he will be seized by the king of Babylon. The fourth consequence—that the city would be burned[153]—was the one substantive thing that Zedekiah could avoid by surrendering (cf. vv. 17–18). In the vision in vv. 22–23 the ambiguity of the word יצא is evident. If Zedekiah surrendered (יצא) he would be surrendering his whole family; if he chose not to surrender, his women and children would still be led out (יצא) to the Babylonians. If either action (surrendering or holding out) had the same result, one wonders why Zedekiah would be persuaded to surrender instead of hoping for divine rescue. There is no salvation even if he were to surrender. Capitulating would lead only to another, perhaps more tolerable kind of captivity, namely, in Babylon rather than the besieged Jerusalem—much like Jeremiah had twice been transferred from one life-threatening confinement (Jonathan's prison and the pit) to another (the court of the guard). The lives of prophet and king mirror one another in their limited choices and freedom.

---

151. McKane, *Jeremiah XXVI–LII*, 959.

152. Although most commentators render it passively, the active plural participle, מוצאים ("they are leading out"), is noteworthy. While its subject is not stated, grammatically the "trusted friends" (men of peace) are the logical referent and thus they are the ones who are leading out the women and children. Abrego mentions the active translation as a possibility, but does not consider its implications (*Jeremías y el Final del Reino*, 77). The direct object marker ואת at the beginning of v. 23 links it with the previous verse, which points to an active translation. The active reading also forms a symmetrical structure with two verbs (deceive and overcome) preceding the subject (the men of peace) and two verbs (turn back and lead out) after it.

153. The verb תשרף is active, "you (Zedekiah) will burn this city with fire," although most translate passively, "this city will be burned with fire." The active translation has a more powerful effect rhetorically, for it unequivocally places the responsibility for the city's destruction on Zedekiah.

In response to the prophet's message, Zedekiah changes the subject (v. 24). If initially Jeremiah was the one who counseled (יעץ) Zedekiah, the roles are reversed at the end of the conversation as Zedekiah advises the prophet. The answer that Jeremiah is instructed to give to the officials—I was presenting my plea to the king not to send me back to the house of Jonathan to die there (v. 26) —is quite perplexing. Two things, however, are evident. First, it thematically connects this meeting with their earlier one (37:17–21) and, second, it is a deceptive statement. At best, the reply was a half-truth because in their first encounter the prophet had in fact petitioned not to be returned to Jonathan's prison. The king, then, does not instruct the prophet not to talk to the officials, but rather to dispense inaccurate information. Interestingly, the previous conversation between Jeremiah and Zedekiah had transpired in "secret" (37:17), but now the contents of that conversation are revealed in order to hide the contents of the current meeting. It is ironic that in order to avoid death, Jeremiah must inform the officials that he was pleading with the king not to put him to death in Jonathan's prison. Further, Jeremiah's scripted answer may have been designed to help the king gain favor with the officials, for it would appear as though the king was pondering eliminating the prophet by death in Jonathan's prison (or at least handing him back over to the officials). The narrative, however, provides only sufficient detail to speculate on what lay behind the words that the king orders Jeremiah to speak.

Zedekiah's rhetorical approach can be further elucidated by observing that Jeremiah's scripted answer does not address what the king had related to him. In fact, in the king's quotation of the officials' words (v. 25), their threat to kill Jeremiah regards only the words that the prophet spoke to the king, not what the king said to the prophet. Although Zedekiah anticipated that the officials would at least inquire about his words, Jeremiah's answer does not address this issue. The prophet's response suggests that the king did not say anything (at least anything significant) because the meeting was about Jeremiah's desire not to be sent back to Jonathan's prison. The ramification is that the officials would not be apprised of the king's fear of those who had deserted. The reader is left to speculate on how the officials would have reacted to that information. In comparison to Jeremiah, Zedekiah had not spoken much during the interview (vv. 14–23), but at its conclusion he has much to say about what supposedly was said.[154]

Contextual Analysis

This interview scene reshapes themes and motifs from the first meeting (37:17–21). In both instances Zedekiah sends for (שלח) and takes (לקח) Jeremiah,[155] initiates the conversation with a question (שאל), or at least a statement that he is

---

154. There may be some irony in that by answering the officials with the words that the king had given him, Jeremiah actually tells the officials what the king had said; that is, since the instructions to prevaricate were literally the king's words, Jeremiah's response is at least part of what Zedekiah had said in their conversation.

155. Verse 38:14 reports that Zedekiah "took Jeremiah the prophet to himself (אליו)," which may suggest a more personal, intimate meeting.

going to pose a question, and there is an element of "secrecy." The nature of their conversation in the third episode may explain, in part, Zedekiah's demand that Jeremiah not conceal any information in this interview. There Jeremiah offered only a brief five-word reply in response to Zedekiah's question—before launching into a forty-three word defense of his behavior—which may have left the king thinking that there was more to be discerned. Jeremiah, however, uses a similar tactic in the present episode. In reply to Zedekiah's command not to withhold anything from him, Jeremiah turns the focus of the conversation to matters regarding his own personal well-being.

The contents of Jeremiah's vision (v. 22) develop earlier images. If previously Jeremiah declared that even the wounded Babylonians "who remained" (נשארו) would defeat Jerusalem, now he says that the "women who remain (נשארו)" will come out taunting the king. In both instances, a remnant brings humiliation on the king. The image of "sinking in the mud" is reminiscent of 38:6 where Jeremiah literally sank in mud in the pit.[156] Here the king figuratively does so. The image of the king with shaky footing may reflect his constant wavering between various views. If Jeremiah had been rescued from the mud by his "friends" (vv. 7–13), the king's friends turn their back on him when he is stuck in the mud.[157] What is more, in his judicial role Zedekiah had declared Jeremiah guilty and said that he was powerless (יכל) against the officials (v. 5). Now if the king does not surrender, the women, as "from a judicial throne,"[158] proclaim that his trusted men—perhaps the officials—have in fact overpowered (יכל) him. This rhetoric suggests, perhaps, that Jeremiah is eager to see Zedekiah suffer as he had—which would be particularly interesting since Zedekiah's fear was that he would be abused by Judeans as Jeremiah had been (v. 19). Is there an element of revenge against Zedekiah in Jeremiah's vision?

Zedekiah's claim that he feared the Judeans who had deserted is crucial for understanding the complexities of the plot as it relates to the narrator's evaluative point of view (37:2). Quite simply, the king's statement introduces the reader to another group of people who apparently have considerable clout—those who have listened to Jeremiah and decided to surrender.[159] This stands in obvious

---

156. The word for "sink" (טבע) is the same in both places, although the word for "mud" differs. The word for mud in v. 22, בץ, is a *hapax*. Of course, many have pointed out this connection between the two texts. This palpable link serves as an invitation to look for more subtle ones.

157. The trusted friends—literally "men of peace"—may be more specifically identified because the narrative has associated two groups with peace. The officials object to Jeremiah's message because it does not seek "peace" for the people (v. 4); and the prophets who opposed Jeremiah claimed that the Babylonians would not come against Zedekiah and Jerusalem, that is, there would be peace for the city (37:19). One is reminded that previously Jeremiah had asked the king where these prophets were; now that question takes on an added dimension, for according to the words of the women in the vision, they have deserted the king.

158. Calvin, *Commentaries on the Book* 4:413.

159. According to Lohfink ("Die Gattung der 'Historischen Kurzgeschichte,'" 335) this group, which probably included Gedaliah, was organized and powerful and prepared to take control once the Babylonians took over. Further, Siegfried Hermann writes that v. 19 indicates that "there were, in the midst of the people, upright individuals, personalities of high rank, who allowed themselves to be

tension with the narrator's assertion that no one listened to Jeremiah. It also creates deep irony in the story, for the king refuses to surrender because of potential problems not from those opposed to surrender, but from those who have already capitulated. Paradoxically, then, the success of Jeremiah's message was preventing the king from surrendering. The king did not listen to/obey Jeremiah's words because of the many people who had. Indeed, Zedekiah's world is uniquely challenging, the complexities and pathos of which the narrator's introductory statement does not capture. As the story of the final days of Jerusalem comes to a close, the narrative's ironies and subtleties evoke in the reader sympathy for all characters involved in the city's tragic end.

The Plot: The Second Scene
In the second scene the narrator does not present the conversation between Jeremiah and the officials; instead this discussion is reported (v. 27). The king has correctly anticipated the words and actions of the officials. Zedekiah's ability to control the prophet and the officials stands in ironic tension with his inability or unwillingness to control other matters, namely, the city's fate. Put differently, the king's passivity, as witnessed in certain aspects of the previous two episodes, contrasts with his active control in this final scene before the fall of Jerusalem. Similarly, he is bold and strong enough to aid Jeremiah, but too weak or stymied to follow Jeremiah's guidance (even if it did not promise much). The king is a paradox.

Jeremiah and Zedekiah cooperate, forming their own community of secrets to hold the officials at bay. While this scenario may generally reflect well on the king who is now collaborating with the prophet of Yahweh, it may have the reverse effect on Jeremiah precisely because he is a prophet of Yahweh. The question that arises is whether Jeremiah has compromised his commitment to and community with Yahweh by joining with Zedekiah. If loyalty and fidelity mandate reporting fully and accurately what others ask you to report, then is the prophet exhibiting faithfulness to Zedekiah instead of Yahweh when he misleads the officials? Is Jeremiah being a spokesperson for the human king Zedekiah instead of the divine king Yahweh? Several ironic features of this final scene seem to suggest this. The most obvious one is that this episode concludes with Jeremiah speaking Zedekiah's words, not Yahweh's. If the prophet began by claiming to speak for Yahweh (vv. 17, 20), he ends by declaring the words of Zedekiah. The king had commanded Jeremiah not to let anyone know of "these words" (v. 24); so the prophet obediently tells the officials "these words" (v. 27) that the king had instructed him to say.[160] The grammar of the text underscores this: "and he told them according to all these words which the king had

---

influenced by the prophetic word, who 'became afraid,' who protected Jeremiah, and who justified the authenticity of his prophetic speech on the basis of tradition referring back to the century old message of the Judean prophet Micah" ("Overcoming the Israelite Crisis," in *A Prophet to the Nations* [ed. L. Perdue and B. Kovacs; Winona Lake, Ind.: Eisenbrauns, 1984], 299–311 [310]).

160. Each time in these stories that the king makes a command (צוה) the instructions are followed and each time it is to Jeremiah's benefit (37:21; 38:10).

commanded him."[161] The prophet is not "the voice of the Lord (יהוה)," as he had professed earlier (v. 20); rather he announces the words of his lord (אדני), as he had previously referred to Zedekiah (37:20). Jeremiah's depiction, too, is paradoxical. At times he is confident and pro-active; at others he is passive and apprehensive. Sometimes he speaks the word of Yahweh or skillfully argues his own case; in other instances he heeds instructions to hide the word and deceive the officials.

Additional tensions and ironies in Jeremiah's portrayal revolve around the word שׁמע. Earlier when the officials "heard" the words that Jeremiah was preaching (38:1), it led to the prophet's life being jeopardized as he was thrown into the cistern. Here Jeremiah's life is secured because, although the officials "heard" (שׁמע, v. 25) about the conversation between the king and prophet, they had not "heard" (שׁמע, v. 27) its contents. Jeremiah, then, is granted one final opportunity to proclaim his message to the officials, but he declines it. The officials do not literally "hear" the word because Jeremiah does not speak the word. It is ironic that immediately before the fall of the city, the narrator reports that the "word (דבר) had not been heard." This carries the connotation that "the word of Yahweh" had not been heard.[162] The conversation began with prophet and king not trusting one another; now it ends with prophet and king collaborating in deception of the officials. The prophet of Yahweh does not announce the words of Yahweh for all to hear; instead he intentionally conceals the deity's message. If no one "listened to" the voice of Yahweh spoken through the prophet (37:2), it is due, in this final episode at least, to Jeremiah's failure to announce it.[163] Jeremiah apparently was willing to compromise and accommodate his message.[164] Indeed, the uses of שׁמע in 37:2 and 38:27 frame the story and draw attention to the complexities and nuances surrounding this word.

Jeremiah's speaking a word of the king, instead of Yahweh, does not negate his being a prophet; in fact, it is understandable in the context of the interviews between the king and prophet. In this final scene Jeremiah and Zedekiah are loyal to one another as they protect each other from potential harm by the officials. Jeremiah's loyalty to Zedekiah is ironic in view of the officials' charge of treason and sedition in 38:1–6. Nonetheless, in view of Jeremiah's role as a prophet of Yahweh, discernible irony exists in the exchange between Jeremiah and the officials. Carroll has rightly observed: "The image of the ranting prophet reduced to

161.   This contrasts with the more general report that the officials "came to Jeremiah and asked him." That is, it is not as clear that the officials said precisely what Zedekiah had anticipated they would say as it is that Jeremiah did say exactly as the king had advised him.

162.   The Greek, in fact, reads, "for the word of the Lord had not been heard."

163.   Brueggemann remarks, "It is as though, in this moment, the prophet is concerned for his own well-being. . . . Apparently he had yet another chance to sound his word to the princes; but he declines" (*To Build, to Plant*, 153).

164.   This is not to sound a note of moral disapproval, for the moral demands of the context are very complex. The point here is simply to note how Jeremiah negotiates the situation; he accommodates to his circumstances by choosing to conceal the truth (which could be understood as the morally upright course of action).

'lying' to protect the king and himself from the hostility of the princes is ironic within the context of the whole tradition, but hardly so from the viewpoint of the exchange between king and prophet in 37.17–20 and 38.14–23."[165] The "context of the whole tradition" cannot be ignored, especially in view of the highly intertextual nature of the book; it thus creates elements of irony and ambiguity in Jeremiah's interaction with the officials.[166]

Zedekiah's ruse protects the prophet from threatened death. It is not a dramatic rescue as Ebed-melech's in the previous episode or even as Zedekiah's first rescue of the prophet in which he moved him from Jonathan's prison. Rather, this deliverance requires the duplicity of both prophet and king. Thus, this final scene plays on the motif of prophetic rescues. If the previous two concluded with Jeremiah being moved to the court of the guard (37:21; 38:13), here the prophet is saved by being permitted to remain in the court of the guard.[167] This time, however, the added phrase, "until the day that Jerusalem was captured," prepares for the ensuing narration of the city's fall. Jeremiah's personal struggles are over for now; he and the city await the inevitable defeat.

Intertextuality
This episode contains several echoes of other texts within the book of Jeremiah. First, Jeremiah hesitates to converse with Zedekiah, expressing concern that he will be killed. This perceived threat on his life recalls, as did the previous episode, ch. 26 where the officials and the people declared that Jeremiah should be put to death. There, despite the threat on his life (26:11), the prophet boldly proclaimed that he had been sent by Yahweh, called the people to repentance, and gave them permission to treat him as they saw fit (26:12–14). This underscores by contrast Jeremiah's behavior in this sixth episode in which he is reluctant to speak at all until he acquires assurance from the king, and in which at the end of the episode he is still sufficiently concerned about his safety not to reveal his message to the officials. Perhaps this comparison depicts Jeremiah in a more negative light as a prophet who is no longer able to announce confidently the word of Yahweh; conversely, it may paint a sympathetic image of him as a man on whom adversity has taken its toll.

Verse 22 also links to other passages within the book. In Jeremiah's final lament, he accused Yahweh of "enticing" (פתה) him and "prevailing" (יכל) over him (20:7). He also asserted that his trusted friends (אנוש שלום) were waiting for him to stumble so that they could prevail (יכל) against him (20:10). These exclamations have thematic and verbal connections with the quoted speech of the women, who observe that the king's "trusted friends" (אנוש שלום) have deceived

---

165. Carroll, *Jeremiah: A Commentary*, 689.

166. Calvin comments that Jeremiah "cannot be excused" from this falsehood or "wholly exempted from blame" (*Commentaries on the Book* 4:419).

167. In each of the three scenes, a different person views the prophet's life as being endangered—Jeremiah himself (37:20), Ebed-melech (38:9), and the king (38:24–25). Also, all three rescues are by dint of human effort.

(or seduced) him (פתה) and overpowered him (יכל) and turned their back (סוג) on him (v. 22). Thus, in his last lament Jeremiah expresses sentiments that are similar to ones that he associates with Zedekiah in the king's final hours.[168] Jeremiah felt deceived by Yahweh, a concept that is not expressly mentioned concerning Zedekiah in 38:22. However, another text within the book hints that Yahweh was in fact behind the "men of peace" who deceived Zedekiah. The prophet voices anguish over Jerusalem's plight and says that Yahweh has "deceived this people and Jerusalem saying, 'peace' even while the sword is at the throat" (4:10). As the prophets were preaching, "peace, peace, when there is no peace" (6:14; 8:11), so Jeremiah accuses the deity of doing the same thing. Has Yahweh become the "deceptive stream" behind the officials (15:18)? In connection with these other texts, the notion of being deceived, abandoned, or overcome by Yahweh may resound in the women's words in v. 22. Zedekiah, indeed, may have envisioned that he was misled by Yahweh, for the deity had declared in ch. 21, a closely related text, that he would fight against Jerusalem.[169] Furthermore, the theme of divine deception finds another nexus in the vision of Micaiah in 1 Kgs 22, a text standing closely in the background (see above).[170] Micaiah describes a heavenly court scene in which Yahweh schemes to send a lying spirit to deceive (פתה) Ahab. Via these intertexts, the motif of divine deception may reverberate in Jeremiah's vision.

The quoted direct speech of the women in v. 22 also links with other texts in the DH.[171] The Rabshakeh urged the citizens of Jerusalem not to let Hezekiah persuade (פתה) them not resist because their deity would not save the city (2 Kgs 18:32 = Isa 36:18). In Jeremiah's vision, the women taunt the king by saying that the "trusted men" have seduced/persuaded (פתה) him not to surrender. Both the Rabshakeh and Jeremiah advocate surrender, and in the process both ridicule their respective Judean kings. Further, the image of the women speaking as they are led out recalls episodes where a chorus of women sing in honor of the king. One thinks specifically of Saul and David whose victories in battle were celebrated by singing women (1 Sam 18:7; 21:11). Jeremiah's vision represents a reversal of this image. Zedekiah is not returning home victorious to receive the praises of the women, but leaving home defeated hearing the laments and mocking of the women.

The phrase "do not hide a word from me" ties to 1 Sam 3:17 where Eli instructs Samuel not to hide (כחד) the word (דבר) from him and then repeats the

---

168. The image of women lamenting the fate of the king may also recall 34:5 where Jeremiah promised Zedekiah that he would die in peace and people would mourn for him. Martens ("Narrative Parallelism and Message," 39) sees this image functioning as an *inclusio* for chs. 34–38.

169. One could extend this link further by noting that in 29:7 Jeremiah exhorts the Babylonian exiles to pray for the peace of Babylon. There is no peace for Jerusalem, as Babylon has replaced Zion. See Jonathan Sisson, "Jeremiah and the Jerusalem conception of Peace," *JBL* 105 (1986): 429–42 (440).

170. They are not specifically called visions, but both begin with "I saw."

171. Scholars typically discuss v. 22 in reference to Obad 7. While there are certainly verbal connections with this verse, no substantive thematic connection emerges.

instruction prefaced by an oath. Likewise, David commands the woman of Tekoa "do not hide a word from me" (2 Sam 14:18). These scenes exemplify the motif of the reluctant speaker withholding the word (cf. also Jer 26:2; 42:4).[172] In both cases bad news is expected by the one making the request. This suggests that Zedekiah, too, anticipated a message of defeat or judgment from Jeremiah, but as Eli and David, he needed to be apprised of the word nonetheless.

Finally, one small word, מָאֵן ("refuse"), may carry complex intertextual overtones. The word appears only three other times in the Hebrew Bible in this form and all three times it refers to Pharaoh's refusal to listen to the word of Yahweh spoken through Moses (Exod 8:2; 9:2; 10:4). Zedekiah and Pharaoh are issued a mandate and if they "refuse" certain consequences would follow—the plagues for Pharaoh, exile and Jerusalem's destruction for Zedekiah.[173] As Pharaoh is commanded to "send out" (שַׁלַּח) the children of Israel, so Zedekiah is commanded to "go out" (יָצָא) to the Babylonians.[174] In both instances, it is imperative to free the people; both monarchs are told "let my people go." Paradoxically, for Zedekiah this requires submitting to, not escaping from, the enemy. Thus, the radical nature of Jeremiah's message is again underscored, much as it is highlighted by its similarity to the Rabshakeh's message. These echoes of the Exodus narrative cast Jeremiah in the role of Moses, but Jeremiah calls for a reverse Exodus, one that leads to loss of land and freedom. Jeremiah is not only an anti-Isaiah figure, but an anti-Moses one as well (see above).

172. See Janzen, "Withholding the Word," 97–105.

173. A correlative notion perhaps in play here is that Yahweh hardened Pharaoh's heart in order to demonstrate his power. Perhaps this notion resonates in the stories of Zedekiah—is God somehow manipulating the king to make a point? See Chapter 5 for a discussion of Zedekiah's connections to Saul and the resulting implications for understanding the role of the deity in the Zedekiah narratives.

174. The overall characterizations of Pharaoh and Zedekiah are remarkably similar. Barbara Green's description of the Egyptian monarch could also be applied to Zedekiah. She notes "his consistent if bumbling resolve to take charge and do well by his people; his narrative characterization as not only powerful but also highly responsive to the suggestions and manipulations of others; and the graded leeway given readers in interpreting and understanding both Pharaoh and ourselves." She demonstrates how Pharaoh has "apparent power and discernible weakness. . . . His power is patent, but he is also manipulated in ways he seems not to suspect. . . . Pharaoh is most subtly characterized . . . by his paradoxical blend . . . simultaneously powerful and powerless" ("The Determination of Pharaoh: His Characterization in the Joseph Story [Genesis 37–50]," in *The World of Genesis: Persons, Places, Perspectives* [ed. P. R. Davies and D. J. A. Clines; JSOTSup 257; Sheffield: Sheffield Academic Press, 1998], 150–71 [150–52]).

Chapter 4

OF PROPHETS, KINGS, AND DESTRUCTION: PART 3

Seventh Episode: 39:1–10

(1) In the ninth year of Zedekiah king of Judah, in the tenth month, Nebuchadrezzar king of Babylon and all his army came against Jerusalem and besieged it. (2) In the eleventh year of Zedekiah, in the fourth month, on the ninth day of the month, the city was breached. (3) All the officials of the king of Babylon came and sat in the middle gate, Nergal-sharezer, Samgar-nebo, Sarsechim the Rabsaris, Nergal-sharezer the Rabmag,[1] and all the rest of the officials of the king of Babylon. (4) When Zedekiah king of Judah and all the soldiers saw them, they fled and went out from the city at night through the king's garden through the gate between the two walls; and they went out toward the Arabah. (5) The army of the Chaldeans pursued after them and overtook Zedekiah in the plains of Jericho. They took him and brought him up to Nebuchadrezzar king of Babylon at Riblah, in the land of Hamath, and he passed judgment on him. (6) The king of Babylon slaughtered the sons of Zedekiah at Riblah before his eyes, and the king of Babylon slaughtered all the nobles of Judah. (7) He gouged out the eyes of Zedekiah and bound him in chains to take him to Babylon. (8) The Chaldeans burned with fire the king's house and the house of the people, and destroyed the walls of Jerusalem. (9) Nebuzaradan the captain of the guard exiled to Babylon the rest of the people who remained in the city and all those who had deserted to him, and the rest of the people who remained. (10) Nebuzaradan the captain of the guard left in the land some of the poor people who had nothing, and gave to them vineyards and fields[2] on that day.[3]

Following an introduction (vv. 1–2), this episode divides into three sections: the fate of Zedekiah (vv. 3–7), the fate of Jerusalem (v. 8), and the fate of the people (vv. 9–10).[4] Accordingly, this episode, unlike the previous six, does not divide into two scenes. This episode functions as a narrative summary rather than a set of scenes. It is the pivotal episode in the story.

Contextual Analysis

The story of the fall of Jerusalem is also recounted in Jer 52 and 2 Kgs 25. Most studies of Jer 39 have compared it to these other reports, focusing on source-critical and redactional questions.[5] An analysis of Jer 39:1–10, however,

---

1. This list of names and titles has generated much debate. See McKane, *Jeremiah XXVI–LII*, 973–76; Holladay, *Jeremiah 2*, 291. The rendering given here follows the NRSV.

2. יְגֵב is a *hapax*; its meaning is somewhat uncertain.

3. Verses 4–10 are absent from the Greek.

4. Willis ("'They Did Not Listen to the Voice of the Lord,'" 79) suggests that "39:1–40:6 is to be read as a continuation of, or sequel to, chapters 37–38."

5. Verse 3 is the only unique verse to this account. For a discussion of the sources and theories of redaction of ch. 39, see McKane, *Jeremiah XXVI–LII*, 989–92; Doug R. Jones, *Jeremiah* (NCBC; Grand Rapids: Eerdmans, 1992), 45–54; and Seitz, *Theology in Conflict*, 264–69.

reveals several features that connect it thematically to chs. 37–38. For instance, the appearance of four named Babylonian officials (39:3) provides a foil for the four named Judean officials (38:1) who have now been defeated by their Babylonian counterparts.[6] These foreigners sit in the city gate, an image which serves to make use of symbolic space—the gate being a place of legal proceedings and where one enters and leaves a city. Earlier Zedekiah sat (ישׁב) at the city gates as the judge (38:7), but now the Babylonian officials sit (ישׁב) in the place of judicial authority. If previously Zedekiah pronounced Jeremiah guilty of infidelity (38:5), Zedekiah is now the defendant, rather than the judge, and he is guilty of the same crime—disloyalty. Further, the Judean officials had control of Jerusalem's gates, as they successfully prevented Jeremiah from leaving the city (37:11–16). Now the Babylonian officials control the gate; consequently, the Judean king and officials must themselves try to escape.

The depiction of the king and army fleeing at "night" (לילה) expands the theme of secrecy. Formerly, the king had questioned Jeremiah in secret (37:17), had instructed him not to hide anything from him (38:14), had sworn an oath in secret (38:16), and had commanded Jeremiah to conceal the contents of their last conversation (38:24–25). Now the king tries to escape secretly at night. Zedekiah and the army flee when they "see" (ראה) the Babylonian officials sitting in the gate, unlike the accounts in 2 Kings and Jer 52 where their fleeing is connected to the famine conditions in the city or to the breach in the wall.[7] Here Zedekiah "sees" what is happening and attempts to flee without being seen. In addition, earlier Yahweh had shown (ראה) Jeremiah a vision of the king's wives and children (בן) being "led out" (יצא) to the Babylonians (38:22–23); now the king himself and his army "see" (ראה) the Babylonians and depart (יצא), but they are captured and Zedekiah is compelled to watch his children (בן) killed.

The king's fate in this episode parallels—and is foreshadowed by—that of Jeremiah in 37:11–16. Both Jeremiah and Zedekiah attempted to leave (יצא) the city, but do not succeed. Jeremiah was arrested (תפשׂ) by Irijah and Zedekiah was captured (תפשׂ) by the Babylonians. Irijah brought (בוא) Jeremiah to the officials who strike him. The Babylonians take (לקח) and bring (עלה) Zedekiah to Nebuchadrezzar who blinds him. The officials confine Jeremiah to prison and he came (בוא) into the cistern house. Nebuchadrezzar binds Zedekiah in chains to bring (בוא) him to Babylon. In short, both king and prophet try to exit the city, but instead are returned for a trial and judgment and are then taken into captivity.[8]

6. There may not be four different names, depending on how one reads the list. The names in v. 3 are different from the ones in v. 13, which has generated many solutions; but narratively it causes little problem.

7. The version presented in Jer 39 is somewhat difficult to imagine historically. Bright (*Jeremiah*, 242), for instance, argues that "saw them" should be read "saw this," that is, the breach of the wall. He concludes that "Zedekiah did not wait to see the Babylonian officers seated before fleeing." The unexpected scenario in this scene could be understood as an ungrammaticality (see on Riffaterre above) that directs the reader elsewhere for its full significance.

8. Another possible parallel between the king and prophet is that Zedekiah went down to the plains of Jericho in an attempt to avoid his punishment for infidelity, and he was "brought up" (עלה)

If Jeremiah had been accused of desertion, both literally (37:13) and ideologically (38:4–6), in the end, ironically, it is the king and army who desert Jerusalem by fleeing instead of attempting to defend it.[9] The text states that the Babylonians pursued "after them"—Zedekiah and the army—but it reports only that they captured Zedekiah. This implies that the army deserted the king. Reading intertextually, this is confirmed in the accounts in 2 Kgs 25 and Jer 52 which indicate that the army "scattered" (נָפֻצוּ) from Zedekiah. After abandoning the city, Zedekiah's army abandoned him. This also connects to the notion in Jeremiah's vision (38:22) that the king would be deserted by his trusted friends. The events in 39:1–10, then, sustain the themes of desertion and fidelity that marked chs. 37–38.

Finally, the *leitwort* יָצָא ties this episode to previous scenes. As with the two distinct meanings of שָׁמַע, there is a play on the two different meanings of יָצָא: the king "goes out" of the city instead of "surrendering." Zedekiah does יָצָא as Jeremiah had advised, but it is the wrong kind of יָצָא.

While there are a number of linguistic and thematic links between the seventh episode and the previous ones, there is also a crucial difference, namely, in the style of narration. With the specification of dates and the length of the siege in 39:1–2, the text moves to a historical mode of narration, akin to that in the introduction (37:1–2). The seventh episode is the only one of the ten that features neither any direct speech nor the appearance of the prophet Jeremiah. The absence of direct speech allows readers only an external perspective on the action; they do not glimpse events through the eyes of the characters. While readers witness a story of great pathos, they are also distanced from the characters in the story, particularly Zedekiah, because of the limited (i.e. external) point of view.

One motif that has animated the story thus far is the extent of Zedekiah's agency. In "reality," what action can the king take? What choices does he have? Like much of the king's depiction, these questions have had indistinct answers. At times he claims little or no agency (38:5), while at others he has appeared in control (37:21; 38:10). In this seventh episode, Zedekiah has one final opportunity at agency, as he "sees" and acts, but he quickly becomes acted upon by the Babylonians. Henceforth, the Babylonians are in control. They choose what transpires; they make the decisions; they are the agents and they determine to whom they will grant agency. The external style of narration, then, reflects the manner in which Zedekiah's diminishing agency is constructed and communicated. One no longer views events from the king's perspective and considers how he might elect to handle the situation (as was sometimes the case in chs. 37–38); rather one watches as actions are performed on the king. The shift in the mode of narration occurs in conjunction with a shift in the portrayal of agency.

to Nebuchadrezzar at Riblah. Jeremiah, as punishment for suspected infidelity, was thrown down into the cistern and was rescued by being "brought up" (עלה) to the court of the guard.

  9.   Cf. Brueggemann (*To Build, to Plant*, 155), who remarks, "Zedekiah abdicates his royal office and his royal responsibility, leaving his people in the lurch." Brueggemann also suggests the possibility that Zedekiah was trying to escape with the hopes of forming a "government in hiding." If so, this would contribute to the secrecy theme.

Point of View

The preceding discussion touched on questions of point of view, but there are a few other matters to examine. First, it has been observed that the naming of a character by the narrator or another figure is an important element in assessing point of view. The opening verse of this episode is the first time since 37:1 that Zedekiah has been identified as "king of Judah," and, as in 37:1, here Zedekiah and Nebuchadrezzar are mentioned together. In 37:1, Zedekiah's kingship is dubious as he has been appointed "king" by King Nebuchadrezzar. At the time of his demise, Zedekiah is, mockingly it seems, again called "king of Judah."

Second, the verb ראה is a "verb of perception" which expresses Zedekiah's point of view.[10] The king departs when he sees (ראה) the Babylonian officials occupying the gates. Zedekiah has struggled to view the situation correctly so that he could act appropriately. Ultimately, he is forced to "see" the reality of defeat, which leads to the termination of any agency he may have had. The king's "seeing" the Babylonian officials in the gate may also introduce some tragic irony in that Zedekiah's children are slaughtered "before his eyes" (v. 6). If Jeremiah had seen a vision of Zedekiah's wives and daughters being led into exile (38:22–23), Zedekiah would have an everlasting vision of his children's death. If Zedekiah attempted to escape under cover of darkness, now he would have a life of perpetual darkness. Further, Zedekiah's punishment by Nebuchadrezzar results in the loss of his sight (v. 7). If in chs. 37–38 the narrator had sparingly revealed the king's point of view, here Nebuchadrezzar literally removes Zedekiah's (point of) view. The narrator focuses the reader's attention on Zedekiah's terrible fate. The audience is forced to watch Zedekiah being forced to watch the execution of his children and the nobles prior to having his own eyes gouged out.

It is as though the narrator wishes the reader to ponder the horrific nature of this scene, for the narrator withholds his point of view. One might expect the narrator to make a didactic point or insert a moral explanation, but there is none—no explicit denunciation of Zedekiah or his actions, no connection between his failures and the city's debacle. There is no theological word or interpretive comment; rather one only watches the tragedy unfold.[11] If the narrative is designed to illustrate the consequences of the rejection of the word of Yahweh, it does so quite laconically, unlike, for instance, 2 Kgs 17 where the narrator inserts an extended theological explanation for the fall of the Northern Kingdom. The narrator's reticence, the lack of expressed point of view, at this juncture is remarkable and is, it seems, a reflection of the messiness and complexity of the tragedy which no single point of view could succinctly or adequately summarize.

The Plot: Fulfillment of Jeremiah's Message?

Most commentators assert that this episode is the fulfillment of Jeremiah's word against Jerusalem. The prophet had foretold that Jerusalem would be handed over

---

10. Cf. Berlin, *Poetics and Interpretation*, 62.
11. Cf. Brueggemann, *To Build, to Plant*, 157.

to the Babylonians and this materializes. There are, however, some discrepancies between Jeremiah's message and the events as reported in this episode. The most salient issue is in v. 9, which states that Nebuzaradan exiled "the rest of the people who remained in the city and all those who had deserted to him." Here is the initial appearance of Nebuzaradan, "the captain of the guard," or literally, "the chief butcher" (רב־טבחים). His title ironically draws attention to the issue at hand. It was King Nebuchadrezzar who was the "chief butcher" as he "slaughtered" Zedekiah's children and the nobles. Nebuzaradan, by contrast, is the one who exiles people. Both those who deserted and those who remained in Jerusalem experience the same fate—they are deported by Nebuzaradan. This undercuts the accuracy of Jeremiah's message, for he had proclaimed that those who remained in the city would die and those who submitted to the Babylonians would live (38:2–3; cf. 21:8–9). The repeated phrase, "the rest of the people who remained," frames the words, "those who deserted." Thus, both literally and syntactically those who had stayed in the city surround those who had already deserted to the Babylonians as all prepare to go to Babylon.

Although this plot development is central for an overall understanding of the story, few commentators address it. Carroll is one who recognizes the issue, but he does not attribute much significance to it. He writes, "The irony of v. 9 should be noted: both those who deserted and those who remained in the city were deported, whereas the options proclaimed by Jeremiah offered survival only to those who deserted and death to those who remained in the city." And later he remarks, "The deportation of all the people, deserters from the city and survivors of the siege, to Babylon undermines the claim attributed to Jeremiah that remaining in the city would lead to death whereas deserting would secure life." Carroll, however, concludes that this "discrepancy . . . underline[s] the nature of the material in the book as a collection of diverse stories associated with Jeremiah but lacking a coherent and harmonious unity."[12] Reading the final form of the text, however, it is difficult to miss the irony, as Carroll recognizes, of Jeremiah's inaccurate message. Similarly, John Bracke perceives that v. 9 is "somewhat puzzling," but he decides that "despite some discrepancies, the overall intention of the these verse [*sic*] is to stress that God's word of judgment announced by Jeremiah was fulfilled."[13] It is nearly unimaginable, however, how the narrator could allow "discrepancies" of this magnitude to remain if the primary objective were to demonstrate the reliability of the word of Yahweh as delivered through Jeremiah.

The question of the fulfillment of Jeremiah's word is especially noteworthy given that this issue—fulfilled prophecy—has already been raised in the context of distinguishing true from false prophets. In Jeremiah's earlier conversation with Zedekiah (37:19), he based the argument for his freedom on the principle that the words of true prophets are fulfilled, whereas the words of false prophets are not. Thus, Jeremiah himself endorses the fulfillment of the prophetic word as

---

12. Carroll, *Jeremiah: A Commentary*, 692, 693.
13. Bracke, *Jeremiah 30–52*, 77.

a standard of measurement when evaluating prophets (cf. Deut 18). Earlier Jeremiah's word against the prophet Hananiah is reported as precisely fulfilled (28:16–17), which is verification that he and not Hananiah is the prophet of Yahweh. Now, however, the events reported in 39:9 challenge Jeremiah's own status as a true prophet.

There are some additional discrepancies between Jeremiah's message and what unfolds. In light of Jeremiah's conflict with the "officials" (שׂרים) in chs. 37–38 and their prominence as characters in the story, a report of their fate—or any mention of them at all—is noticeably absent. The Babylonians killed the sons of Zedekiah and the nobles (חֹר), who could perhaps include the "officials."[14] Nonetheless, the officials, more than Zedekiah, rejected the word of the prophet; yet there is no clear indication that they died, as Jeremiah predicted for those who did not surrender (38:2). In addition, Jeremiah had foretold that the city would be burned (37:8, 10; 38:18).[15] It is reported, however, that the Babylonians burned "the king's house and the house of the people," which is quite different from burning the whole city.

The "king's house" presumably refers to the palace, but the referent for the "house of the people" (בֵּית הָעָם) is less obvious. Nicholson suggests that it may indicate a general assembly hall or a council building,[16] and Franz Landsberger argues that it refers to the temple.[17] Others, however, emend "house of the people" to "houses (pl.) of the people" to accord with 52:13 and 2 Kgs 25:9, and understand the phrase to signify total destruction. This is dubious, however. The phrase "burn the city" (שׂרף עיר) occurs six times outside of the book of Jeremiah and each time it denotes complete destruction.[18] There is no text in the Hebrew Bible where the notion of burning houses is tantamount to burning the city. The phrase "burn the city" is also found nine times in the book of Jeremiah, all part of the prophet's warnings of the city's fate. In Jer 32:29 the prophet predicts that the Babylonians will burn the city *and* the houses in it, implying that these are two different acts. "The house of the people" may quite possibly denote one specific building (as Nicholson and Landsberger argue), and even if one emends to "houses (pl.) of the people," it would not seem to signify the total destruction that Jeremiah foretold. It is true that one could understand the phrase "the king's

14. The "nobles" (חֹר) make one other appearance in the book of Jeremiah (27:20) where it is reported that Nebuchadrezzar deported all the nobles along with Jehoiachin. Thompson (*Jeremiah*, 647) points out the difference between the שׂרים and the חֹרים, but others (Holladay, *Jeremiah 2*, 292) think that the officials are included within the designation "nobles." The version in 2 Kgs 25 does not indicate that the nobles or the officials are killed, only the king's sons. The account in Jer 52 states that the king's sons and the officials are killed, but does not mention the nobles.

15. One might connect the non-mention of the officials with Jeremiah's vision (38:22) which said that Zedekiah's "trusted friends" would desert him. Perhaps the officials successfully fled, or else agreed to cooperate with the Babylonians?

16. Nicholson, *Jeremiah 26–52*, 128.

17. Franz Landsberger, "The House of the People," *HUCA* 22 (1947): 149–55. Abrego (*Jeremías y el Final del Reino*, 83) finds this suggestion attractive; he says it is the Babylonian attempt to destroy the civil (palace) and religious (temple) centers of Jerusalem.

18. Cf. Num 31:10; Deut 13:16; Josh 6:24; Judg 18:27; 1 Sam 30:3; Isa 1:7.

house and the house of the people" as defining the whole (city) by naming its parts. However, in view of the other apparent discrepancies (see below for additional ones) between Jeremiah's word and reported events, one can, at the very least, appreciate the tension between "burning the city" and burning "the king's house and the house (or houses) of the people."

As Seitz has observed, "when the city is actually taken, no reports of destruction or widespread violence are included" and thus it is "an odd and sparse report."[19] The horror of the destruction is not mentioned. There is nothing that matches the phrasing of Jeremiah's predictions of death by "sword, famine, and pestilence" (38:2) when describing the city's fall; nor is there any kind of formulaic phrase that what occurred was "according to the word of Yahweh that he spoke through the prophet," as one might expect given its use in similar contexts.[20]

Furthermore, v. 10 reports that Nebuzaradan left some of the poor people in the land of Judah and provided them with vineyards and fields.[21] This concluding image contrasts with the closing images in previous scenes where Jeremiah "remained" in the court of the guard (37:21; 38:13, 28). Not only are there no indications of widespread violence or death for those who did not desert, but some were also permitted to remain in the land and supplied with the resources to thrive. This represents another incongruity, for the scope of Jeremiah's message did not allow the possibility for continued residence or the acquisition of fields and vineyards.[22]

There are too many such discrepancies to ignore, and, when combined, one must consider that the narrative has been constructed so as to question Jeremiah's reliability.[23] Some might argue that Jeremiah is "close enough" to be considered

---

19. Seitz, *Theology in Conflict*, 239, 266. Seitz argues that the target of the Babylonian invasion was not the city, nor the temple, nor the general populace, but only the Davidic house represented by Zedekiah. It is to be noted, however, that according to the archaeological record there seems to have been fairly widespread destruction of Jerusalem. See Gösta Ahlström, *The History of Ancient Palestine from the Paleolithic Period to Alexander's Conquest* (JSOTSup 146; Sheffield: JSOT Press, 1993), 798.

20. See 1 Kgs 12:15; 15:29; 16:12, 34; 2 Kgs 1:17; 23:16; 24:2. Cf. Alter's discussion (*Art of Biblical Narrative*, 180) on the "avoidance of repetition." Alter also observes that "the reader's attention is drawn to the lack of specific information in one passage because of its presence in a second context that is similar to the first." It is the "there but not here" effect (18). One may also note that the narrative has tried to impress the reader with omissions—the omission of Zedekiah's response to Jeremiah's message in episodes three and six, the omission of Jeremiah's defense in scene four, etc. The same may be said of the present scene—the omission of any comment by the narrator that affirms the unfolding of events as Jeremiah predicted is significant.

21. If Zedekiah fled "at night" (v. 4), Nebuzaradan prospers the people who remain "on that day."

22. It is evident from the continuing story in chs. 40–44 that many people remained in the land. The image that one gets from 39:3 and 10 is that the Babylonians were intent on maintaining economic and social order and stability, which does not exactly cohere with Jeremiah's message.

23. Another possible discrepancy is that Zedekiah is blinded and not killed, which contradicts Jeremiah's message that all who remained in the city would die (38:2). Boadt remarks that "Zedekiah's fate seems especially cruel, even though it was not exactly what Jeremiah had predicted" (*Jeremiah 26–52*, 100). While Zedekiah's not being killed could be listed as another incongruity,

correct or that nothing is "intended" by the discrepancies because predictions are not meant to be taken literally. This position not withstanding, it cannot be gain-said that significant disparity exists between Jeremiah's message and the account of the fall of Jerusalem. One may thus conclude that the narrator is undermining Jeremiah's image as a prophet.[24]

Intertextuality
The image of the officials sitting in the gate (v. 3) points to Jer 1:15 where Yahweh declares, "I am calling all the tribes of the kingdoms of the north, and they will come and all of them will set their thrones at the entrance of the gates of Jerusalem." This connection reminds one that Yahweh is behind the Babylonians who have now taken control of the gates. Chapter 1 also links with forensic issues associated with "sitting at the gate." Yahweh proclaims in the next verse (1:16), "I will utter my judgments against them" (ודברתי משפטי אותם). This phrase establishes a direct linguistic link to 39:5 in which Nebuchadrezzar "spoke judg-ment on him" (וידבר אתו משפטים). This allusion insinuates that Yahweh executes his judgments through Nebuchadrezzar. These two ties to Jer 1 invite one to explore yet a third connection. In 1:18 Yahweh tells Jeremiah that Yahweh will make the prophet a "fortified city, an iron pillar, and a bronze wall." The meta-phor of Jeremiah as a divinely protected city contrasts with Jerusalem as a vul-nerable, Yahweh-forsaken city which has fallen.[25]

A second intertext that is even more palpable is found in 32:4 and 34:3. In a warning to Zedekiah in 32:4, Jeremiah prophesies that Zedekiah will be given into the hand of the king of Babylon and that "you will speak with him face to face and see him eye to eye."[26] Similarly in 34:3, Jeremiah informs Zedekiah "you will see the king of Babylon eye to eye and speak with him face to face."[27] These prophecies take on a cruel irony as Zedekiah does see Nebuchadrezzar, only to be blinded by him. This unmistakable allusion to 34:3 recalls the larger context in ch. 34, including 34:4–5 in which Jeremiah promises Zedekiah a

Jeremiah also predicted that Nebuchadrezzar would take Zedekiah to Babylon (32:5; 34:3). So some ambiguity exists in the prophet's warnings to the king.

24. The argument proffered here is literary, not sociological. The proposition is that as a character in the story, Jeremiah's depiction as a prophet of Yahweh may be challenged. The sociological phenomenon of prophecy in which inaccurate predictions may have been of little consequence (and perhaps even expected) is not the focus of this analysis.

25. See Harry Nasuti, "A Prophet to the Nations: Diachronic and Synchronic Readings of Jeremiah 1," *HAR* 10 (1986): 249–66. Nasuti observes the contrast between Jeremiah and Jerusalem, but makes no connection with ch. 39.

26. Chapter 32 may also be echoed by v. 10 in which Nebuzaradan gave the poor people "vineyards and fields" (כרמים ויגבים). In 32:15, Yahweh declares to Jeremiah that "houses and fields and vineyards will again be bought in this land." Thus, Nebuzaradan's actions may be interpreted as a foreshadowing of future blessings. If so, it is a foiled foreshadowing since the Palestinian community soon experiences their own debacle with the death of Gedaliah.

27. Likewise, Jeremiah had apprised the king that he would be given into the hand of the king of Babylon (37:17), whereas he had told "this city" that they will be given into the hand *of the army* of the king Babylon (38:3). This distinction does, in fact, come to fruition as Zedekiah is brought directly to Nebuchadrezzar (39:5) while the military officials seize the city.

peaceful death: "Thus says Yahweh concerning you: You will not die by the sword; you will die in peace. And as there was burning (of spices) for your fathers, the kings who were before you, so will they burn (spices) for you and lament for you." Zedekiah witnesses the execution of his sons, is blinded, exiled in chains to a foreign land, and, as is reported later (52:10–11), dies there; the king does not experience a good death.[28] This disparity between prophecy and narrated events is often handled by understanding an implicit conditional clause so that the king is promised a peaceful death only if he obeys the voice of Yahweh.[29] However, in light of the observations made above, this may be interpreted as another instance of incongruity between prophetic word and reality.

Other items in 34:4–5, however, warrant attention. First, the two references to burning (שׂרף) in 34:5 produce an ironic allusion which is significantly strengthened by the fact that קטר ("to burn incense") or בשׂם ("spice") are only implied, not expressly stated. That is, spices are not "burned" for Zedekiah; rather parts of Jerusalem are "burned" for the king's refusal to surrender. The intertextual wordplay is again brutally ironic at Zedekiah's expense.[30] Secondly, the phrase in 34:5, "your fathers, the kings who were before you," reminds one of a similar prophecy of a good death conveyed to Josiah by the prophetess Huldah (2 Kgs 22:19–20). This did not come to pass as Josiah was murdered by Pharaoh Neco (2 Kgs 23:28–30). Both Josiah and Zedekiah were promised peaceful deaths but neither received them.[31] The wording of Huldah's oracle is also of note: "You will be gathered to your grave in peace; your eyes (עין) will not see (ראה) all the disaster that I will bring on this place." Josiah, of course, did not witness the ultimate destruction of the city and people. Zedekiah, however, does "see" (ראה) the Babylonians sitting in the gate and then watches "before his eyes" (עין) part of the disaster that Yahweh brings—the slaughtering of his sons and the nobles. He then personally suffers a portion of the evil as his eyes (עין) are gouged out.[32]

Zedekiah's blindness resonates on two intertextual levels beyond the book of Jeremiah. First, it recalls Samson, the only other character in the Hebrew Bible

---

28. Calvin (*Commentaries on the Book* 4:428) captures the pathos of Zedekiah's suffering, which prevents a "peaceful" death: "Nebuchadrezzar intended to kill him a hundred and a thousand times, and not once to put him to death, for death removes man from all the miseries of the present life. That Zedekiah remained alive was then a much harder condition." This kind of "slow death" is reminiscent of the officials' attempt to kill Jeremiah in the pit and of the slow death of besieged Jerusalem.

29. Cf., for example, Bright, *Jeremiah*, 216.

30. However, שׂרף was also a theme word in ch. 36 (vv. 25, 27, 28, 29, 32) where Jehoiakim burned the scroll containing Jeremiah's words. The palace is now burned because Jehoiakim burned the scroll—a connection which may shift the focus away from Zedekiah or make him less culpable.

31. This connection is strengthened by the fact that these are the only two such promises of a peaceful death made to Israelite or Judean kings. Also, the prophecy of a peaceful death for Josiah was simply not fulfilled—that is, context does not allow one to read an implied conditional element into the prophecy. This unfulfilled prophecy suggests the appropriateness of evaluating Jeremiah's message to Zedekiah as similarly incorrect.

32. One might note another connection between the events surrounding the deaths of Josiah and Zedekiah: Pharaoh's headquarters were apparently at Riblah, as that is where he confined Jehoahaz (2 Kgs 23:33). Likewise, Nebuchadrezzar stationed himself at Riblah (39:5), which is where he met with Zedekiah.

to be blinded by an enemy as punishment. Blindness links the end of the monarchy to the closing of the period of Judges; the final king and judge can no longer see the way. However, perhaps Samson's concluding victory over the enemy provides some echoes of hope for Zedekiah. Secondly, Exod 23:8 and Deut 16:19 instruct leaders never to accept a gift because it "blinds" (עָוַר) the eyes of the wise; the connection is tightened by the fact that the verb עָוַר appears only in these two laws and in the three texts referring to Zedekiah (Jer 39:7; 52:11; 2 Kgs 25:7). Zedekiah's eyes have been blinded literally because he accepted the gift of kingship from the Babylonians. Jeremiah does take a gift from the Babylonians (40:1–6; see below), which invokes speculation on whether he too has been blinded by the Babylonians, not literally as Zedekiah was, but figuratively so as to obscure his judgment, as the laws warn.

This episode also resonates with stories in the Pentateuch and the DH. There are echoes of the Exodus story in that as Zedekiah and his army "went out" (יָצָא) at "night" (לַיְלָה), so too the Israelites "escaped" (יָצָא) from Egypt at "night" (לַיְלָה, Exod 11:4; 12:31: 12:42; Deut 1:16). Similarly, the Egyptians "pursued" (רדף) and "overtook" (נשׂג) the fleeing Israelites (Exod 14:9; 15:9); so too the Babylonians "pursued" (רדף) and "overtook" (נשׂג) the fleeing Zedekiah. Further, while Zedekiah and his army tried to escape between the walls (חומה, 39:4), the Israelites were able to escape from the Egyptians by passing between the walls (חומה) of water as the sea parted (Exod 14:22–29). The recollection of the exodus from Egypt is relevant in a story that narrates the people's exodus from their homeland.

Similarly, it is fitting to recall the accounts of the entrance into the promised land at the time when the Judeans are exiled from their homes. Specifically, there are verbal and thematic associations with the narratives of the spies at Jericho—enhanced by the fact that the city of Jericho is specifically mentioned in 39:5. Rahab tells the men of Jericho, "when it was time to close the gate (שׁער) at dark, the men [the spies] went out (יָצָא). . . . Pursue (רדף) them, for you can overtake (נשׂג) them" (Josh 2:5). The spies, one recalls, had not departed at night but remained hidden in the city until they could be safely deposited outside the walls (2:15). Zedekiah, by contrast, when he saw the Babylonians in the gate (שׁער), went out (יָצָא) at night through the city walls, only to be pursued (רדף) and overtaken (נשׂג). Both stories feature images of gates, city walls, darkness/night, going out/escaping, secrecy, and pursuit and capture (foiled or successful).

Finally, Zedekiah's "going out" (יָצָא) from the city at "night" (לַיְלָה) recalls that the angel of Yahweh "went out" (יָצָא) at "night" (לַיְלָה) to kill the Assyrians, thereby delivering Hezekiah and Jerusalem (2 Kgs 19:35). This link underscores the fact that there is no salvation for Zedekiah and the city: they flee from the Babylonians at night instead of being the recipients of nocturnal divine intervention.[33]

---

33. The verb שׁחט ("slaughter") in v. 6 may also resonate intertextually. It appears eighty-one times in the Hebrew Bible and all but five times it refers to killing an animal in a sacrificial context. The exceptions are notable. Twice it refers to killing/sacrificing children—Abraham killing/sacrificing Isaac (Gen 22:10), and the Israelites killing/sacrificing children under every green tree (Isa 57:5).

Eighth Episode: 39:11–14

(11) Nebuchadrezzar king of Babylon commanded concerning Jeremiah through Nebuzaradan the captain of the guard, saying, (12) "Take him, look after him and do not do him any harm, but do with him according to what he says to you."[34] (13) Then Nebuzaradan the captain of the guard, Nebushazban the Rabsaris, Nergal-sharezer the Rabmag and all the officers of the king of Babylon (14) sent[35] for and took Jeremiah from the court of the guard and gave him to Gedaliah son of Ahikam son of Shaphan to bring him out to the house.[36] So he remained among the people.

After detailing the fate of the king, city, and people, this brief episode attends to Jeremiah's circumstances. The style of narration changes as there is once again direct speech. As in the first six episodes, this one contains two scenes—Nebuchadrezzar's instructions concerning Jeremiah (vv. 11–12) and the subsequent execution of those instructions (vv. 13–14).

Contextual Analysis

Nebuchadrezzar speaks "by the hand" of Nebuzaradan. As has been pointed out, יד is a key word that appears repeatedly in these chapters, often representing or symbolizing agency. Here and in the introduction (37:2) it is used in the context of speaking through another agent. As Yahweh spoke "by the hand of" Jeremiah, now Nebuchadrezzar speaks "by the hand of" Nebuzaradan. This signals the new situation: Nebuchadrezzar, like Yahweh, is the one who controls and delivers messages through the agency of others. Instead of being the intermediary agent, now Jeremiah himself is the subject of the message.

Nebuchadrezzar's instructions regarding Jeremiah link verbally to the previous episode; the connections function to contrast the agency granted to Jeremiah vs. that given to Zedekiah. The Babylonian king enjoins Nebuzaradan to "take" (לקח) Jeremiah, "put your eyes (עין) on him," and "do with him according to what he says (דבר) to you" (v. 12). This is a reversal of Zedekiah's treatment by Nebuchadrezzar. Zedekiah was taken (לקח) to the Babylonian king who declared (דבר) judgment on him and slaughtered his children "before his eyes" (עין) and

---

Given the rarity of שחט to refer to the killing of people, Jer 39 may echo these two other contexts which refer to sacrificing/killing children. If so, then the cultic, sacrificial notions contribute undertones to Jer 39—Zedekiah's sons are sacrificed because of the sins of the people and the failure of their father. Twice שחט refers to killing other Israelites—those from Gilead killing Ephraimites (Judg 12:6), and Jehu killing Ahab's descendants (2 Kgs 10:7, 14). In a sense, the actions of Zedekiah and the officials have led to the slaughtering of their fellow Israelites. The one remaining exception is in 1 Kgs 18:40 where Elijah killed the prophets of Baal, which may also reverberate in Jer 39 since it too is about the "fulfillment" of the prophetic word.

34. Verses 11–13 are absent from the Greek.

35. The two uses of שלח are awkward grammatically. Verse 13 has שלח (singular), so it is possible to read "Nebuzaradan the captain of the guard sent Nebushazban the Rabsaris," as the NEB does. However, it seems better, as *BHS* suggests, to read the שלח in v. 13 as a duplicate since v. 13 is likely serving as a bridge between vv. 3 and 14.

36. The words אל הבית are not represented in the Greek. Nicholson (*Jeremiah 26–52*, 128–29) suggests that "the house" refers to a "Governor's Residence," a building designated by the Babylonians as the headquarters for Gedaliah's new administration. Cf. also Thompson, *Jeremiah*, 648. The use of the definite article implies an official location of some sort.

then gouged out his "eyes." Indeed, Zedekiah loses his eyes, while Jeremiah receives the benevolent eye of the Babylonians. Furthermore, if Zedekiah unsuccessfully attempted to יצא from his prison (the city), the Babylonian king mandates that Jeremiah יצא (v. 14) from his prison.

The extent of the agency that Nebuchadrezzar grants to Jeremiah, however, becomes more complex by its similarities to Zedekiah's earlier treatment of the prophet. Nebuchadrezzar orders (צוה) his officers to take (לקח) Jeremiah (v. 12) in the same way that Zedekiah commanded (צוה) that Jeremiah be placed in the court of the guard (37:21) and that Ebed-melech remove Jeremiah from the cistern (38:10). While these verbal parallels point to scenes in which Zedekiah ameliorated Jeremiah's conditions, they also recall situations in which Jeremiah was not an agent, but rather was acted upon, and in which Jeremiah was confined in the court of the guard (37:21; 38:28), in lieu of being freed. If previously Jeremiah was in one king's hands (Zedekiah), now he is in the hands of another (Nebuchadrezzar). The nature of the prophet's agency remains in question—a question which can be better explored by a consideration of point of view.

Point of View
In the previous episode the narrator focused attention on the fate of Zedekiah (39:4–8); in this episode, it is on Jeremiah. Yet there is no direct speech attributed to the prophet, which is surprising since Nebuchadrezzar had commanded his officers to handle Jeremiah as the prophet "spoke" (דבר) to them. It is conceivable that a gap exists in the narrative between vv. 12 and 13 and that the reader must supply the conversation between the Babylonian officers and Jeremiah. On this reading, the prophet does express his view and thereby exercises the agency that is apparently granted to him. The actions in v. 13, then, are in response to Jeremiah's directives. Alternatively, one could interpret the officials as not soliciting Jeremiah's preferences, and opting instead simply to commit him to Gedaliah. Read in this fashion, Jeremiah's perspective is not revealed and his agency is severely limited as he has no choice in the matter.

Thus, there is a certain ambiguity regarding Jeremiah's point of view and the measure of his freedom. However, even if Jeremiah does communicate his wishes, the verbal description of the Babylonian treatment of Jeremiah underscores the limitations of the prophets agency, particularly when likened to his treatment in chs. 37–38. The Babylonian officers send for (שלח) the prophet (vv. 13, 14) and take (לקח) him, just as earlier Zedekiah twice "sent for" (שלח) and "took" (לקח) Jeremiah to conduct a meeting with him (37:17; 38:14). Nebuzaradan and the other officials "gave" (נתן) Jeremiah to Gedaliah (v. 14). This is reminiscent of Jeremiah being "put" (נתן) in prison (37:15; 38:7). Further, Gedaliah is "to bring him out to the house" (להוצאהו אל הבית). While this is an ambiguous phrase for which there have been a number of different translations, the word בית ties to the third episode in which בית is found four times to describe the place where Jeremiah was incarcerated by the officials (37:15–16). Consequently, a reference to "the house" (39:14) yields some menacing notions. Similarly, the Babylonians burned the king's "house" and the people's "house," so when they take Jeremiah to "the house," unsettling undertones exist. In addition, this episode culminates with Jeremiah "remaining among the people." In four previous instances (37:16, 21; 38:13, 28) יָשַׁב is employed in the closing note of a scene to indicate Jeremiah's "remaining/staying" in confinement.

Read in its narrative context, 39:11–14 subtly suggests that with the Babylonians in power, no one is "out of prison" and everyone's agency is constrained. Indeed, Jeremiah is "sent for," "taken," and "given" into the hands of Gedaliah and is to be "brought out" to "the house" where he is to "stay." Since Jeremiah was passively shuffled back and forth between Zedekiah and the officials, the reader wonders if the prophet has simply been transferred from one place of confinement (the court of the guard) to another ("the house"), from one jurisdiction (Zedekiah's) to another (Gedaliah's).[37]

Although Nebuchadrezzar expresses concern for Jeremiah's well-being, the narrator does not reveal how the Babylonians acquired knowledge of Jeremiah. This represents an additional gap in the story. Perhaps those who deserted would have apprised the Babylonians of the circumstances in Jerusalem.[38] If this is the case, then ironically the deserters would be responsible, not for Zedekiah's demise (as he feared, 38:19), but for Jeremiah's benevolent (?) treatment. The narrator also passes over in silence the question of why Nebuchadrezzar singles out Jeremiah for preferential treatment, which is a much more troubling and complex issue. In a sense, Jeremiah's treatment by the Babylonians vindicates the officials' point of view: Jeremiah had been a traitor who advocated "evil" (רָעָה) for the city (38:4); appropriately, now the Babylonians declared that no "evil" (רַע) is to be done to him. Is Jeremiah a prophet of Yahweh or a Babylonian diplomat? The Babylonian officials, as might be expected, never refer to Jeremiah as a "prophet," and neither does the narrator in these post-fall episodes.[39]

It indeed appears that Jeremiah's treatment by the Babylonians is his reward for siding with them.[40] But this introduces multiple questions: If Zedekiah had deserted his people by fleeing, is Jeremiah now deserting his people by permitting himself to be rescued by the enemy? Is this admission of collaboration? If Jeremiah was true to his people, should not he insist on sharing their fate? Can one be pro-Babylon and yet not betray one's people? If so, how would this be enacted? The narrator offers no answers, no perspective, just as there was no interpretive comment on the fall of Jerusalem. This stimulates readers to form their own perspective on the situation.

The Plot

Many commentators see this episode as depicting the liberating reward for Jeremiah, but a closer examination reveals a more complicated situation. The

---

37. At his point, the reader only knows Gedaliah from intertextual connections (see below), since the narrative has not introduced him. One may also note that Gedaliah is not instructed to take care of Jeremiah and there is no indication that Gedaliah has any special concern for the prophet.

38. Cf. Thompson, *Jeremiah*, 648.

39. Jeremiah is named as a "prophet" seven times in chs. 37–38 but not again until ch. 42.

40. Cf. Carroll, *Jeremiah: A Commentary*, 694.

structure of the narrative encourages comparison between the fates of Zedekiah (vv. 4–7), Jerusalem (v. 8), the people (vv. 9–10), and Jeremiah (vv. 11–14). The treatment of Zedekiah and Jeremiah is, of course, quite distinct. But the Babylonian treatment of the poor people—who are permitted to remain in the land and are given fields and vineyards (39:10)—and of Jeremiah is not noticeably different. A linguistic link prompts comparison between the fate of "the poor" and Jeremiah. Nebuchadrezzar assigned land to those who had "nothing" (מאומה), and he orders that "nothing" (מאומה) harmful be inflicted on Jeremiah. Nebuzaradan assists the poor by commissioning material goods, and he helps Jeremiah by omission of ill treatment. Jeremiah is hardly getting special treatment, at least when compared to the poor. Verse 10 holds out the possibility for continued life in Judah, and Jeremiah will merely be a member of that community. Ironically, the prophet who himself did not desert to the Babylonians is taken care of by the enemy and permitted to stay in the land along with the poor, while those who heeded his message and deserted are exiled to Babylon. In a strange sense, Jeremiah's own fate undermines his message.

There is another peculiar facet in the plot. The Babylonians find Jeremiah in the court of the guard. On the one hand, this makes sense, since that is where he was last seen (38:28). On the other hand, it is unclear why he was still there even after the king, nobles, and officials had abandoned the city. It is possible that he was physically restrained (i.e. fettered), but this does not seem plausible, since conditions there appear tolerable (cf. 37:21). Thus, it remains uncertain as to why Jeremiah did not take some sort of action when the city was captured. In this sense, Jeremiah is passive and indecisive, the same features for which Zedekiah might be criticized. When the Babylonians arrive, Zedekiah moves out, the Babylonians move in, and Jeremiah does not move at all.

Intertextuality
While neither Gedaliah's position nor the purpose of Jeremiah being discharged to him is unveiled, the narrator does provide his patronymic—he was the son of Ahikam the son of Shaphan. Shaphan was a scribe under Josiah and was an instrumental figure in finding the law book which became the basis for Josiah's reforms. In fact, according to 2 Kgs 22:10, Shaphan was the one who read the book to Josiah. Ahikam also served under Josiah and was appointed to the delegation which consulted Huldah about the newly discovered book (2 Kgs 22:12, 14). Ahikam has also made an appearance in the book of Jeremiah, as he protected the prophet from death, in contrast to Uriah's fate (26:24).[41] These intertextual relationships lead one to believe that Gedaliah—following his father and grandfather—will support and protect Jeremiah. The prophet is in good hands. There are, however, a number of instances in the Hebrew Bible where sons do not follow in the footsteps of their father (e.g. Eli, Samuel), so there are no

---

41. Micaiah, the son of Gemariah, is another grandson of Shaphan; he brought the news of Baruch's reading of the scroll to Jehoiakim (Jer 36:11). His father Gemariah encouraged Jehoiakim not to destroy the scroll (36:25). Elasah, a third son of Shaphan, accompanied Gemariah when he delivered Jeremiah's letter to the Babylonian exiles (29:3). Cf. Thompson, *Jeremiah*, 653.

guarantees. Furthermore, 26:24 reminds one that prophets who preach destruction and submission do sometimes die, as did Uriah. Yet another factor suspending the reader's judgment of Jeremiah's security is that according to 26:24, "the hand of Ahikam was with Jeremiah so that he was not given into the hand of the people to be put death." In 39:14, Jeremiah is placed under Gedaliah's jurisdiction, but he then remains "among the people." Do "the people" still represent a threat to Jeremiah as they did previously?[42]

The phrase "set your eyes" (עֵין שִׂים) reflects 24:6, where Yahweh declares regarding the Babylonian exiles: "I will set my eyes on them for good, and I will bring them back to this land, I will build them up and not tear them down; I will plant them and not pluck them up."[43] Both 24:6 and 39:13 address the future of the people after Jerusalem's fall. On the one hand, it may demonstrate that both the Babylonian exiles and Jeremiah will be "looked after" during this crisis. On the other hand, it may indicate that Yahweh will bless only the Babylonian exilic community of which Jeremiah is not a member; while those in Babylon receive a hopeful word from Yahweh, Jeremiah receives assurance only from the Babylonians. The intertextual connection adds ambiguity to Jeremiah's circumstances.

Ninth Episode: 39:15–18

(15) The word of Yahweh came to Jeremiah when he was confined in the court of the guard, saying: (16) Go and say to Ebed-melech the Cushite saying: Thus says Yahweh of hosts, God of Israel: Look, I am bringing my words against this city for evil and not for good, and they will be fulfilled before you on that day.[44] (17) But I will save you on that day, says Yahweh, and you will not be given into the hands of the men whom you fear. (18) For I will surely save you, and you will not fall by the sword; but you will have your life as a prize of war, for you have trusted in me, says Yahweh.

Framed by two accounts of Jeremiah's "release" from prison (39:11–14; 40:1–6) is an oracle given to Ebed-melech. If 39:1–10 chronicled the fates of the king, city, and people and 39:11–14 of the prophet, then this scene appropriately focuses on the only other character who played a significant role in events leading up to the fall.[45] The scene—set when Jeremiah "was confined in the court of the guard"—is clearly a flashback since it breaks the chronological sequence of the narrative. This episode is also unique in that it is the only one that depicts only one scene.

---

42. There is nothing to suggest that "the people" are supportive of Jeremiah. If "the people" are associated with "the people of the land" in 37:2, there is reason to suspect some hostility toward Jeremiah. The people who remain in the land (v. 10) are permitted to do so not because they submitted to the Babylonians (i.e. agreed with Jeremiah), but because they were poor.

43. The expression עֵין שִׂים is found only three other places in the Hebrew Bible: Gen 44:21, Amos 9:4, and Jer 40:4 (see below).

44. This phrase does not appear in the Greek. Perhaps it is dittography from v. 17 (cf. *BHS*).

45. If this scene functions somewhat like a postscript that reports what became of the main characters when the city fell, then the lack of an explicit account of the officials' fate is all the more conspicuous (see above).

Contextual Analysis

There are several thematic and verbal elements of this episode that relate it to earlier ones.[46] The scene in which Ebed-melech rescued Jeremiah from the pit (38:11–13) was the only one in the six episodes prior to the fall in which a single person spoke—Ebed-melech spoke to Jeremiah. In the present episode it is as if that earlier "conversation" is now completed as Jeremiah responds to Ebed-melech.

The previous episode began with Nebuchadrezzar speaking through Nebuzaradan concerning Jeremiah (39:11); this episode begins with Yahweh delivering a message through Jeremiah concerning Ebed-melech. The content of the message—"I am bringing my words against this city for evil and not for good, and they will be fulfilled before you on that day"—also relates to earlier scenes. It recalls that the officials charged Jeremiah with weakening morale in the city by "speaking these words," which, according to the officials, Jeremiah intended for "evil" (38:4). Here it is Yahweh himself who plans "evil" for the city. Paradoxically, then, the officials were correct about Jeremiah, but they did not recognize that Yahweh too was targeting "words" against the city for "evil." The phrase "they will be before you on that day" is somewhat awkward, but it establishes a connection with v. 10, where "on that day" Nebuzaradan bestows land and vineyards to the poor people.[47] Thus, the repetition of the phrase in v. 16 reminds one that "on that day" Yahweh did bring evil, but some are spared and blessed with the opportunity to prosper. Similarly, if Yahweh designs "evil" for the city, Nebuchadrezzar instructed that no "evil" be done against Jeremiah (39:12). Yahweh intends evil, but Nebuzaradan wills benevolence. Finally, the phrase "before you" conjures the image of Zedekiah's children being killed "before his eyes." Yahweh literally enacts evil "before you"—that is, before both Ebed-melech and Zedekiah. Ebed-melech, however, "escapes" (מלט, v. 18) while Zedekiah does not "escape" (מלט) from the Babylonians, as Jeremiah had foretold (38:18, 23).

Jeremiah's oracle consists of two promises to Ebed-melech which recall the prophet's message in earlier scenes. The phrase "You will not be given into the hands of the men whom you fear" is reminiscent of the one conveyed to Zedekiah if he chose to surrender (38:19–20).[48] Zedekiah did not surrender and was given into the hands of the Babylonians. Ebed-melech did not surrender either, but he is informed that he will not be handed over because he trusted in Yahweh. In biblical narrative, analepsis (a flashback) is sometimes employed to create sharp contrast and irony.[49] Such is the case in this episode. The word of hope to Ebed-melech contrasts with the fates of Zedekiah's sons, Zedekiah himself, and the

---

46. The phrase "court of the guard" functions to unite this episode with the previous one (cf. vv. 14 and 15).

47. The idea of the evil coming "on that day" connects ironically to the image of Zedekiah fleeing "at night."

48. Cf. Carroll, *Jeremiah: A Commentary*, 695.

49. Donald Tolmie (*Narratology and Biblical Narratives: A Practical Guide* [San Francisco: International Scholars Publications, 1999], 90–91) cites several examples from the Jephthah story (11:1–3) and the Absalom story (2 Sam 18:17–18) where analepsis is used for this purpose.

nobles. While they are the Babylonians' prizes of war, Ebed-melech maintains his life as his own prize of war.

The phrase in v. 18, "you will have your life as a prize of war," links to 38:2 where Jeremiah extended the same promise to the people if they would surrender. Ebed-melech, however, did not surrender, but he was spared.[50] A word-play underscores this. Ebed-melech will not נפל by the sword even though he did not נפל to the Babylonians as Jeremiah had indicated was necessary to survive (21:9). The placement of this episode (i.e. the analepsis) also sparks comparison between the fate of Ebed-melech and that of Jeremiah and the poor.[51] Of course, Ebed-melech, Jeremiah, and the poor all survive the capture of Jerusalem. However, some of the poor acquire not only their lives but also new land as prizes of war. Thus, Ebed-melech, who saved Jeremiah from death in the pit and who "trusted" in Yahweh, ironically receives less than some people for whom faith in Jeremiah or the deity is never mentioned.[52]

Point of View
First, this scene features, as did earlier ones, an instance of double voicing as the prophet Jeremiah is instructed to speak the message of Yahweh. Since the entire oracle is in the first-person, Jeremiah is expressing the view of the deity. Secondly, Yahweh names Ebed-melech as a Cushite. Previously the narrator had identified Ebed-melech as such (38:7, 10, 12), and here Jeremiah/Yahweh follows the narrator's lead. This is important because the notion of foreigners speaking or acting for Yahweh continues in the next episode. Thirdly, the use of הנה at the head of the oracle serves to focus attention on its contents. Fourthly, Jeremiah/Yahweh twice identifies Ebed-melech's internal point of view. It is stated that Ebed-melech fears a certain group of people (v. 17) and that he has trusted in Yahweh. Thus Ebed-melech's views are refracted through the words of Jeremiah who is speaking for Yahweh.

Intertextuality
This scene is virtually a midrash constructed from phrases and motifs from the Jeremiah tradition.[53] Intertextual allusions uncover a tension in the oracle to Ebed-melech. In v. 17 Jeremiah promises Ebed-melech that he will not be

---

50. Carroll, seemingly unaware of its significance, remarks, "Ebed-melech and Jeremiah are two figures who did not desert to the Babylonians during the siege, yet survived the ordeal of those days" (*Jeremiah: A Commentary*, 697).

51. It is true that the poor people are not characters in the story in the same way as Jeremiah, Zedekiah, and Ebed-melech. Nonetheless, the reporting of what happened to the poor cannot be dismissed, for they are, after all, still in the story. In a similar fashion, the fathers and grandfathers of the various officials are not characters in the story, but the references to them add an important dimension to the narrative.

52. Baruch is also promised his life as a prize of war in ch. 45. This text represents an instance of analepsis (set in the fourth year of the reign of Jehoiakim). Chapters 43–44 narrate the events in the lives of the Egyptian community; thus, the oracle to Baruch which promises his life as a prize of war seems a bit banal because the whole Egyptian community survives as well.

53. Carroll, *Jeremiah: A Commentary*, 696, following Duhm, *Das Buch Jeremia*, 312–33.

handed over to those whom he fears (יגור).[54] This implies that Ebed-melech will be free, liberated.[55] The word יגור ("fear") is found one other time in the book in 22:25 where Yahweh says, "(I will) give you (Jehoiachin) into the hands of those who seek your life, into the hands of those whom you fear (יגור)."[56] The word יגור is employed in a context of exile (cf. 22:26), which hints that Ebed-melech, who—in contrast to Jehoiachin—would not be given into the hand of those he "feared," could expect to escape exile and to be granted full freedom. The phrase "you will have your life as prize of war," however, suggests something different. It parallels 21:9 where Jeremiah conveys the same promise to those who surrender (יצא) and desert (נפל) to the Babylonians.[57] There the phrase signifies escaping death, not escaping from the hand of the enemy altogether. That is, one will survive, but there is no promise of plenary freedom. Similarly, in 39:18 the promise to Ebed-melech that he will have his life as a prize of war is placed directly after the promise that he will not die by the sword; so it appears that, as in ch. 21, it indicates that Ebed-melech will live, not that he will have compete freedom. Therefore, the oracle to Ebed-melech is not as salvific as it might first appear. The phrase is idiomatic and its meaning is not explicit, but as Jones observes, "what is certain is that it does not mean a joyous and rich salvation. Ebed-melech will be among the things that are not destroyed in the general carnage and pillage. He will be, so to speak, up for booty. But at the very least this means that he will be alive."[58] When this notion is combined with the fact that the report of general pillaging and carnage is quite minimal, then Ebed-melech's "salvation" becomes even less significant. In short, a certain tension exists in the oracle in ch. 39 which is best seen in light of the intertextual connections with 22:25 and 21:8–10.

There is another dimension to this subdued element in the oracle to Ebed-melech as it relates to its context in ch. 39. Ebed-melech may have risked his life to save Jeremiah's life; therefore, Yahweh promises to save Ebed-melech's life. However, just as Ebed-melech did not (or was not able to) give the prophet full freedom—Jeremiah simply remained in the court of the guard (38:13)—so

54. The identity of those he fears is unclear. The two most likely candidates are the Judean officials, as Bright (*Jeremiah*, 232) suggests, or the Babylonians.

55. The verbs נצל (v. 17) and מלט (v. 18) seem to suggest more than "saving" from death. Cf. Jer 1:19; 15:20, 21.

56. The phrases are the exact same in both verses: אשר אתה יגור מפניהם.

57. There are also other verbal connections between 21:8–10 and 39:15–18 that invite comparison. In ch. 21, Yahweh declares, "I have set my face against this city for evil and not for good," which is similar to the phrase "I am bringing my words against this city for evil and not for good" in 39:16. Jerusalem "will be given into the hands of the king of Babylon" (21:10), but Ebed-melech will "not be given into the hands" of those he fears (39:17). Ebed-melech will not "fall by the sword" (39:18), but those who do not surrender and desert will "die by the sword" (21:9).

58. Jones, *Jeremiah*, 466. Similarly, Carroll (*Jeremiah: A Commentary*, 744–45) writes of the phrase, "This is an ironic figure of speech which assures the recipient of survival but nothing else." He does argue, however, that in 21:9, 38:2, and 45:5 the phrase is associated with survival, but in 39:18 it is linked to escape. Holladay (*Jeremiah 1*, 574) explains this phrase as "an ironic soldier's joke" that conveys the idea that "when a soldier is defeated and escapes, having barely saved his life, he has at least that as booty." Cf. also Calvin, *Commentaries on the Book* 4:386–87.

Jeremiah does not promise Ebed-melech full freedom, only that he will not die. In a similar light, Yahweh had promised to נצל ("save") Jeremiah from the hand of his enemies (1:8, 19; 15:20, 21), but either Yahweh had failed to do so or else "saving" (נצל) meant only saving him from death, for, indeed, Jeremiah is imprisoned in the court of the guard when he utters the oracle to Ebed-melech. Thus, Yahweh's promise to נצל Ebed-melech is lessened by the very conditions of the one who delivers the oracle to him.

Ebed-melech's trust (בטח) in Yahweh produces some complex intertextual linkages with the stories of Hezekiah and Isaiah. There the Rabshakeh exhorted the people of Jerusalem not to trust (בטח) in Yahweh to save the city (2 Kgs 18:22, 30; 19:10). Hezekiah, supported by Isaiah, of course, did trust in Yahweh to save Jerusalem and was rewarded for it. During the Babylonian crises, Zedekiah and the officials are the ones who "trusted" in Yahweh, which they enact by not surrendering to the enemy. Their trust, however, is not requited by the deity. It is ironic, then, that Ebed-melech is praised for "trusting" in Yahweh when Zedekiah and the officials presumably would have forwarded the same claim about themselves, citing Hezekiah's "trust" as a successful precedent. Unfortunately for Zedekiah, "trusting" in Yahweh paradoxically meant trusting the deity to wreak "evil" against Jerusalem, rather than sheltering it from evil. Thus, it is not a matter of who trusts in Yahweh, but who understands which of Yahweh's intentions to trust.

Finally, there are unmistakable thematic and verbal similarities between the oracle to Ebed-melech in 39:15–18 and the message to Baruch in 45:1–5. Observing these parallels, Seitz proposes that Ebed-melech and Baruch are modeled after Joshua and Caleb.[59] Seitz's analysis strengthens and elaborates the network of connections (explored above) between Jer 37–40 and the stories of the exodus and the conquest.

Tenth Episode: 40:1–6

(1) The word that came to Jeremiah from Yahweh, after Nebuzaradan the captain of the guard had let him go from Ramah, when he took him bound in chains among all the exiles of Jerusalem and Judah who were being exiled to Babylon. (2) The captain of the guard took Jeremiah and said to him, "Yahweh your God spoke this evil against this place, (3) and Yahweh has brought it about and done as he said, for you all have sinned against Yahweh and did not listen to his voice; so this thing has happened to you all. (4) Now look, I have released you today from the chains that are on your hand. If it seems good to you to come with me to Babylon, come, and I will look after you. But if it seems bad to you to come with me to Babylon, stay here. See all the land that is before you; wherever it seems good and right to go, go there." (5) He had not yet answered when Nebuzaradan said, "Return[60] to Gedaliah son of Ahikam son of Shaphan whom the king

---

59. Seitz, "The Prophet Moses," 16–27.

60. The meaning of these words has been variously understood. The Hebrew is וְעוֹדֶנּוּ לֹא־יָשׁוּב וְשֻׁבָה אֶל־גְּדַלְיָה. McKane (*Jeremiah XXVI–LII*, 993, 1000–1001) and Nicholson (*Jeremiah 26–52*, 131) also understand the sense to be "he had not yet answered." Cf. also the NEB. The shift to the third person (יָשׁוּב) makes it difficult to render "if you remain" (NRSV).

of Babylon appointed over the cities of Judah, and stay with him among the people or wherever it seems right to go, go." So the captain of the guard gave him rations and a present and let him go. (6) And Jeremiah came to Gedaliah son of Ahikam at Mizpah, and he remained with him among the people who were left in the land.

In this final episode, the story resumes chronicling Jeremiah's fate. If the previous scene consisted of an oracle delivered from Yahweh through Jeremiah, this episode features a lengthy speech from Nebuzaradan to Jeremiah. While the preceding episode was unmistakably a flashback, this one is fashioned to be one as well insofar as the narrator had already reported Nebuzaradan's exiling of the people to Babylon (39:9); here, however, the narrator backtracks to portray the deportees as they are being gathered. The sixth and final occurrence of the phrase "and he remained" serves to bring section one (37:1–40:6) to a close.

Time
Scholars are divided over whether this episode represents a second version of Jeremiah's release or whether 39:11–14 and 40:1–6 are to be read sequentially.[61] This scenario is not unlike that regarding the relationship between the stories in chs. 37 and 38. As with the accounts of Jeremiah's imprisonments and his interviews with Zedekiah before the fall, these two stories of his release reflect one another, inviting comparison—which does not preclude a linear reading. That is, these stories resist an easy linear or circular read, which calls the reader to consider both options.

If one reads the two stories of Jeremiah's release (39:11–4 and 40:1–6) linearly, then it seems that after having been freed from the court of the guard, Jeremiah is (mistakenly?) detained by Babylonian soldiers and taken to Ramah where others were being gathered for deportation.[62] Clues in the account in 39:11–14 do not assure the reader that all will be well for the prophet; thus one may not be surprised to learn in 40:1–6 that, rather than being liberated, the prophet has again found himself fettered and his circumstances in need of amelioration. As before the fall, Jeremiah is shuffled from place to place (the court of guard, freed to Gedaliah, taken to be with the exiles at Ramah, and freed to Gedaliah again).

Such a linear reading may also explain the curious phrase in 39:14, "to bring him out to the house." The "house" would then denote the place where the exiles

---

61. Bright (*Jeremiah*, 245–46) and Thompson, (*Jeremiah*, 651), for example, read it sequentially. Carroll (*Jeremiah: A Commentary*, 699) and Nicholson (*Jeremiah 26–52*, 131) read it as a second account of the same events. Likewise, Wanke (*Untersuchungen zur sogenannten Baruchschrift*, 89) maintains that both accounts of Jeremiah's release from prison (39:11–15; 40:1–6) cannot be original since they both end with the same formula ("Jeremiah remained with the people"). He concludes that the version in 40:1–6 is a *Legenbildung*, an insertion from the time of the exile made by the editors. Other commentators—among them Huey (*Jeremiah, Lamentations*, 344, 348)—reserve judgment, admitting both possibilities. Rofé (*Prophetical Stories*, 210) considers the possibility that Jeremiah was released and again detained several times because "Jeremiah had already demonstrated that in situations of this kind—false or mistaken arrests—he was quite incapable of taking care of himself (37:12–15)."

62. Is it possible that after being released the first time, Jeremiah voluntarily joined the exiles?

were being held before the journey to Babylon.[63] Indeed, Nebuchadrezzar said nothing about freeing Jeremiah (39:12), only about not harming (רע) him. Submitting Jeremiah to Gedaliah (39:14) would simply suggest that Gedaliah was responsible for separating and organizing those who were to be deported. As a final point in favor of a linear reading, a distinction could be made between Jeremiah "remaining among the people" in 39:14 (those being gathered for exile) and his "remaining among the people who were left in the land" in 40:6.

Contextual Analysis

The final three episodes depict the fates of Jeremiah and Ebed-melech as they contrast to that of Zedekiah and the nobles. Especially important is the contrast between the Babylonians' eliminating of Zedekiah's agency and their granting a certain extent of autonomy to the prophet—a contrast which is underscored by the verbal nature of the text. The image of Jeremiah "bound in fetters" (באזקים אסור) is reminiscent of Zedekiah being "bound in chains" (ויאסרהו בנחשתים) in preparation of deportation. The king, however, is exiled to Babylon while the prophet is released and remains in Judah. If Zedekiah has his eyes gouged out by Nebuchadrezzar, Nebuzaradan invites Jeremiah to do what is right "in your eyes"—to exercise his agency—and to "see all the land that is before you." The six references to Jeremiah's "eyes" and his "seeing" distinguish the fortunes of prophet and king. If Jeremiah is allowed to decide his own future, Nebuchadrezzar "spoke judgment" against Zedekiah and blinded him. Jeremiah is released "today" (היום) while Zedekiah attempted unsuccessfully to escape at "night" (לילה). If Jeremiah told Zedekiah that he and Jerusalem would be given (נתן) into the "hand" (יד) of the Babylonians (37:17; 38:3, 18), Nebuzaradan removes the fetters from Jeremiah's "hands" (יד). While Jeremiah's autonomy is to be contrasted with Zedekiah's, it is not altogether unlimited.

Rather, as was true for the eighth episode (39:11–14), many of the elements that link the tenth episode to the previous ones revolve around the theme of constrained agency. Before the fall, the Judean officials twice imprisoned Jeremiah (37:15–16; 38:6), and the Judean king (Zedekiah) and his servant (Ebed-melech) released him (37:21; 38:12–13); after the fall, the Babylonian king (Nebuchadrezzar) and his servant (Nebuzaradan) twice free Jeremiah. However, as Jeremiah's releases in chs. 37–38 involved limited freedom (in the court of the guard), so do his Babylonian emancipations.

The appointment of Gedaliah by Nebuzaradan connects with the introduction in 37:1–2 and casts doubt on the level of freedom and security Jeremiah will experience. In the introduction, the narrator reported that Zedekiah had been made king by Nebuchadrezzar. In 40:5, another Babylonian leader designates another Judean, Gedaliah, to govern Judah. In view of the tragic events that unfolded during Zedekiah's "kingship," the idea of another Judean ruling the

---

63. The commentators who read the two accounts sequentially do not point this out. The definite article, "*the* house," is problematic (and militates against reading "to be brought home"), but in view of the events in 40:1–6, it emerges as the location where the deportees are being assembled.

land under Babylonian authority strikes an unpromising note for Jeremiah and others. This sense of uneasiness plays itself out as Gedaliah is murdered, which leads to yet another exile, this time to Egypt.

Furthermore, as was mentioned above, Gedaliah may have been part of a significant contingent of Judeans who had deserted to the Babylonians (cf. 38:19). If prior to the fall, Jeremiah had been under the control of those who advocated resistance, now he is in the hands of those who had surrendered. Will the prophet's agency be constrained by the new ruling party? Zedekiah had expressed considerable apprehension about how those who had surrendered would treat him even if he too were to surrender. One may then ask if this group also represented a threat to Jeremiah. His advice to surrender may not appease them, especially since he himself never deserted, and in fact, explicitly denied this intention (37:14).

Other elements generate ambiguity concerning the extent of the agency granted to Jeremiah. The verbs used to describe Nebuzaradan's treatment of the prophet—שלח and לקח (vv. 1, 2, 5)—are the same verbs that describe the prophet's treatment by Zedekiah (37:17; 38:14) and the Judean officials (38:6). In addition, Nebuzaradan gives (נתן) the prophet "an allowance of food and a present" and he "remains" (ישב) with Gedaliah "among (בתוך) the people who were left (שאר) in the land" (v. 6). Although this is an improvement in Jeremiah's conditions, echoes of 37:4–5, 12, 21, and 39:10 temper the uniqueness and optimism of his condition. In 37:12, Jeremiah attempted to go out "among the people," and although he was apparently free to "come and go among the people" (37:4), he was detained by Irijah—his freedom short-lived. As the loose chiastic structure to 37:1–40:6 demonstrated (see above), Jeremiah's state of freedom in 37:4–5 parallels his freedom in 40:4–5. However, since his earlier freedom terminated with imprisonment, the prospects of his freedom "among the people" in this scene remain dubious.

In 37:21 Zedekiah moved Jeremiah from Jonathan's prison (37:16) to the court of the guard and gave (נתן) him food; thus when Nebuzaradan supplies the prophet with provisions (40:5), it is reminiscent of a context in which although Jeremiah's conditions improved, he remained incarcerated. Still, a gift would seemingly presage freedom and autonomy for the prophet; Nebuzaradan, however, had given vineyards and fields to the poor people in the land of Judah (39:10), which is substantially more than he gives to Jeremiah. Nebuzaradan is generous to all those he leaves behind—Jeremiah is no one special in this regard. This connection is highlighted by clever word-play: Jeremiah is told that he can חדל ("cease," i.e., stay in Judah, 40:4), which means he will be remaining with the הדל ("the poor", 39:10).

Finally, the episode concludes with Jeremiah "remaining" (ישב) among the people. The close verbal ties with the four parallel phrases in which Jeremiah "remained" (ישב) in prison (37:16) or the court of the guard (37:21; 38:13, 28) implies some constraint on Jeremiah's agency as he "remains" among the people. The prophet is, at least, alive, undermining his assertion that those who ישב would die.

The juxtaposition of the last three episodes also encourages comparison between the agents of Ebed-melech's and Jeremiah's salvation. Jeremiah survives as a friend of Babylon, whereas Ebed-melech survives because of his "trust" in Yahweh; neither survives because of their surrendering to the Babylonians. A word-play highlights their two different modes of rescue: Ebed-melech is saved because of his בטח ("trust") in Yahweh, while Jeremiah is saved by the actions of Nebuzaradan, the chief טבחים (lit. "butcher"). Yahweh is the agent of Ebed-melech's salvation; the Babylonians are the agent of Jeremiah's salvation. The effectiveness of the word-play is underscored by the contrast between the divine first-person oracle to Ebed-melech—"I (Yahweh) will surely save you . . . because you have trusted in me"—and Nebuzaradan's speech to Jeremiah—"Now look, I have released you today." The apparent absence of, or lack of direct involvement by, Yahweh in Jeremiah's fate—a feature that is more prominent when compared to Ebed-melech's rescue—is remarkable given the deity's promise in ch. 1 to protect the prophet. Indeed, in neither of Jeremiah's two "releases" is there any reference to Yahweh, *contra* Ebed-melech's rescue. It is possible, however, to interpret Nebuzaradan as the agent of Yahweh's rescue of Jeremiah, as earlier Ebed-melech could be deemed as functioning in the same capacity. On this reading, there are multiple levels of "agency" as the Babylonians enact Yahweh's will, rather than their own.

Point of View

This episode features several complex issues regarding point of view, which can best be seen by close analysis of the characters' speech, or their reticence. Opening the narrative is the formulaic phrase, "The word that came to Jeremiah from Yahweh." There is, however, no subsequent oracle, only a lengthy speech by Nebuzaradan. This gap evokes several interpretive possibilities.[64] One option is to ascertain that the deity's view is not presented, which is perplexing since the text sets up the reader to expect it. A second way of understanding the gap is to imagine that there is no gap; that is, the text is playing on the opening formulaic phrase. The word of Yahweh "to Jeremiah" is, in fact, what follows in the form of Nebuzaradan's speech—which is, after all, in prophetic parlance.[65] Yahweh communicates to Jeremiah through Nebuzaradan, in contrast with speaking to someone else—most recently Ebed-melech—through Jeremiah. If this is the case, there may be irony at the expense of Jeremiah.

In all of his previous appearances (39:9, 10, 11, 13) and in his first appearance in this scene (40:1) Nebuzaradan is identified by name and title (captain of the guard). By contrast, when Nebuzaradan speaks to Jeremiah, he is referred to only by his title (40:2, 5). This deviation points to the idea that Nebuzaradan stands in relationship to Jeremiah as a Babylonian officer, not as a personal friend or acquaintance. This distances Jeremiah from his liberator, which may reflect well

---

64. Some commentators explain this by suggesting that the oracle has fallen out. If so, it is difficult to imagine the final redactor not being aware of this gap.

65. Keown, Smothers, and Scalise, *Jeremiah 26–52*, 235, read the text this way, as does the NEB, which renders: "The word which came from the Lord concerning Jeremiah."

on Jeremiah by implying that he had no personal relationship with Babylonian authorities. However, the Babylonians—as well as the narrator in these post-fall episodes—never name Jeremiah as a prophet, which suggests that they view him as a spokesman for their political propaganda (hence their benevolent treatment of him?).

The narrator provided no interpretive perspective on the fall of Jerusalem in 39:1–10; similarly, Jeremiah does not at any point comment on the significance of the debacle. Instead, it is a Babylonian official who interprets the events. Recalling the narrator's introduction in 37:2, Nebuzaradan draws a lesson by attributing the fall to a lack of obedience.[66] According to Nebuzaradan's point of view, the Babylonian hegemony is a result of the people's sin against Yahweh. Thus, the Babylonians broker both Yahweh's punishment and the message that interprets the punishment. Earlier the officials had accused Jeremiah of seeking "evil" (רעה) against Jerusalem by "speaking" (דבר) words of discouragement (38:4); now Nebuzaradan asserts that Yahweh "spoke evil" (דבר את־רעה) against this city. Nebuzaradan's standpoint confirms, in a sense, the officials' view of Jeremiah: the prophet, like the Babylonians, had sought evil for the city, ostensibly in the name of the deity to validate his position.

Attributing this speech to Nebuzaradan, not Jeremiah or the narrator, raises a number of questions: Did Nebuzaradan know the details of Jeremiah's message? How did he come to hold this view of the catastrophe? Is Jeremiah surprised to hear Nebuzaradan's statement? Why did Jeremiah omit in his message before the fall that even the Babylonians themselves understand that the siege and inevitable destruction were punishment from Yahweh? Why does Nebuzaradan separate Jeremiah from the group of deportees and then speak directly to him? What sort of speech-act is this? Furthermore, Nebuzaradan does not exempt Jeremiah from the statement that "you all sinned" and "you all did not listen." In this vein, there may be a play on Nebuzaradan's instructions to Jeremiah to שוב: Is he to "repent" or "return"? These questions remain unanswered, the ambiguity and uncertainty calling the reader into the conversation.

The lesson which Nebuzaradan outlines is somewhat in tension with Jeremiah's message to Zedekiah in chs. 37–38—surrender and live, rebel and die. Jeremiah's words had not focused on submitting to the Babylonians because their ascendancy was punishment for sin.[67] One can note what Nebuzaradan does not say, namely, that Yahweh had brought about this disaster because Zedekiah and the Judeans did not capitulate to the Babylonians. Nonetheless, it is logical to conclude that Jeremiah would be in general agreement with Nebuzaradan's

---

66. Perhaps the narrator ascribes these words to Nebuzaradan to demonstrate that even the Babylonians correctly perceive the theological situation. In this sense, there is biting sarcasm and irony at the expense of all of Judah. These words on the lips of a foreign conqueror may be a bit unpalatable.

67. In some places there is no connection whatsoever between Babylonian rule and Yahweh's punishment for disobedience. For instance, in ch. 27 Jeremiah preaches submission because Yahweh had relinquished all the land—including Edom, Moab, Amon, Tyre, and Sidon—into the hand of Nebuchadrezzar. This approach is difficult to reconcile with interpreting the destruction as punishment for the sins of Judah (cf. 27:3).

assessment, but, and this is crucial, the reader does not know if he is in agreement because the prophet remains taciturn throughout this episode. Jeremiah never expresses his point of view.

Nebuzaradan's speech contains a הנה clause that focuses Jeremiah's attention on his liberated conditions and presents him with three different options based on the prophet's perspective (come to Babylon; return to Gedaliah; or go wherever he wanted, vv. 4–5). Two idioms that use עין play off one another. Nebuzaradan recommends to Jeremiah that "if it is good in your eyes to come with me to Babylon, come, and I will put my eyes on you." Nebuzaradan also directs Jeremiah's and the reader's view when he encourages the prophet to "see (ראה) all the land that is before you." One may speculate—given the apparent destruction of the land—if there were any suitable places for Jeremiah to go.[68] It is not surprising, then, that Nebuzaradan advises Jeremiah more specifically to go to Gedaliah, for this may be the only "good" (טוב) possibility if he were to remain in the land.

Nebuzaradan's choice of verbs betrays his Babylonian perspective and may be understood as an attempt to influence Jeremiah's view. He informs the prophet that he may בוא ("come") to Babylon or he may הלך ("go") wherever he wished. From a Babylonian standpoint, one indeed would "come" ("home or back") to Babylon or "go" to Judah. But from Jeremiah's perspective the actions would be reversed: he would "go" (הלך) to Babylon or "come" (בוא) to Judah. The narrative, appropriately then, adopts Jeremiah's perspective when it reports that Jeremiah בוא ("came") to Gedaliah. Finally, although Nebuzaradan expresses his view about the theological significance of Jerusalem's fall, he tenders no reason for releasing Jeremiah. Thus, as in 39:11–14, the Babylonian perception of Jeremiah lacks clarity.

While the prophet does not speak in this episode, the first four words of v. 5 may make his taciturnity more explicit: "He had not yet answered when Nebuzaradan said, 'Return to Gedaliah.'" Jeremiah, then, fails to express—or does not get the opportunity to express—whether he would prefer to stay in Judah or go to Babylon. Moreover, Nebuzaradan has essentially reneged on the option to travel to Babylon and has instead instructed that he return to Gedaliah, or go somewhere else in Judah. A secure life in Babylon is no longer an alternative for Jeremiah, only life in Judah, about which Nebuzaradan makes no felicitous promises. Again Jeremiah's choices are limited, his agency constrained.

Furthermore, Jeremiah's silence—or at least his delaying a response to Nebuzaradan—is reminiscent of Zedekiah in that both characters are indecisive when confronted with choices. Zedekiah could have יצא to the Babylonians or ישב in Jerusalem, while Jeremiah could בוא to Babylon with Nebuzaradan or הלך to Gedaliah in Judah. Both end up staying in Judah/Jerusalem.[69] If Jeremiah can

---

68. Alternatively, this could be taken as another indication that the destruction was not widespread. Similarly, Nebuzaradan states that Gedaliah has been appointed over "all the cities of Judah" (v. 5), which implies that there were other viable options for Jeremiah.

69. In view of what happens to Jeremiah in chs. 42–44, one could say that he, like Zedekiah, made the wrong decision.

be likened to Zedekiah in this manner, then Nebuzaradan assumes the role of the prophet as the one presenting the choices, which incidentally links nicely with the notion that Nebuzaradan's speech represents the oracle of Yahweh to Jeremiah.[70]

Even if one does not follow this rendering of v. 5a, it remains evident that Jeremiah's perspective is not revealed. The prophet does not explain his reasons for staying (if he even had a choice). Again one can draw parallels to Zedekiah's perspective prior to the fall and Jeremiah's after it. If Zedekiah was caught between two groups with opposing views (the officials and Jeremiah), here one imagines that Jeremiah is somehow trapped between loyalty to those who were being exiled and those remaining in Judah. Like Zedekiah's predicament, to ally with one group meant betraying the other. Thus one can ask if (by staying) Jeremiah is loyal to Judah or if he is deserting the exiles.[71] The answer may very well depend upon whom one asks—that is, whose perspective one seeks. Incidentally, if one assumes, as many commentators do, that Jeremiah remained to help guide the new government under Gedaliah, then his absence in the next section (40:7–41:18) is all the more salient.

Although no character expresses a perspective on it, a pertinent question here is how Jeremiah, the exiles, and those Judeans who remained viewed Jeremiah's treatment by the Babylonians. Brueggemann speculates that "to be well treated by the occupying army can hardly be a popular outcome. It is the treatment given to someone who has become a traitor."[72] Seeing Jeremiah as a traitor and his preferential handling by the Babylonians as evidence of that seems a rather justifiable opinion. Further, one may wonder how Jeremiah evaluated being labeled a friend of the enemy. Thompson hypothesizes,

> He was treated as a "friend" of Babylon. No doubt he would have been just as unhappy about such an assumption of his loyalty as he had been when he was accused by the Jewish military authorities of going over to the enemy (37:13). He would not have found it any easier to explain his theological position to the Babylonians than to the people of Jerusalem and Judah.[73]

This is a reasonable answer, albeit not the only reasonable one. For instance, if Thompson is correct, one may question why Jeremiah does not at least attempt to articulate his perspective. His quiet acceptance of their treatment may easily be (mis?)interpreted as affirming his friendship with the Babylonians. Further, if as Thompson implies, no one comprehends the prophet's perspective, whatever it may be, then perhaps the problem lies with the communicator and not with those to whom he is communicating. In short, point of view functions in a complex manner in this episode. Specifically, Jeremiah's reticence precludes sure

---

70. It also connects with the fact that Nebuchadrezzar gave commands "by the hand of Nebuzaradan" (39:11)—that is, Nebuzaradan is serving as the intermediary/prophet.

71. Jeremiah's not going to Babylon where he is promised special treatment should have eliminated all accusations that he was a Babylonian collaborator, but it did not (cf. 43:4).

72. Brueggemann, *To Build, to Plant*, 162.

73. Thompson, *Jeremiah*, 652.

conclusions about his perspective—giving readers multiple interpretive options and leaving them peering into the shadows as the prophet journeys to Gedaliah.

Intertextuality

Nebuzaradan's assertion that Yahweh has brought about the destruction revisits the Rabshakeh's speech (2 Kgs 18:25) in which he says, "Is it without Yahweh that I have come up against this place to destroy it. Yahweh said to me, 'Go up against this land and destroy it.'" In addition to the phrase common to both, הוה הקום, both the Rabshakeh and Nebuzaradan—foreign military officers—appeal to Deuteronomistic theology which explains that destruction is the result of sin.[74] Two other key factors emerge in the comparison of these speeches. First, Nebuzaradan addresses Jeremiah, not the people at large to whom it would be more appropriately directed. This peculiarity is underscored by the fact that the Rabshakeh speaks to the people of Judah in their own language, which is precisely the matter to which the Judean officials object (2 Kgs 18:26).

Second, Nebuzaradan utters his statement after Jerusalem has been captured, whereas the Rabshakeh's speech is during the siege, designed to persuade the people to surrender. The Rabshakeh is wrong; Nebuzaradan is correct. However, the echo of the Rabshakeh's speech reminds one that sometimes enemy commanders who appeal to Deuteronomistic theology are misguided. Indeed, it is easy for Nebuzaradan to make his claims after the fact. While, on the one hand, the intertextual connections highlight the disparity in the outcomes of the Assyrian and Babylonian crises, on the other hand, it evokes sympathy for Zedekiah and his refusal to surrender by calling attention to the fact that hindsight is always better than foresight (cf. above). Further, since Jeremiah articulated basically the same position as the Rabshakeh, the narrator's placing this speech on Nebuzaradan's lips, instead of Jeremiah's, may bolster Jeremiah's image. At least it is not the prophet saying, "I told you so." However, given that Jeremiah has been cast in the role of the foreigner, the Rabshakeh, it is ironic (seemingly at Jeremiah's expense) that here the foreigner Nebuzaradan plays the role of the prophet Jeremiah.

One may also recall the story of Rahab and the spies, a story echoed by previous episodes, for it is another example of a Deuteronomistic speech in the mouth of a foreigner (Josh 2:8–14). Rahab declares that she is aware that Yahweh has given the land to the Israelites, contrary to the Rabshakeh and Nebuzaradan who assert that Yahweh has taken away the land and conferred it to Assyria and Babylon. Accordingly, Rahab, one foreigner, petitions special treatment from the Israelite conquerors, whereas Jeremiah, one Judean, receives special treatment from the foreign conquerors. In a sense, Rahab's and Nebuzaradan's speeches frame the history of Israel and Judah to demonstrate that Yahweh is in control of

---

74. They do so, however, in slightly different ways. The Rabshakeh states explicitly that Yahweh authorized the Assyrians to destroy the land, but he only implies that it is punishment for the people's sins. By contrast, Nebuzaradan explicitly claims that the Babylonian destruction was a consequence of disobedience, but he does not overtly contend that Yahweh sent the Babylonians.

history, giving and taking as he sees fit. The key, as Zedekiah learned, is to know when he is doing what.

The use of שׁלח in the piel meaning "let go," in 40:1 and 5, points to the Exodus story where this verb appears in the piel numerous times.[75] Here Jeremiah is "let go," which enables him to stay in the land; ironically, the people who are not "let go" are forced to make a reverse exodus—out of the land and into captivity. However, שׁלח here in this episode does not occur with חפשׁי, "free," as it does in Jer 34:9, 10, 11, 14, and 16 where it refers to the people letting their slaves "go free." In this sense, one wonders if Jeremiah is "let go" by Nebuzaradan, but will not be truly free under Gedaliah's governorship—not entirely unlike the servants in ch. 34 who are set free, but only temporarily. These intertextual links reinforce the motif of Jeremiah's limited agency.

There are several other intertextual connections that feature ostensibly positive ideas but carry ominous undertones—suggesting constraints on Jeremiah's freedom. First, in Gen 13:9, Abraham says to Lot, "Is not the whole land before you?" (כל הארץ לפניך). This is the exact same phrase—כל הארץ לפניך—that Nebuzaradan speaks to Jeremiah (40:4). The relationship between the two contexts is strengthened by the fact that these are the only two times that this phrase occurs in the Hebrew Bible. Both Lot and Jeremiah are granted choices regarding their destination. Lot's decision appears to be a good and reasonable one, but the presence of wicked people (those in Sodom, Gen 13:12–13) renders it ultimately fatal. Jeremiah's choice, too, looks as though it is an auspicious one, but it also leads to misfortune because of the deeds of wicked people (Ishmael and those who flee to Egypt). After Lot chooses his portion of land, Yahweh promises Abraham land and descendants. Again, a text which features the initial acquiring of the land is linked to the story in which the people lose the land. Furthermore, as Abraham's fortune is contrasted to Lot's, so too the fate of the Babylonian exilic community can be contrasted to that of Jeremiah and those who remained in the land and subsequently migrated to Egypt. In short, כל הארץ לפניך may subtly presage the difficulties that lie ahead for Jeremiah because of the constraints imposed upon him by Babylonian hegemony.

Moreover, the image of Jeremiah "seeing" (ראה) the land may recall Moses being instructed to "see" the land that Yahweh was about to bestow to the people (Deut 3:27; 32:49). In both of these contexts, Yahweh rebukes Moses and his seeing the land is only a consolation for not being able to enter it (Deut 3:26; 32:50–51). As with Lot, negative connotations accompany "seeing the land." Indeed, both Jeremiah and Moses see the land, but die outside of it.

Second, Nebuzaradan furnishes Jeremiah with "rations and a present" (ומשׂאת ארחה) as he departs for Gedaliah. This is reminiscent of the Israelites receiving provisions when they depart from Egypt (Exod 3:20–22; 11:1–2; 12:35–36).[76] Jeremiah receives material goods and embarks on his own type of Exodus, while

---

75. For example, Exod 3:20; 4:23; 5:1, 2; 6:1, 11; 7:2, 14, 16; 8:1, 2, 8, 20, 21, 28, 32; 9:1, 2, 7, 13, 17, 28, 35; 10:3.

76. See David Daube, *The Exodus Pattern in the Bible* (London: Faber & Faber, 1963), 55–61, for a discussion of receiving provisions at the time of release. He does not mention Jer 40.

the exiles gather at Ramah to prepare for a reverse Exodus. This image also reflects Jehoiachin's treatment by the Babylonians recorded in 2 Kgs 25:27–30 and Jer 52:31–34. In fact, the word ארחה appears only in the text at hand (Jer 40:5), these two parallel accounts concerning Jehoiachin, and Prov 15:17.[77] The significance of the brief account of Jehoiachin at the conclusion of 2 Kings has been a matter of scholarly debate. Some perceive in the text an element of hope for the future restoration of the Davidic dynasty, whereas others see nothing that ameliorates the book's pessimistic view of the future of Israel as Yahweh's people.[78] The ambiguity—evidenced by the debate—illustrates that Jehoiachin's treatment, including his receiving ארחה from Evil-merodach, contains some negative reverberations, particularly since his death is narrated. Thus, Jeremiah's receiving ארחה from Nebuzaradan carries with it some ambivalent resonances. Furthermore, the word משאת is related to משא, "oracle." This may be an ironic play on the idea that Nebuzaradan did give Jeremiah an "oracle" (משא) from Yahweh as well as a "gift" (משאת).

The offering of a gift to Jeremiah recalls several scenes in the DH in which prophets are granted rewards for their services. The crucial difference, however, is that these other prophets refuse the gifts on religious grounds. The man of God from Judah rejects the food and gift offered by King Jeroboam for healing the king's hand—citing a command from Yahweh as the reason for his refusal (1 Kgs 13:7–9). Similarly, the Syrian general Naaman is healed by Elisha and then presents a gift which the prophet rejects with reference to his fidelity to Yahweh (2 Kgs 5:16–17). Both of these may be compared to Daniel's rejection of Belshazzar's offer to position him third in the kingdom (Dan 5:16–17). In the ancient world of reciprocity, the gift in all three instances is something owed to the prophet for the performance of a service.[79] In each case the basis for rejection was to affirm the prophet's allegiance to Yahweh and to eschew identifying with the gift-giver and what he represented or becoming a part of an illegitimate regime.[80] Of course, from one viewpoint Jeremiah too had performed a service for the Babylonians by advising Zedekiah to surrender. The fact that he readily accepts the gifts suggests some relationship with the conquering enemy. The Babylonians compensate Jeremiah for his loyalty in the past and to ensure his fidelity in the future, a notion which elicits questions about Jeremiah's ultimate allegiance and calls his actions into doubt. Should prophets of Yahweh accept gifts from a foreign ruler? The analogous instances suggest not.

This episode also constructs links to other texts within the book. First, after saying that Yahweh has brought רעה against this place, Nebuzaradan relates to

---

77. Proverbs 15:17 reads, "Better a dinner (ארחה) of herbs where love is than a fatted ox and hatred with it." Here ארחה is contrasted with a sumptuous or rich meal; hence, it denotes limited rations. If the term is related to ארח ("to journey"), it would likely indicate fairly light provisions.

78. See the recent overview and discussion in Donald Murray, "Of All the Years the Hopes—Or Fears? Jehoiachin in Babylon (2 Kings 25:27–30)," *JBL* 120 (2001): 245–65.

79. Cf. Victor Matthews, "The Unwanted Gift: Implications of Obligatory Gift Giving in Ancient Israel," *Semeia* 87 (1999): 91–104.

80. Cf. "The Unwanted Gift," 100.

Jeremiah that he has "released" (פתח) him. This ironically recalls 1:14 where Yahweh proclaimed that the enemy from the north would "pour forth evil" (פתח הרעה) on the people. Indeed, the Babylonians פָּתַח evil on the people, but Nebuzaradan פָּתַח Jeremiah from his chains. This intertextual connection contrasts the fate of the people and Jeremiah. Second, in chs. 30–33 Jeremiah delivers a series of salvation oracles in which he indicates a future for the people in the land of Judah. While this view conflicts with the one put forth in ch. 24—which places all hope with the Babylonian exiles—it can shed light on Jeremiah's remaining in the land: the prophet stayed, or was instructed to stay, because there was hope for the Judean community. Perhaps Nebuzaradan, acting on Yahweh's behalf, encouraged or ordered Jeremiah to remain in order to help nurture this hope. In light of this connection, Jeremiah's limited choices and his remaining in the land can be interpreted in a more constructive light.

Chapter 5

Jeremiah, Zedekiah, and Prophet–King Narratives

The intertextual nature of Jer 37–40 can be explored at greater length. Chapters 2, 3, and 4 began to study some of the ways in which the stories of Jeremiah and Zedekiah are linked to other narratives featuring the interaction of a prophet and king. Comparisons were drawn mainly with the stories of Hezekiah and Isaiah in 2 Kgs 18–20 (= Isa 36–39) and Ahab–Jehoshaphat and Micaiah in 1 Kgs 22. This chapter presents a more sustained comparison of three other prophet–king narratives: the stories of Samuel and Saul, of Nathan and David, and of the unnamed man of God from Judah and Jeroboam.

The first two of these three narratives (Samuel–Saul, Nathan–David) warrant further consideration if for no other reason than that they are the most elaborate accounts in the Hebrew Bible of the interactions between a prophet and a king (along with the stories of Jeremiah and Zedekiah,).[1] In the Hezekiah/Isaiah stories, by contrast, the relationship between the prophet and king and the portrayal of each character is less developed because these stories are characterized by long speeches by the prophet (and the Rabshakeh) and prayers by Hezekiah. In fact, there is no direct, face-to-face interaction between prophet and king during the Assyrian crisis. The only such contact concerns Hezekiah's reception of the envoys from Babylon, and even that is relatively brief (2 Kgs 20:1, 8–11, 14–19). Thus, two of the three most detailed prophet–king relationships occur with the first two kings of Israel at the beginning of the monarchy, and the third occurs with Jeremiah and Zedekiah at its close. The fact that the story of the monarchy is framed by extended prophet–king interaction is another signal to study them in tandem. The third prophet–king text to be examined—the man of God from Judah and Jeroboam in 1 Kgs 13—is also about beginnings, namely, the beginning of the Northern Kingdom.

Various elements in Jer 37–40 recall other important moments of "beginnings," such as the accounts of Abraham and Lot dividing the land (the beginning of the deity's relationship with the patriarchs), of Moses and the exodus (the beginning of the "nation" of Israel), of the stories of the Israelite's entrance into the promised land (the beginning of life in Palestine), and of David's initial capture of Jerusalem (the beginning of the united monarchy). It is not surprising, therefore, that the narratives in Jer 37–40 are reminiscent of prophet–king stories set at the inauguration of kingship.

---

1. The stories of Moses and Pharaoh are exempted here because they do not deal with an Israelite king.

Samuel and Saul

The accounts of Saul and Samuel have been studied at length, and one can lean on the results of those studies in an effort to compare them to Jer 37:1–40:6. Some compelling similarities exist between Samuel and Jeremiah and between Saul and Zedekiah; there are also a variety of interfaces in the stories about them.[2] First, as with the Jeremiah–Zedekiah stories, the ambiguity of the prophet's image contributes to the complexity of the prophet–king relationship and to the interpretation of the characters and events. The reader of 1 Samuel, for instance, anticipates that Samuel will be the "faithful priest" for whom God will build a "sure house" (1 Sam 2:35), but this does not materialize. Instead, Samuel's sons turn out to be as evil as Eli's children, and Samuel apparently makes no attempt to rebuke them, casually ignoring their wickedness (1 Sam 12:2). Samuel's repeated trips to Eli in 1 Sam 3 may reflect his dullness and lack of perception, not a devotion to the elderly priest.[3] Even though Samuel is called a "seer," he does not really "see" who Saul is until Yahweh speaks to him. Similarly, when he is sent to anoint David, Samuel errs and needs Yahweh's correction.[4] His assertion that God has not changed his mind (1 Sam 15:29) places him in contradiction to both the narrator (15:35) and God (15:11).

Furthermore, an analysis of Samuel's speeches reveals him to be ill-tempered and ungracious. He manipulates his audience through a one-sided description of kingship (1 Sam 8:11–17). He is selective in what he reveals of Yahweh's intentions by mentioning neither Yahweh's objection to kingship, nor the deity's willingness, nonetheless, to grant the people a king. At no point in Samuel's speech does he acknowledge that the wickedness of his own sons was a principle motivating factor in the people requesting a king (1 Sam 8:3–5).[5] He is "opaque" and "inconsistent," giving ambiguous instructions to Saul in 10:7–8: "Do whatever you see fit to do . . . wait, until I come to you and show you what to do."[6] Even in Samuel's final scene in which he is summoned from the dead (1 Sam 28), he appears hostile and insensitive in contrast to the kind hospitality of the medium at Endor.[7] With good reason Martin Buber refers to the "delinquency of Samuel,"[8] for there are a number of narrative clues which suggest that Samuel is to be seen as "imperceptive, insensitive, self-seeking, and manipulative."[9] This

2. Peter Miscall ("The Jacob and Joseph Stories as Analogies," *JSOT* 6 [1978]: 28–40 [29]) proposes that comparing long portions of Hebrew narrative "increases the amount of biblical material pertinent to the study of a given section. The added material raises and clarifies issues that might otherwise be underemphasized or even missed."

3. Polzin, *Samuel and the Deuteronomist*, 49–51.

4. Alter, *Art of Biblical Narrative*, 149; Sternberg, *The Poetics of Biblical Narrative*, 94–97.

5. Lyle Eslinger, *Kingship of God in Crisis: A Close Reading of 1 Samuel 1–12* (Bible and Literature 10; Sheffield: Sheffield Academic Press, 1985), 386.

6. Barbara Green, *How Are the Mighty Fallen? A Dialogical Study of King Saul in 1 Samuel* (JSOTSup 365; London: Sheffield Academic Press, 2003), 219.

7. T. R. Preston, "The Heroism of Saul: Patterns of Meaning in the Narrative of Early Kingship," *JSOT* 24 (1982): 27–46 (36).

8. Martin Buber, *Kingship of God* (trans. R. Scheimann; New York: Harper & Row, 1967), 76.

9. George Ramsey, "Samuel," *ABD* 5:956.

description of Samuel—the last two words in particular—is reflective of the characterization of Jeremiah.

In addition to the portrayals of Samuel and Jeremiah, an intertextual analysis of their respective kings uncovers further insights.[10] Saul and Zedekiah are naturally linked simply because they are the first and last monarchs of Israel.[11] To begin, both Saul and Zedekiah are explicitly granted their kingship by another— Saul by God and Zedekiah by the Babylonians. Neither one inherits the kingdom from his father. Both kings have their position removed by the same agent that granted it—Saul because of his rebellion against God (at least according to Samuel) and Zedekiah because of his rebellion against the Babylonians. Thus, neither one passes on the throne to an offspring.[12] Furthermore, both Saul and Zedekiah find themselves in the role of a puppet king. In the narratives in 1 Samuel, Saul remains the king even though God has rejected him and chosen David. Similarly, Zedekiah wields no genuine power other than that given to him by the Babylonians. Put differently, David is the true king, even though Saul occupies the throne; Nebuchadnezzar is the true king even though Zedekiah holds the throne. Moreover, both kingships evoke competing ideological groups within Israel. It is evident that some supported Saul as king while others did not (1 Sam 10:27; 11:13); of course, Zedekiah too had those who remained loyal to him—his "officials" (e.g. 38:4)—and those who opposed his policies and kingship and sided with the Babylonians (38:19). Both Saul and Zedekiah must do their best to navigate between the two parties.

Neither Saul nor Zedekiah sought kingship, and neither was positioned for any success. Nevertheless, both Saul and Zedekiah cling to their kingdoms at all costs. David Gunn's analysis of Saul is instructive for a comparison to Zedekiah:

> Saul knows that he and his house are rejected. He 'knows', however, nothing else concerning either his designated successor or the appointed manner of his removal from office. He knows everything yet he knows nothing! . . . Why—to repeat our question— does Saul refuse to surrender his kingdom gracefully? One simple answer, therefore, would be that he does not know when, and to whom, and how, he should surrender it.[13]

---

10. Hopefully the ensuing discussion begins to address Josiah Derby's observation that "a comparison between King Saul and King Zedekiah would make a most interesting study" ("The Tragic King," *JBQ* 29 [2001]: 181–85.) The stories about Saul seem to call for intertextual reflection. For instance, Robert Alter observes that the story in 1 Sam 9 depicting Saul looking for his father's lost donkeys is a play on the betrothal-type scene which involves meeting girls at a well in a foreign land (*Art of Biblical Narrative*, 60–61). Many have compared Saul and David; see Mark K. George, "Yhwh's Own Heart," *CBQ* 64 (2002): 442–59; or Preston, "The Heroism of Saul."

11. Interestingly, Thomas Paine (*Age of Reason*, Part 2, Section 11) connects the double story of Zedekiah's imprisonment with the double story of Saul learning about David. To that could be added the two stories of Saul being appointed king. Both the stories of Saul and Zedekiah have a cyclical and linear sense.

12. The close connection between Saul and Samuel is represented by the similarity of their names and the context in which Samuel is named, as has been well documented. See, e.g., Sara R. Mandell, "Reading Samuel as Saul and Vice Versa," in *Approaches to Ancient Judaism* (ed. J. Neusner; Atlanta: Scholars Press, 1996), 13–32. Zedekiah and Jeremiah are also linked via naming, as Zedekiah's maternal grandfather is named Jeremiah (2 Kgs 24:18; Jer 52:1).

13. David Gunn, *The Fate of King Saul* (JSOTSup 14; Sheffield: JSOT Press, 1980), 121.

The same inquiry can be posed regarding Zedekiah: Why does he refuse to relinquish his kingdom gracefully? Zedekiah and Saul are in similar predicaments: they lack the proper knowledge or practical insight regarding the mechanics of capitulating. Although Zedekiah has been told to whom to surrender the kingdom—the Babylonians—when and how are totally different matters. It was too late to surrender, so the possibility of acquiescing presents a messy and complex scenario about which little is known. Indeed, like Saul, Zedekiah knows everything—that he has been "rejected" and that it would be advantageous to yield his kingdom—but he knows nothing about exactly how that might be done or what the result would be.

The issue of surrendering also joins the stories of Saul and Zedekiah in another way. At the beginning of his kingship, Saul refuses to allow the people of Jabesh-gilead to surrender to Nahash the Ammonite. The verbal link is made by יצא (1 Sam 11:3, 7). Instead of capitulating Saul marshals the Israelite forces and defeats Nahash. Unlike Zedekiah, Saul's tenacity is honored by God, a fact which the text makes explicit: "And the spirit of Yahweh came upon Saul in power" (11:6). Later, the people of Jabesh-gilead rescue Saul's corpse from the Philistines, preserving (some of) his dignity and honor; even posthumously Saul profits from his unwillingness to surrender (1 Sam 31:11–13). For all of Saul's failures and for all of God's silence and tormenting of Saul (see below), it is noteworthy that his initial and only complete success in battle arises from a divinely blessed refusal to surrender. Saul's victory, as with Hezekiah's, stands in the background of Zedekiah's decision not to surrender—a backdrop which tends to elicit sympathy for the last king.[14] Ironically, Saul's non-compliance saved the people of Jabesh-gilead from being blinded by Nahash, whereas Zedekiah himself is blinded by the enemy for his failure to acquiesce.

Saul's successful defense of Jabesh-gilead builds a bridge between Zedekiah and the end of the book of Judges. Saul's cutting up an ox and employing it to call the tribes of Israel to battle recalls Judg 19 in which the Levite dismembers his concubine and sends the pieces out as a summons to war against the tribe of Benjamin. Zedekiah and the close of the monarchy are linked via Saul's actions to the stories of chaos that marked the end of the period of the judges. This in turn reinforces the connection between the last king Zedekiah and the last judge

---

14.   Zedekiah and Pharaoh are connected in several ways—for example, both are instructed to let the people go (יצא). Other interpreters have made connections between Pharaoh and Saul, thereby creating an intertextual thread linking three prophet–king relationships: Moses–Pharaoh, Samuel–Saul, and Jeremiah–Zedekiah. An analogy between Saul and Pharaoh is set up by the similarity of 1 Sam 15:24–25 and Exod 10:16–17. Saul declares to Samuel, "I have sinned, for I have transgressed the command of Yahweh and your instructions. . . . Now please forgive my offense and return with me, so that I may worship Yahweh." Pharaoh declares to Moses, "I have sinned against Yahweh and against you. . . . Now please forgive my offense just this once and plead with Yahweh your God that he remove this deadly thing from me." In both instances the king admits his sin and implores the prophet to facilitate forgiveness. See Amos Frisch, "For I Feared the People and I Yielded to Them (1 Sam 15:24)—Is Saul's Guilt Attenuated or Intensified?," *ZAW* 108 (1996): 98–104; and Ralph W. Klein, *1 Samuel* (Waco, Tex.: Word Books, 1983), 153.

Samson, both of whom are blinded. Blindness, dismemberment/disfigurement, and chaos characterize the final days of judges and kings.

In addition to comparing the prophets Samuel and Jeremiah and the kings Saul Zedekiah, one can also consider the nature of each prophet–king relationship. In a recent article, Stanley Nash translates a poem written by Judah Loeb Gordon (1831–1892).[15] Nash writes that Gordon "adduces the view of Yosef Ibn Caspi that 'there was no man like Zedekiah among all the kings of the House of David who was so harshly stricken by the hand of God.'"[16] Gordon's work is powerful and captures many of the subtle nuances and challenges of Zedekiah's predicament, including the challenges of dealing with Jeremiah. Strikingly, Gordon also makes a direct comparison between Zedekiah and his prophet Jeremiah and Saul and his prophet Samuel. Gordon's poem addresses the struggle between kings and prophets since the beginning of the monarchy:

> Always the prophesying seers have sought
> To have the kings submissive beneath them.
> Thus did the first prophet Ben Elqanah [Samuel] do
> To the first king five hundred years ago,
> For Ben-Kish [Saul] was a warrior of great strength,
> Who refused to surrender, who would not lower himself.
> So the seer looked for a pretext and found one
> To degrade his honor and defame him.[17]

Gordon's poem then rehearses how Saul sacrificed when Samuel failed to arrive at the appointed time (1 Sam 13). On the eve of their demise, both Saul and Zedekiah are confronted with a dwindling army due to some aspect of the prophet's behavior. Saul is waiting for Samuel and the delay influences some members of the army to abandon camp (1 Sam 13:8), and Zedekiah expresses fear over the Judeans who have deserted, presumably because of Jeremiah's message (38:19). Gordon then writes:

> Thus did every seer and prophet, each in his respective era,
> Strive to bend his king to his controlling will!
> What befalls Saul has also befallen me
> At the hands of this Anatot seer.[18]

The conflict between prophet and king is captured in Gunn's comments on Saul, which are again germane to Zedekiah as well: "Why should the king be browbeaten by the fulminations of a religious functionary and the dictates of an inscrutable God? Here, then, we have an important element in the story which is plainly ambiguous in value. Its moral/theological evaluation depends ultimately not on the text, for the text offers no independent evaluative judgments, but on the stance of the reader."[19] The narrative in Jeremiah does not offer an independent

---

15. Stanley Nash, "Y. L. Gordon: Zedekiah in the Prison House," *CCAR* (Spring 2003): 33–48.

16. Nash, "Y. L. Gordon," 33. The use of Gordon illustrates the intertextual nature of interpretation: Nash translating Gordon reading Yosef Ibn Caspi.

17. Nash, "Y. L. Gordon," 42–43.

18. Nash, "Y. L. Gordon," 45.

19. Gunn, *Fate of King Saul*, 123.

evaluative judgment either, apart from the narrator's introduction (37:1–2), which is only one perspective (and one that is challenged by the events that unfold in chs. 37–39). Gunn's insights also raise the issue of God's role in the Jeremianic narratives. The comparison with the stories of Samuel and Saul highlights the fact that the deity is not immediately involved in the stories of Jeremiah and Zedekiah. Unlike the narratives of 1 Samuel, Yahweh does not speak directly in the Jeremianic narratives; rather the deity speaks only through the prophet Jeremiah (i.e. the formulaic phrase, "The word that came to Jeremiah from Yahweh").[20] Yahweh's absence is conspicuous. There is no independent report of Yahweh communicating with the prophet Jeremiah, as there is in Samuel (cf. 1 Sam 8:7, 22; 9:17; 16:1, 2, 7, 12). Therefore, Gunn's questions can be modified to fit Zedekiah's situation by asking: Why should the king be browbeaten by the fulminations of a religious functionary who speaks for an absent (and inscrutable) God? Of course, God is also not present at important points in the Saul narratives, for instance, when the deity refuses to answer the king (e.g. 1 Sam 28:6). In the stories of both Saul and Zedekiah, God is either absent or malevolently present. Gordon's poem from Zedekiah's perspective is again instructive:

> Was it out of capriciousness that I did this,
> That I attempted to throw off the yoke of Babylon's king?
> Was it not that I feared for the honor and liberty of my people . . .
> And if indeed as a human being I erred, is that a sin?
> Why, therefore, wrathful God, have you lashed out at me
> And pursued me angrily like an avenging enemy
> And handed me over to those who seek to kill me? . . .
> For a man like me, fallen before his enemies
> There is no help even from God in his high heavens![21]

Again Gunn's remarks on Saul's struggles against God are relevant for the understanding of Zedekiah:

> Is struggle against God (or 'Fate'), in such circumstances, positive or negative according to one's own set of values? The phrase 'in such circumstances' is important to my point; for, as we have seen, the story makes clear that Saul operates not in some theological vacuum where simple and abstract questions may be met with simple and abstract answers, but in 'real-life' situations of moral complexity and theological obscurity. The story allows a range of responses to Saul's 'refusal to accept', including a significant degree of positive identification (by the reader) with Saul in his struggle. This is not just because human beings have so often had a soft spot for the underdog but because the story in chapters 13–5 has opened up the possibility of viewing Saul as essentially an innocent victim of God, and thus of seeing God in negative as well as in positive terms.[22]

Zedekiah is also facing complex "real life" situations for which facile solutions are not forthcoming. As with the character of Saul, the text allows for a variety of responses to Zedekiah, including a significant degree of sympathy for him as an innocent victim.

---

20. God does occasionally speak directly to Jeremiah in chs. 1–20; cf. 1:7, 9; 11:9; 14:14.
21. Nash, "Y. L. Gordon," 36, 47.
22. Gunn, *Fate of King Saul*, 123.

In fact, reading broadly intertextually, the Hebrew Bible as a whole encourages a sympathetic reading of both Saul and Zedekiah; for it is replete with characters who "struggle against God." For example, Jacob's name is changed to Israel after he literally wrestles against God (Gen 32:22–32); accordingly, the name Israel itself means "one who strives with God."[23] One thinks of other characters too, such as Abraham who argued with God about the fate of Sodom and Gomorrah, challenging God to reconsider the decision to destroy the cities (Gen 18:16–33). Moses and Gideon resist God's actions by questioning and demanding signs of assurance (Exod 3–4; Judg 6). The poet of the book of Lamentations not only bewails the destruction of Jerusalem, but in so doing protests that God has been an enemy, destroying his own people (Lam 1). Many of the lament psalms register objections against God (cf. Pss 39; 88). The prophet Habakkuk openly questions the justice of God (Hab 1). Job, of course, is the quintessential example as he rails against God at length. Remarkably, in the end, God not only restores Job's fortunes two-fold, but also declares that Job has spoken what is right of God (Job 42:7). Minor characters too can be included, such as Zipporah who fends off God's attempts to kill her husband Moses (Exod 4:24–26). Other characters and stories could be mentioned. Indeed, the Hebrew Bible preserves many traditions of protest, complaint, challenge, and struggle against God. Saul and Zedekiah, then, can minimally receive a sympathetic reading precisely because, like their eponymous ancestor Jacob, they dared to struggle against God.

In addition to the intertextual linkages between Saul's and Zedekiah's struggles with their respective prophets and with God, there are a number of other thematic and verbal connections between their stories which have not heretofore been examined. Many of these are found by examining 1 Sam 28 and 31.

Saul's and Zedekiah's final encounters with their prophets are connected in a variety of ways (1 Sam 28; Jer 38:14–28). Each king appears to take the right action by consulting a prophet in difficult times. Assisted by the medium at Endor, Saul seeks the counsel of the deceased Samuel concerning an impending battle with the Philistines. Likewise, Zedekiah summons Jeremiah on the eve of the destruction of Jerusalem (38:14–28). Both prophets must be brought up (עלה) from the ground to be consulted—Jeremiah from the pit (38:7–13), Samuel from the realm of the dead. Also, in both scenarios (1 Sam 28:8–11; Jer 38:10) royal orders are dispensed for a "servant" of the king to bring up the prophet—Ebed-melech ("servant of the king") pulls up Jeremiah and the medium twice refers to herself as Saul's "servant" (28:21–22).

If Samuel is brought up from the realm of the dead, Jeremiah is saved from entering that abode. Unlike Jeremiah, Samuel is annoyed that he has been summoned—appropriate perhaps, since he is dead!—but his response nonetheless is somewhat unexpected since in his last appearance with Saul the narrator reports that "Samuel grieved over Saul," prompting Yahweh to ask Samuel, "How long will you grieve over Saul?" (1 Sam 15:35; 16:1). Here Samuel shows pity for the bewildered king. He is not antagonistic or judgmental. Rather, he partners with

---

23. As with many names in the Hebrew Bible, the meaning of "Israel" is debated; the one proposed here is a common interpretation.

the king in mourning the tragedy of the monarchy. Something similar occurs in the final meeting between Zedekiah and Jeremiah as the king and prophet scheme together to protect one another from the officials, namely, by giving misinformation to them (38:24–28). As with the final scene of Samuel and Saul (when both are alive), the narrative evokes a sense of pity for both the prophet and the king.[24]

First Samuel 28 and Jer 38:14–28 both contain an element of secrecy. Saul disguises himself and travels under cover of night to the medium (1 Sam 28:8), while Zedekiah swears an oath "in secret" to Jeremiah (Jer 38:16) and then takes measures to be sure that no one discovers their meeting (38:24). In fact, the element of "secrecy" connects the two sets of prophet–king relationships on a broader level. Jeremiah and Zedekiah meet in secret (37:17; 38:16) to discuss the future of the king and nation. Similarly, Samuel sends away Saul's servant in order to inform him in private that Yahweh had elected him king (1 Sam 9:27–10:1). Later, Saul explicitly does not apprise his uncle of Samuel's pronouncement (10:16).[25] Saul does not want it revealed that he has been anointed as the first king, while Zedekiah does not want it revealed that Jeremiah has warned him that he will be the last king.[26] The monarchy, then, is framed by secret dialogues between prophet and king.

Furthermore, in the final meeting between Samuel and Saul and between Zedekiah and Jeremiah it is not clear what information the king is seeking. The reader is not privy to what Saul asked when he inquired of Yahweh (1 Sam 28:6). When Saul dialogues with the prophet, he explains that the Philistines are waging war against him and that God will not answer, but he does not indicate what specific information he anticipates Samuel will render. Does he want to know why Yahweh will not answer him? Does he hope Samuel will inquire of Yahweh for him? Does he want to know if he should attack the Philistines? Similarly, when Zedekiah meets Jeremiah, he states that he has a question to ask the prophet (Jer 38:14), but the conversation turns to other matters and the king never poses the inquiry. In this way, both narratives generate mystery and suspense.

Both the medium and Jeremiah express fear of death as a result of deceit by the king. The woman points out the Saul has banned mediums from the land and so she inquires of him, "Why are you laying a trap for my life to bring about my death?" (1 Sam 28:9). Likewise, Jeremiah asks rhetorically, "If I tell you, you will put me to death, will you not?" (Jer 38:15). To alleviate the mistrust, both kings swear an oath of assurance using the same formula. Saul replies, "As Yahweh lives, no punishment will come on you for this matter" (1 Sam 28:10). Zedekiah responds, "As Yahweh lives, who made for us this life, I will not put you to death or give you into the hand of those men who are seeking your life"

---

24. An alternative interpretation might observe by way of contrast that Jeremiah does not display any grief for the fate of Zedekiah. He does not mourn the demise of his king. First Samuel 15:35 provides a poignant element not present in the stories of Jeremiah and Zedekiah.

25. One also recalls the image of Saul "hiding" among the baggage (1 Sam 10:22).

26. Similarly, both sets of prophet–king stories play on the public–private distinction. Saul is anointed privately by Samuel (10:1) and later publicly proclaimed king (10:17–25). Zedekiah and Jeremiah, as the above analysis demonstrated, move between the private and public realms.

(Jer 38:16). Both kings assure the intermediaries that the king themselves will not harm them. Ironically, however, in both scenes, it is the life of the king, not the intermediary, which is in danger. The phrase "As Yahweh lives" develops the irony because Zedekiah's life as he knows it is about to end and Saul uses the phrase to conjure a dead prophet who will announce his death. While it is part of a standard oath formula, in both of these contexts it emphasizes an ironic element which underscores the tragedy of each king's demise.

The fact that Jeremiah is analogous to the medium could be understood in a variety of ways. It may function to characterize Jeremiah more negatively—is there any difference between a medium and a prophet, for they both serve as intermediaries? In a different vein, it highlights that Zedekiah is only one intermediary removed from God, not two as is Saul, needing the medium to invoke Samuel who would then have a word from the deity. The iterated absence of God in the story of Saul (28:6, 15) underscores the concept that for Zedekiah God is still accessible through Jeremiah. However, perhaps Saul's calling on Samuel because God has abandoned him suggests that Zedekiah is forced to consult Jeremiah because God has deserted him too. The reading develops earlier observations that Jeremiah speaks more for himself than for God who is silent.

In both final prophet–king encounters the plot is driven largely by the multiple effects of knowledge or lack of it. In 1 Sam 28, Saul is in need of information but cannot obtain it from God. The medium is not cognizant of Saul's presence, but she conjures a character who she subsequently realizes is Samuel, which then causes her to recognize the concealed identity of Saul. Samuel wants to know the reason he has been bothered (28:15); he then asks why Saul inquires of him if Yahweh will not answer. Samuel then reveals the knowledge of Saul's impending death. In Jer 38:14–28, the king states that he has a question for the prophet, but he never asks it. Jeremiah discloses information, which may or may not have been what the king desired. After the meeting, Zedekiah and Jeremiah conspire to keep their meeting a secret. In both of these prophet–king encounters prior to the king's demise, obtaining and managing the flow of information is a crucial aspect of the story.

Both kings have difficulties not only with information management but also with food management. Saul deprived himself of food before seeing the medium, thus causing his weakened condition (1 Sam 28:20). Lack of food in Jerusalem was also a problem for Zedekiah (Jer 37:9). Thus both kings find themselves enfeebled—Saul personally, Zedekiah corporately. The motif of food creates an intertextual thread with 1 Sam 14 where Saul's ordering that his army eat nothing until evening wreaks havoc among his men. If Saul created trouble by forbidding his army to eat, Zedekiah found himself in trouble because the people could not eat.

The reason behind Saul's fasting has evoked much speculation. Barbara Green offers some insight: "Why he had fasted seems not the point. . . . It seems rather that we are redirected back . . . to the fasting/feasting of Hannah and her prayer (1.15–16; 2.5), [and] to the banquet which initiates Saul's kingship (9.22–24)."[27]

---

27. Green, *How Are the Mighty Fallen?*, 432.

Not only is Green reading 1 Sam 28 intertextually, but she is also tying it specifically to texts at the beginning of the life of Samuel and the beginning of Saul's kingship. As the end of the Samuel and Saul stories recalls their beginning, so the stories of the final days of the monarchy are linked to its commencement. In fact, Green also connects the scene of Saul's final meal to events surrounding the end of the kingdom, namely, the concluding scene in 2 Kings in which Jehoiachin is given food (2 Kgs 25:27–30).[28] First Samuel 28 is bristling with intertextuality, pointing both forward to the kingdom's end and backward to its very beginnings.

שמע is a key word in Jer 37:1–40:6 and in the sixth episode in particular (38:14–28). It is also a *leitwort* in the last meeting between Samuel and Saul. Saul had not "listened" to the voice of Yahweh concerning the battle against Amalek (1 Sam 28:18), so now Yahweh will not listen to him. Because the medium had "listened" to Saul and brought up Samuel, she petitions him to "listen" to her (28:21–22). Saul refuses until his servants urge him to "listen" to the woman (28:23). It is ironic that Saul had failed to "listen" to Yahweh's command to kill all the Amalekites, whereas Zedekiah is informed that he can save his own life and the lives of the people in Jerusalem if he "listens" to Jeremiah and submits to the enemy army. Saul is guilty of not killing the enemy; Zedekiah is guilty of not surrendering to the enemy.[29] Saul killed the women and children but is guilty of not killing the enemy king; Zedekiah is told that his women and children will be led out to the enemy king if he does not surrender to them (Jer 38:23). The kings fail to listen to opposite commands, but the result is the same: loss of kingdom and life.

Both prophets foretell of future destruction not only for the king, but also for his family. Samuel apprises Saul that "tomorrow you and your sons will be with me" (1 Sam 28:19), while Jeremiah warns that "all your women and children" will be led out to the Babylonians (Jer 38:23). Samuel's poetic words underscore that the prophet and king will receive the same ultimate fate—both will reside in the realm of the dead. This notion calls attention to the fact that, by contrast, Jeremiah and Zedekiah find themselves in two very different places. Zedekiah is blinded and taken to Babylon, but Jeremiah remains in Judah with his needs met. This comparison may cast suspicious light on Jeremiah's loyalty. Why does he not experience the same fate as his king?

Prior to informing Saul of his impending death, Samuel declares to Saul that "Yahweh has become your enemy." Not only has the deity abandoned Saul, but he now opposes him. This creates a link with Jer 21:3–7, another Jeremiah–Zedekiah meeting, in which God declares that he will fight against Jerusalem and its king. For the first and last kings of Israel God becomes a malicious foe.

---

28. Green, *How Are the Mighty Fallen?*, 433.

29. Prophets and enemy kings relate differently: Samuel killed King Agag (1 Sam 15:33), but Jeremiah is saved by Nebuchadrezzar. Samuel's execution of Agag ties with Zedekiah's treatment by Nebuchadrezzar. Samuel "hewed Agag in pieces"; Nebuchadrezzar gouged out Zedekiah's eyes. Before killing Agag, Samuel says, "As your sword made women childless, so your mother will be childless among women"; Zedekiah's children are killed in his presence. Agag's position as a son and Zedekiah's as a father are highlighted.

Indeed, Samuel's announcing God's ultimate rejection of Saul in 1 Sam 28 ("Yahweh has become your enemy") recalls the time when God first stated his rejection of Saul. There the deity said to Samuel, "I regret that I made Saul king" (1 Sam 15:11). God changes his mind about making Saul king. This has two effects on the stories of Zedekiah. First, Zedekiah's indecisiveness and waffling can be evaluated more sympathetically when it is realized that God too struggles with major decisions. Secondly, if God is capable of changing his mind about Saul, perhaps God will change his mind about Zedekiah and Jerusalem and decide to save the king and city (as he had done during the Assyrian crisis). Zedekiah's connections with Saul shed additional sympathetic light on his decision not to surrender.

Previous analysis of the Jeremianic narratives demonstrated the narrator's employment of differing points of view to create a complex scene. Kenneth Craig makes a similar observation about 1 Sam 28: "The narrator does, of course, have the option to tell the story straight—what happens, why, what the characters think, how their actions square with the narrator's evaluative system, and so forth. The option that the narrator chooses, namely, to bring speaking characters on stage, produces an orchestration of voices, a systematic interplay of perspectives."[30] In both Jer 38:14–28 and 1 Sam 28, then, the reader engages a polyphonic text.

The tragic death of Saul narrated in 1 Sam 31 echoes the fate of Zedekiah in Jer 39 in several respects. First, there are verbal resonances. In Saul's final battle with the Philistines, the people of Israel see (ראה) that Saul's army is defeated and that Saul was dead; they flee their towns and the Philistines occupy (ישב) them (1 Sam 31:7). The scenario is reversed in the story of Zedekiah's defeat. The Babylonians occupy (ישב) the gates, and when Zedekiah and his army see (ראה) them, they flee the city (Jer 39:3–4).

Both Saul and Zedekiah are surrounded by loyal supporters to the very end. Saul dies fighting alongside his sons and his armor bearer who refuses Saul's request to kill him (1 Sam 31:4). Zedekiah is surrounded by his sons and the nobles. Saul's sons are killed prior to his death, and it is implied that Saul witnessed their deaths (31:2). Similarly, Zedekiah's sons are slaughtered in front of him. Saul is severely wounded in battle and commits suicide to avoid being killed by the Philistines. His corpse is beheaded and his armor and body are displayed by the enemies as a sign of victory. The fate that Saul had desperately sought to avoid—his enemy making sport of him (31:4)—comes to fruition nonetheless. Likewise, Zedekiah was subject to humiliation and physical mutilation as he is blinded, shackled, and taken to Babylon.[31] Like Saul, Zedekiah cannot escape the

---

30. Kenneth Craig, "Rhetorical Aspects of Questions Answered with Silence in 1 Samuel 14:37 and 28:6," *CBQ* 56 (1994): 221–39. Craig is reading intertextually.

31. L. Daniel Hawk ("Saul as Sacrifice: The Tragedy of Israel's First Monarch," *BRev* 12 [Dec 1996]: 20–25, 56) writes that "Saul's determination to *know* in response to divine opacity" has much in common with Oedipus, whose "compulsion to discover the cause of the plague suffered by Thebes leads to the revelation of his guilt. When he then blinds himself, divine wrath is averted and the plague is lifted." Hawk's observation draws intertextual lines beyond the Hebrew Bible and invites

tragic end that he could see coming and wanted dearly to evade. Of course, the actual death of Zedekiah is not reported, but he perhaps experiences something worse: the death of the kingdom, the end of Judah and the Davidic dynasty. Both Saul and Zedekiah die with their sons and both in a sense cause the death of their sons by their (in hindsight) ill advised actions. Because their sons are killed, there is no possibility for their kingship to continue. The only two kings who die with their sons, Saul and Zedekiah mark the tragedy of the monarchy and its finality. Again one can turn to Gordon's poem to capture the poignancy of Zedekiah's fate:

> What then, Heavenly Power, is my crime against You?
> That You have landed such blows upon me and my entire family?
> If I have acted wickedly and done what is evil in your eyes,
> Would that I alone had met my doom:
> But what have these lambs done, what have they sinned?
> Jealous and vengeful God, the God of Jeremiah!
> I, if I sinned, transgressing your word—
> Why were my children put to death—in violation of your Torah?
> My dear children, comparable to fine gold . . . !
> Oh my heart, my heart, oh how strong is my pain!
> Is there another man as unfortunate as I?
> I wish that day could be erased from my memory,
> I wish I could sever it together with the brain in my head!
> Ah, the nightmarish picture, ah, the horrific sight,
> With burning vividness I see it still now,
> I see it without my eyes, I visualize it in my soul.
> Ah, wreckers of destruction, men of blood and murder!
> Before they extinguished my eyes for me permanently,
> Before they took away from me the light of my eyes—
> They slaughtered my cherished babes before my eyes . . . "
> 'Because I did not surrender before Jeremiah!!' . . .
> Perhaps in death my eyes will be restored to sight,
> And my perished children will I once again see,
> If not—let me lie down and quiet my agitated spirit
> And let my bones have rest from eternal pain.[32]

The demises of Saul and Zedekiah can be interpreted as heroic. Not only did Saul refuse to be killed by the enemy, but also, as Preston argues, Saul was "faithful to the ideal of a military king supporting the covenant. . . . Saul emerges as the narrator's hero—a hero who was also a failure, but a failure who . . . died on the battlefield in defense of Israel, not in his bed [in contrast to David] with the moral fabric of Israel crumbling around him."[33] Similar observations might also be made of Zedekiah: he was faithful to the covenant, at least from his

---

one to ask if the blinding of Zedekiah is be understood as a way to appease divine wrath? Does it serve as the sacrifice that satisfies God and paves the way for a fresh start?

32. Nash, "Y. L. Gordon," 37–39, 47.

33. Preston, "The Heroism of Saul," 44. Cf. also Eben Scheffler, "Saving Saul from the Deuteronomist," in *Past, Present, Future: The Deuteronomistic History and the Prophets* (ed. J. C. de Moor and H. F. Van Rooy; Leiden: Brill, 2000), 263–71 (265).

perspective, by relying on Yahweh to save the people, rather than submitting to a foreign king.[34] Zedekiah too met his fate on the battlefield—like Saul, he was fleeing from the enemy—having held out hope till the end for divine commitment to the covenant in return for his fidelity. Like Saul he was a hero and a failure. Indeed, the final images of both kings contain elements of heroism and ignominy. The ultimate fates of Saul and Zedekiah—framing the monarchy—suggest that the monarchy itself lay somewhere between the absurd and the sublime.

The kingdom was inaugurated when the tribes of Israel desired a king "to be like the nations around them" (1 Sam 8:5). Now at the monarchy's final destruction, Jeremiah ironically councils Zedekiah to be like the nations and surrender to the Babylonians. The Rabshakeh's speech to Hezekiah reverberates here; previously God had saved Jerusalem from the hand of the enemy king so that it would not resemble the surrounding kingdoms which the Assyrians had subdued. Now, however, the people and king tragically witness their wish fulfilled—they are as all the other nations whose king failed to save them. The stories of Samuel and Saul largely revolve around the question of the identity of the nation. Was Israel to be ruled by a king or by God, or did a possible reconciliation between the two alternatives exist? Obviously these would be pressing questions in the exilic and post-exilic periods. By reflecting the accounts of Samuel and Saul, the stories of Jeremiah and Zedekiah raise to the surface these fundamental questions of identity.

The importance of the fall of Jerusalem is evidenced by the number of times it is recorded in the Hebrew Bible. It is appropriate that such a tragic story would not be narrated in a manner to provoke disdain for Zedekiah. Rather, the story attends to the subtle complexities of the events and characters.[35] If Zedekiah is not the scapegoat, the bad guy, then who is to blame or, at least, with whom can Zedekiah share the responsibility? The intertextual connections with Saul underline God's absence during Jerusalem's struggles and defeat; even further, they highlight God's active participation in the city's undoing. To a certain extent, the narrative impugns God. God was ambivalent about the monarchy from the outset, and Saul suffers as a result.[36] With such an unfavorable beginning, the collapse of the kingdom was perhaps inevitable, which lightens the burden of guilt placed on Zedekiah.

This perspective provides an appropriate counter-voice to the view that the idolatry of the king and people is to blame—an explanation that is expressed in a number of places, such as 2 Kgs 17. Juxtaposed to this sin-theodicy, however, is

---

34. According to George, David is different from Saul because he is confident that Yahweh will be with him and act on his behalf ("Yhwh's Own Heart," 456). Zedekiah is confident too, but that is his problem: God will not act on his behalf. Zedekiah is condemned precisely for the actions which, according to George, suggest that David is the man after God's own heart.

35. Yet again, Gunn's insights on the story of Saul fit perfectly for Zedekiah as well: "Saul's failure is not simply a matter of obedience or disobedience; nor is the story presented in simple categories of right and wrong, good and evil" (*Fate of King Saul*, 19).

36. According to Green's analysis of the Samuel and Saul stories, the monarchy "suffers from underdesign," so "God and the prophet must take some responsibility here" (*How Are the Mighty Fallen?*, 218).

an alternative position pointing the finger at God (i.e. the poem by Gordon). Such a divine-theodicy offered a common external "enemy" against which Israel could focus its anger and frustration, an opponent against whom it could wrestle (cf. Jacob). Israel required, paradoxically perhaps, elements of a theodicy which held Yahweh responsible in order for faith in Yahweh to continue. Furthermore, it would have been too simple to blame only themselves, only the king, or only God. In a tragic scenario rarely is only one party culpable. The intertextual features of Jer 37–40, particularly the links to the stories of Saul, cultivate a sophisticated theodicy which could function powerfully for the Israelite exilic and post-exilic community.

Nathan and David

The intertextual links between the Zedekiah–Jeremiah stories and the Saul–Samuel stories has required extended attention, as those ties are the deepest and most compelling. It was not Saul's kingdom, however, which perished with the demise of Zedekiah, but rather the Davidic line. David, the founder of the dynasty which was to rule the kingdom of Judah, also had a close relationship with a prophet, Nathan. The stories of their interaction represent a second prominent prophet–king relationship at the dawn of the monarchy. As with Saul, David is presented as a complex character. Although the biblical tradition considers him the standard by which all other kings are to be measured, David's depiction is not idealistic; he is depicted committing sins, making mistakes, and using poor judgment. The complexity of David's character, of course, is widely recognized.[37] What has not received as much analysis is the ambiguity in the prophet's portrayal and in the prophet–king relationship.[38]

The first encounter between Nathan and David is devoted to the topic of building the temple (2 Sam 7).[39] This text thus has a natural connection with the stories of Jeremiah and Zedekiah and the destruction of the temple. After David expresses concern over the disparity between his palace and Yahweh's dwelling place, Nathan declares to David: "Go and do all that is in your heart, for Yahweh is with you" (2 Sam 7:3). However, immediately after Nathan communicates this message to the king, Yahweh appears to Nathan and instructs him to apprise David that he is not the one to construct a temple (2 Sam 7:4). The juxtaposition of Nathan's message to the king and Yahweh's instructions to the king points to a certain tension between the prophetic word and the divine word. It reveals that

---

37. See, among others, David Gunn, *The Story of King David* (JSOTSup 6; Sheffield: JSOT Press, 1978); Cheryl Exum, *Tragedy and Biblical Narrative* (Cambridge: Cambridge University Press, 1992), 120–52; Polzin, *David and the Deuteronomist*.

38. The most extended study of Nathan is by Gwilym Jones, *The Nathan Narratives* (JSOTSup 80; Sheffield: JSOT Press, 1990). Cf. also Keith Bodner, "Nathan: Prophet, Politician and Novelist?," *JSOT* 95 (2001): 43–54.

39. For close analysis of this text, see Polzin, *David and the Deuteronomist*, 71–72; Lyle Eslinger, *House of God or House of David: The Rhetoric of 2 Samuel 7* (JSOTSup 164; Sheffield: JSOT Press, 1994).

prophets can speak independently of Yahweh, and sometimes their word will differ from Yahweh's. It also unveils that prophets can employ Yahweh's name without Yahweh's approval. Nathan commands David to do whatever he wants because "Yahweh is with you," but Yahweh is not. Thus, in David's first meeting with a prophet, it proves arduous to discriminate a word that is genuinely from Yahweh and one that is not. This, of course, is precisely the issue that confronts Zedekiah in the final days of the Jerusalem. If Nathan essentially said to build the temple, but Yahweh prohibited it, are Jeremiah's instructions to surrender the temple and city from himself or the deity? If Nathan was wrong, maybe Jeremiah is misguided as well. Nathan also promises David an everlasting dynasty in this text (2 Sam 7:8–17). Perhaps that word from Yahweh would stand, and Jeremiah would be wrong? Second Samuel 7 reverberates loudly as the Davidic kingdom comes to a close.

Nathan's third and last encounter with David is in 1 Kgs 1, a story about the appointing of a successor for David.[40] As with the final consultations between Samuel and Saul and Jeremiah and Zedekiah, the one between Nathan and David revolves around information management.[41] David is old and bordering on senility when Nathan and Bathsheba approach him in hopes of having Solomon crowned king, rather than Adonijah who had already claimed the throne. Nathan advises Bathsheba to confront David and "remind" him that he had promised her that Solomon would succeed him. As many commentators have pointed out, one of the intriguing aspects of this incident is that the reader is unaware if David had made such an oath to Bathsheba. This conspicuous gap in the narrative compels the reader to consider the possibility that Nathan has concocted the whole story in order to deceive the aging king. Further, Nathan persuades Bathsheba to approach David in order to save her own life and the life of her son Solomon (1 Kgs 1:12). Yet when Nathan himself interacts with the king, it is evident that his primary motivation is his own well-being. Both of these features—the contrived oath and Nathan's selfish interests—can be elaborated.

When Nathan speaks with David, rather than promoting Solomon, as one might expect, Nathan observes that Adonijah "did not invite me, your servant, and the priest Zadok, and Benaiah son of Jehoiada, and your servant Solomon" (1 Kgs 1:26). Nathan places himself in the emphatic position and joins himself to Solomon with the phrase "your servant." Nathan apparently is trying to incite the king by highlighting the wrong that has been done to Nathan personally. The prophet's only mention of Solomon is buried among a list of four individuals whom Adonijah did not invite. Perhaps Nathan, like Jeremiah, is employing an indirect approach with the king. Nonetheless, Nathan's speech hardly conveys that Solomon should be king; instead, it appears that Nathan's primary interest is his own well-being, which can only be secured if Solomon is named king. If Samuel's anointing Saul was dubious (because of Yahweh's hesitations), and if

---

40. The second meeting is Nathan's confronting David about his affair with Bathsheba (2 Sam 12); it is not as relevant for this study.

41. See Lasine, *Knowing Kings*, 113–17, for an insightful analysis of "information, intrigue, and deniability" in 1 Kgs 1. He explores the manipulative nature of Nathan's behavior.

Samuel the prophet necessitated correction by Yahweh as to which of Jesse's sons to anoint (David), here the crowning of Solomon is also wrapped in uncertainty and prophetic (mis)calculation. Akin to some of the issues raised regarding Jeremiah, Nathan is portrayed as more interested in his personal safety than with national security.

Regarding David's oath, there are strong indications in the narrative to support the view that the oath was, in fact, feigned. In light of its importance for the future of the Davidic dynasty, it is strange that if David had made such an oath, no one had knowledge of it. Adonijah does not appear aware of it, and his claiming of the throne is not presented as an act of rebellion. He simply assumed the authority that would be rightfully his when David could no longer fulfill his duties. It is also evident that Solomon himself knew of no such oath promising him the kingdom.[42] In addition, Nathan's failure to mention the oath to David during their conversation implies that he had prevaricated. If the oath were genuine, Nathan simply would have cited David's pledge as the reason that Solomon should be crowned (as Bathsheba had done). It is difficult to understand why Nathan would conclude his conversation with David by asking who would be king (1 Kgs 1:27) if David has already made such a proclamation. If David had designated Solomon as the successor—even if, or perhaps especially if, in private to Bathsheba—it is quite unclear why the queen would have forgotten and need to be reminded by Nathan.[43] Accordingly, it seems much more likely that the idea of an oath was a hoax propagated by Nathan to deceive the king. As Gwilym Jones concludes, Nathan "appears to have been taking advantage of the king's senility, and was also probably playing on the special affection that David had for Bathsheba." Thus, "Nathan was acting in a very dubious, if not corrupt, manner," and "he was responsible for inventing a false statement and for persuading Bathsheba to present it to the king, which unquestionably renders him guilty of deception."[44] As Jeremiah relayed misinformation to the officials (Jer 38:24–28), Nathan too disseminates fabricated data. In both instances the prophet's main motivation is self-preservation. As for David, like Saul and Zedekiah, he is struggling to manage information. A variety of figures—officials, queens, and prophets—surround the king, but whom he is to deem trustworthy is quite nebulous. Even the reader is unsure.

It can be concluded, then, that Solomon, the first son in David's long line of successors, acquires the throne by means of prophetic chicanery. If the very concept of monarchy had an inauspicious beginning with Saul, here the Davidic

42. Cf. Jones, *Nathan Narratives*, 51–52.

43. Alter suggests that Nathan does not mention the oath because he could not presume to know of a pledge given only to Bathsheba (*Art of Biblical Narrative*, 99). If Nathan is being indirect, he is doing so to a risky extreme.

44. Jones, *Nathan Narratives*, 53; see also Bodner, "Nathan," 50, who writes: "Is Nathan fabricating this scenario? There are grounds for suspecting that he is, not the least being that he has done something similar before." He then points to Nathan's "literary artifice" in 2 Sam 12. See also Tomoo Ishida, *The Royal Dynasties in Ancient Israel* (BZAW 142; Berlin: de Gruyter, 1976), 158. Nathan's playing on David's affections for Bathsheba may be seen as particularly devious since earlier Nathan had forcefully denounced the relationship (2 Sam 12).

dynasty also has a portentous origin—due not to Yahweh's misgivings, but to Nathan's self-interest. Even if one were to disagree with this reading of Nathan, the very possibility that he forged the oath leaves a cloud of doubt surrounding him. The prophet Nathan is in the middle of the palace intrigue that envelops David's final days and the appointment of Solomon. If the founder of the Davidic kingdom can be duped by his prophet, it is easier to appreciate why Zedekiah struggles with Jeremiah's word. Indeed, even the paradigmatic King David's final days are marked by rebellion, strife, internal disputes, deception, and chaos—and those were during the good times when God was with David and his kingdom. How much more social, religious, and political disintegration can be expected during Zedekiah's reign when God has abandoned the city and its king or, worse yet, is fighting against them? In light of their circumstances and in comparison to Nathan and David, the relationship between Jeremiah and Zedekiah is relatively healthy and stable, a tribute, seemingly, to both of them.

The Man of God from Judah and Jeroboam

A third and final prophet–king relationship stands at the beginning of the monarchy. Jeroboam, the first Northern king, experiences three encounters with prophets during his reign, two of them with Ahijah (1 Kgs 11:26–40; 14) which frame one with the unnamed man of God from Judah (1 Kgs 13).[45] The Jeroboam series of prophet–king stories varies from the previous two, for he interacts with two different prophets and there is no extended or developed relationship among the characters.

Although it does not feature direct interaction between a prophet and king, the story of Jeroboam's wife and Ahijah can be associated with the stories of Jeremiah and Zedekiah. For instance, Ahijah's blindness (1 Kgs 13:4) is reminiscent of Zedekiah's blindness. The offer of a gift of food (1 Kgs 13:3) to the prophet recalls the Babylonian offer to Jeremiah (Jer 40:5). The wife's disguise links to the secrecy motif in both the Saul–Samuel and Jeremiah–Zedekiah narratives; the use of clothing to conceal one's identity, of course, directly ties with Saul's effort to disguise himself from the medium (1 Sam 28:8). Other correlations with both Saul–Samuel and Zedekiah–Jeremiah include the fact that Samuel and Ahijah predict the death of the king's son(s) just as Jeremiah foretold the capture of Zedekiah's sons, who are subsequently killed. In all three scenes, the prophet indirectly indicts the father—the king—as the instrument of death for his children by some form of unfaithfulness or disobedience to Yahweh. Nonetheless, all three kings persist in their efforts to consult the prophet, despite expectation of receiving a negative word. Saul acts in the extreme by summoning Samuel from the dead even though the prophet had declared the end of Saul's kingdom; Jeroboam seeks out Ahijah, although he evidently fears a hostile message from the prophet because he conceals his wife's identity; and Zedekiah calls on Jeremiah despite previous messages of defeat.

---

45. The first encounter with Ahijah depicts no dialogue, only the prophet declaring to Jeroboam that he would rule over ten tribes. It will not be considered here.

All three prophets anticipate the word that the king wishes to know before the king voices it. Yahweh apprises Samuel that Saul will be consulting him and Samuel informs Saul of the status of his lost donkeys before he asks (1 Sam 9:15, 20). Likewise, Yahweh reveals to Ahijah that Jeroboam's wife is approaching, and before she speaks the prophet delivers a word from Yahweh concerning her son. For Jeremiah, however, there is no divinely granted foreknowledge, and it is not clear if his response to Zedekiah's unspoken inquiry aligns with the information that the king desired (Jer 38:14–18). Finally, Ahijah's prophecies—like those of Jeremiah—are not fulfilled exactly as stated. Ahijah told the wife of Jeroboam that her son would die when "your feet enter the city" (1 Kgs 14:12); however, the child expires "when she came to the threshold of the house" (14:18). While this may appear to be a small detail, given the biblical narrative's propensity for repetition, variations are often significant.

In sum, the connections between 1 Kgs 14 and the Jer 37–40 tend to complicate the image of Jeremiah and his relationship with Zedekiah. Unlike Ahijah, Jeremiah does not explicitly receive a word from Yahweh; akin to Ahijah, he presents only a partially accurate prediction. Yet, reminiscent of Saul and Jeroboam, Zedekiah adamantly pursues a consultation with the prophet.

In 1 Kgs 13 Jeroboam is confronted by an anonymous man of God from Judah who announces the future destruction of the altar at Bethel, which Jeroboam had set up. In response the king stretches out his hand and says, "Seize him!" But the hand shrivels up, so he beseeches the prophet to intercede with Yahweh on his behalf. The man of God complies and the king's hand is healed. The king then offers a meal and a gift to the prophet, who declines citing specific instructions from the deity. As was noted earlier, the man of God's refusal of the king's benevolence contrasts with Jeremiah's acceptance of it from the Babylonians. Jeroboam's attempt to seize the man of God recalls the physical trials that Jeremiah experienced, albeit under the authority of the officials (37:11–15; 38:6), not the king. In fact, Zedekiah is instrumental in protecting Jeremiah, which accentuates his deference for Jeremiah. For neither prophet, however, is there any mention of divine rescue or protection.[46] The deity's presence and who represents his views are strikingly opaque matters in these prophet–king narratives.

The nature of the prophet–king relationship in this scene is not unlike the stories of Jeremiah and Zedekiah in that the interaction between Ahijah and Jeroboam is marked both by confrontation and assistance. The man of God personally helps the king by healing his hand; yet his word of judgment against him remains. Jeroboam offers hospitality to the anonymous prophet although they remain at odds with one another. Similarly, Jeremiah and Zedekiah also work for the protection of each other (Jer 37:21; 38:10, 24–28) despite their different perspectives on Jerusalem's dilemma. Prophet and king are not always as opposed as it may appear on the surface.

---

46. One may speculate how the prophet managed to avoid being constrained, for the king's hand withering would not have nullified the king's order. Regardless, the text says nothing of divine assistance.

Following this prophet–king encounter is a scene detailing events that befall the man of God on his return home (1 Kgs 13:11–34). It has deep implications for the portrayal of the man of God, and by extension for prophets in general and their relation to kings. On his journey home, an "old prophet" in Bethel asks the man of God to return to his house for a meal. The man of God declines citing the word from Yahweh which prohibited him from eating or drinking in Bethel. The old prophet, however, declares that he too has received a word from Yahweh instructing him to bring the man of God back to his house. The man of God believes him and returns to the old prophet's house to eat. When he does, however, the old prophet condemns him for disobeying the word of Yahweh. Specifically, he tells the man of God that he will not be buried in his proper place. Subsequently, a lion kills the man of God.

First, concerning the prophet–king relationship, it should be noted that the man of God evidently thought that the king was trying to dupe him into staying for a meal, a violation of Yahweh's orders. This is suggested by the prophet's response to the king, "If you give me half your kingdom, I will not go with you" (1 Kgs 13:8). The king, however, could harbor no evil intentions since the prophet does not apprise him of Yahweh's orders until after the king has extended his invitation of a meal. Ironically, of course, it is another prophet (the "old prophet") who beguiles the man of God. Prophets need not worry so much about the malice of kings as of other prophets (cf. Jer 27–29).

While 1 Kgs 13 has been approached from a variety of interpretive angles, it is evident that the man of God's depiction is less than ideal.[47] A number of scholars have noted problematic elements of his characterization and consequently of the role and function of prophets and prophecy.[48] Even a genuine prophet may not be able to discern whether or not another prophet's oracle is from Yahweh. How then could prophets expect kings and others to distinguish true from false prophecy? While the portrayals of Samuel, Nathan, and Jeremiah advance a more subtle critique of prophets, the man of God presents a blatant challenge to the prophetic role.

---

47. First Kings 13 has been read intertextually by other interpreters. For example, the unusual role of the donkey in the story recalls Balaam's donkey in Num 22, also a prophet–king narrative of sorts. Cf. Uriel Simon, "I Kings 13: A Prophetic Sign—Denial and Persistence," *HUCA* 47 (1976): 81–117. Even Balaam, a non-Israelite, could not utter a word that Yahweh had not sent, whereas in 1 Kgs 13 an Israelite prophet (of Yahweh?) delivers a message that Yahweh had not commissioned.

48. See James Mead, "Kings and Prophets, Donkeys and Lions: Dramatic Shape and Deuteronomistic Rhetoric in 1 Kings XIII," *VT* 49 (1999): 191–205. Mead (205) maintains that there is a "close literary and symbolic relationship between the rebellious king and the disobedient man of God." This is not unlike the observation that Jeremiah and Zedekiah parallel each other in certain ways. Further, Mead observes that "the narrator leaves the reader with a profound uneasiness over the connection between these two characters" (205). Again, the same could be said of Jeremiah and Zedekiah. Pamela Tamarkin Reis refers to the man of God's insincerity ("Vindicating God: Another Look at 1 Kings xiii, *VT* 44 [1994]: 376–86 [381–82]); David Marcus cites several examples of parody and ridicule of all the main characters in the text ("Elements of Ridicule and Parody in the Story of the Lying Prophet from Bethel," *Proceedings of the Eleventh World Congress of Jewish Studies, Div A* [1994]: 67–74).

Analyzing this story James Crenshaw writes: "Here one sees the true prophet become false to his commission, and the false prophet take up the genuine word of God and let it fall with shattering force on the erring man of God."[49] This story illustrates the fine line between authentic and fraudulent prophecy. True prophets can be deceived by false ones, and false prophets can speak truths. No one, including the reader, is sure whom to trust. Not surprisingly, perhaps, the episode concludes with the observation that "Even after this, Jeroboam did not turn from his evil ways" (1 Kgs 13:33). Why would the king be prompted to believe the man of God's word and repent?[50] Both prophets have as much need of repentance as the king. The text deconstructs itself, for readers are sympathetic to Jeroboam's disregard of the whole event.

The man of God utters a word of judgment against the king; but then he himself is also judged. The judge becomes the judged, the condemner the condemned, the voice of criticism the object of criticism. Although the prophet has been tricked and is consequently dead, the words he spoke against Jeroboam are fulfilled. Ironically, the "old prophet" who tricked the man of God affirms the truth of the man of God's words (1 Kgs 13:31–32). Evidently, Yahweh's "word can come to Israel and Judah, through wavering men of God and lying prophets."[51] In short, the prophet–king and subsequent prophet-prophet encounter in 1 Kgs 13 present a striking juxtaposition—one that creates a messy and complex story about prophets and their relationship to kings. Set at the beginning of the monarchy, it links with the messy and complex stories of Jeremiah and Zedekiah at the end of Israelite history. Specifically, as one of the prophet–king stories that forms the background against which the accounts of Jeremiah and Zedekiah are read, it draws Jeremiah into the cloud of questions that envelop the prophetic office.

Summary

The stories of Jeremiah and Zedekiah are reminiscent of many other Hebrew Bible narratives featuring the interaction of a prophet and king. Such encounters were a "standard literary form," according to Mary Callaway, one of the few who has devoted attention to the Jeremianic narratives.[52] This literary form, however, has been largely overlooked by scholars. The work in this chapter hopefully has taken some productive initial steps in "analyzing the lineaments of a prophet–king story."[53] Not only are the stories of Samuel and Saul, and Nathan and David two of the most evolved prophet–king relationships, but they also stand at the outset of the monarchy, making them natural intertexts with the account of

49. James Crenshaw, *Prophetic Conflict: Its Effect Upon Israelite Religion* (BZAW 124; Berlin: de Gruyter, 1971), 48.
50. Earlier the king requested and received healing of his hand without repenting in any fashion. Is there a need to repent?
51. Mead, "Kings and Prophets," 205 (italics in original).
52. Callaway, "Telling the Truth and Telling Stories," 263.
53. Callaway, "Telling the Truth and Telling Stories," 264.

Jeremiah and Zedekiah. Indeed, the history of the monarchy is framed by stories portraying a dynamic and complex relationship between prophet and king and in which the images of both figures are ambiguous.

Scholars commonly state that a key ingredient of the prophet's role in relation to the king is to communicate a critical word of judgment; this indeed is a significant aspect of the work of Samuel, Nathan, Ahijah, the man of God from Judah, and Jeremiah, as well as others such as Amos and Micah. Prophets and prophecy, however, are not exempted from criticism, whether it be of the more overt kind, as in 1 Kgs 13, or more nuanced modes. While others have noticed a critique of certain prophets on certain occasions, a critique of prophets and prophecy is much more deeply embedded in the Hebrew Bible than has heretofore been recognized.

Interpreters have witnessed criticism in characters such as Elijah and Elisha, who may be described as charismatic, miracle-working figures—prophets who were not known for calling Israel to a life of faith.[54] If the stories of Elijah and Elisha were composed by prophetic circles who traced their identity to these two figures, as Antony Campbell asserts,[55] then it is a credit to their ability to engage in critical reflection on their tradition.[56] However, the complexity of the stories in Jer 37:1–40:6 and their participation in a network of other equally intricate prophet–king narratives uncovers a sophisticated view of prophets and prophets throughout the Hebrew Bible. By painting complex narratives and images of prophets, the biblical writers solicit readers to weigh various points of view, rather than to side with the religious figure against the royal one. If one speculates that the Jeremianic narratives were written by Jeremiah's disciples or Baruch, then they too have demonstrated a capacity for self-criticism, or at least acknowledged the complexities of the circumstances in which no easy answers resided. One should not be surprised if prophetic circles were capable of self-critical reflection, since, after all, that is primarily what their office entailed. If they could censure the monarchy and the cult, which were part of their own social and religious culture, then it is reasonable to conclude that they could subject their own circles to such judgment. Their appreciation for ambiguity enriches the biblical text.

---

54. Mark Roncace, "Elisha and the Woman of Shunem: 2 Kings 4.8–37 and 8.1–6 Read in Conjunction," *JSOT* 91 (2000): 109–27 (126). See the bibliography provided there.

55. Antony Campbell, *Of Prophets and Kings: A Late Ninth Century Document (1 Samuel 1–2 Kings 10)* (Washington: Catholic Biblical Association of America, 1986). Campbell's thesis is that behind the present text of 1 Samuel–2 Kgs 10 lies a unified work written from a northern prophetic perspective. This "theologically inspired history" originated towards the end of the ninth century among the disciples of Elisha.

56. Cf. Mark O'Brien, "The Portrayal of Prophets in 2 Kings 2," *ABR* 46 (1998): 1–16 (16).

CONCLUSION

Generally, narrative in the prophetic books is not lengthy or sustained, but instead is fragmentary and episodic, concentrating on a small number of actions or on speech. Prophetic narratives have been characterized as "false narrative in which the theological interest . . . supersedes the importance of the narrative elements."[1] Such, however, is not the case with Jer 37:1–40:6. It has been the aim of this study to offer insight into the "narrative elements" of this text through a careful and systematic narratological and intertextual study. It is hoped that much of the value of this book lies in its exegetical insights, which are not easily summarized. Nonetheless, a few concluding remarks are appropriate.

Previous diachronic analyses have shed much light on the possible pre-history of Jer 37–44 and in this way have made important contributions. The synchronic reading proposed in this study adopts another angle of vision in order to uncover additional dimensions. Such a reading, however, does not insist on the unity of the text, nor does it seek to find some way to resolve the questions that served as the basis for the redactional work. Jeremiah 37–40 can fruitfully be read in its final form, in the same manner as many others have generated insightful and varied readings of numerous biblical narratives. Complicating interpretation with new angles of vision leads to a deeper understanding of the text and will assist efforts to deal more faithfully with the "intractable riddle"[2] that is the book of Jeremiah.

The narratological focus included analyzing a number of textual elements, many of which revolve around characterization. This study has demonstrated that the images of Zedekiah and Jeremiah are complex. Characters can be assessed in multiple ways—along a continuum. The biblical narrator's "art of reticence," the "studied effect of opacity" in the presentation of both prophet and king leaves space for readers to draw different conclusions about their speech, actions, and motivations.[3] In this sense, the stories in Jer 37–40 are constructed much like other biblical narratives.

While interpreters have noticed an ambivalence in Zedekiah's portrayal, this study has documented specifically how that is developed in the narrative. The complexity of Zedekiah's image can be seen in light of Lasine's observations regarding information management in the maintenance and exercise of monarchical power. Zedekiah, like all other kings, is a paradox, simultaneously weak and

---

1. Claus Westermann, *Genesis 12–36: A Commentary* (trans. J. Scullion; Minneapolis: Augsburg Fortress, 1986), 214–15.

2. A. R. Pete Diamond, "Introduction," in *Troubling Jeremiah* (ed. A. R. P. Diamond, K. M. O'Connor, and L. Stulman; JSOTSup 260; Sheffield: Sheffield Academic Press, 1999), 15–32 (15).

3. Cf. Alter, *Art of Biblical Narrative*, 119.

strong, independent and dependent on his officials. Many commentators recognize elements of the former (his weakness), but few have pointed out his displays of power. In fact, his power over the officials is witnessed precisely in some of the actions that are commonly witnessed as evidence of his fear and cowardice, namely, in his successfully withholding information from them.[4]

As king, Zedekiah is in a lonely and precarious position in the Babylonian crisis. A recent article by Niels Peter Lemche brings Zedekiah's dilemma into focus. Lemche argues that historically it is unlikely that Zedekiah rebelled against the Babylonians.[5] Regardless of the historical merits of Lemche's position, it underscores that even an issue as fundamental as whether or not Zedekiah surrendered is open to debate—open not only on a historical level, but on a textual one as well. That is, an interpretation of the king's actions depends on one's perspective; the text's opacity calls attention to the importance of point of view. In the account of Jerusalem's fall in Jer 39, the narrator discloses nothing about the motivations behind the Babylonian aggression. The text's conspicuous silence on this subject opens the door for other characters and readers to formulate their own conclusions about Zedekiah. Of course, even if the narrator had cited Zedekiah's rebellion as the reason for the Babylonian attack, that would not have simply resolved the matter.

The issue is this: What constitutes rebellion and what constitutes surrendering? Is "not surrendering" tantamount to "rebellion"? As noted earlier, part of Zedekiah's problem presumably regarded the mechanics of surrendering. What action would be necessary: relinquish the throne? Pay tribute? Hand over the treasuries in the temple (whatever remained after 597)? The narrator, Jeremiah, and the officials are, again, conspicuously taciturn on this question. Similarly, what would constitute "rebellion"? Any degree of "submission" to the Babylonians would have been interpreted as "surrendering" by some and anything short of full compliance would have been understood as rebellion by others. Whatever course of action the king followed, some perspectives would have interpreted it as too much concession to the enemy and others as not enough. A single action could be rendered as either rebellion or submission.[6] Thus, Zedekiah's actions are

---

4. Although Ezekiel, Chronicles, and Kings depict Zedekiah in negative terms, Jeremiah's more nuanced and sympathetic view of him is further developed in post-biblical interpretation. For instance, Josephus' depiction of Zedekiah in his *Antiquities of the Jews* (5:102–54) is quite sensitive. Josephus reports that Zedekiah was receptive to Jeremiah's word, calls Zedekiah "good and righteous," and says that the king was not resentful toward the prophet. Josephus, does, however, hold Zedekiah responsible, at least in part, for the destruction of Jerusalem and the subsequent exile. See Christopher Begg, "Josephus' Zedekiah," *ETL* 65 (1989): 96–104, for a detailed discussion of Josephus' many editorial changes to the biblical account. The rabbinic tradition, too, is ambiguous toward Zedekiah, with plenty of positive interpretations along with negative ones. See Louis Ginzberg, *The Legends of the Jews* (trans. H. Szold; 7 vols.; Philadelphia: Jewish Publication Society, 1909–1938), 4:291–94, 339–46.

5. Niels Peter Lemche, "What if Zedekiah had Remained Loyal to His Master?," *BibInt* 8 (2000): 115–28.

6. The potential ambiguity surrounding Zedekiah's historical "rebellion" could explain, in part, why his literary characterization is sketched in such a complex fashion.

"undecidable" from a historical standpoint and—as a sensitive reading reveals —from a literary one as well.

The ambiguity of Jeremiah's depiction has not heretofore been adequately assayed. Prophetic narratives in the Hebrew Bible frequently emphasize the humanity of prophets by the portrayal of their mistakes, reluctance, anger, despair, loneliness, and alienation. In addition to the images of Samuel, Nathan, and the man of God from Judah, discussed briefly in the previous chapter, one thinks of the images of Moses, Elijah, Elisha, and Jonah. Viewed positively, one might say that the prophets' own personalities are a central part of their ministry. Seen negatively, prophets might be interpreted as "unreliable,"[7] or one may sense some "anti-prophetic satire,"[8] or even "the end of prophetism."[9] A study of prophet–king narratives reveals a number of elements that complicate the image of prophets—including deceptive speech,[10] a difficulty distinguishing between the words of the prophet and the words of Yahweh,[11] misuse of power or failed uses of power,[12] excessive interest in their personal well-being,[13] and incorrect predictions.[14] The point is that many—if not all—prophets in the Hebrew Bible are ambiguous characters who can be read in diverse ways. Jeremiah is no exception. Indeed, the stories in Jer 37–40 involve Jeremiah's human concerns as well as his efforts to carry out his prophetic responsibilities. The tension between these two forms much of the depth of his portrayal.

The attention to characterization is closely related to and influenced by how point of view is deployed in the text. Jeremiah 37–40 is told by a third-person omniscient narrator—a narrator who is not bound spatially or temporally. The story, however, is dominated by dialogue between the characters rather than by narration. After the introduction (37:1–2), the narrator remains neutral, making no further evaluative comments. Events are presented from a detached, external perspective that allows for the presentation of ideologies other than that of the narrator to compete for validity and authenticity. The story, then, is what Shlomith Rimmon-Kenan would label a "more complex case" in which the narrator "gives way to a plurality of ideological positions whose validity is doubtful in principle. Some of these positions may occur in part or in whole, others may be mutually opposed, the interplay among them provoking a non-unitary 'polyphonic' reading of the text."[15]

The main competing ideologies in the story are those of Jeremiah and the officials. One of the primary plot-lines concerns Zedekiah's choice of ideologies. As for the deity's view, it is not clear whether or not Jeremiah speaks for

---

7. Kissling, *Reliable Characters in the Primary History*, 147–48, 198–99. Kissling considers portions of Elijah's and Elisha's portrayal unreliable.

8. Marcus, *From Balaam to Jonah*.

9. Bergen, *Elisha and the End of Prophetism*.

10. First Kings 1:13; 18:11–12; 22:15; 2 Kgs 6:19; 8:10.

11. Second Samuel 7:3–4; 1 Kgs 14:7, 12; 20:13, 22; 21:19–24; 2 Kgs 3:16–21; 7:1–2; 8:10.

12. First Kings 1:1–16; 3:27; 6:23–24.

13. First Kings 1:1–27; 17:1; 2 Kgs 1:1–16; 5:8; 7:1–2.

14. First Kings 14:12; 20:13; 21:19; 2 Kgs 3:18–19; 8:12; 13:19; 19:7; 20:18; 22:20.

15. Rimmon-Kenan, *Narrative Fiction*, 81.

Yahweh. The prophet appears to filter Yahweh's perspective through his own agenda, which is troubling, especially when combined with the discrepancies between Jeremiah's word and events as they are reported, and the prophet's benevolent treatment by the Babylonians after the fall. If it were to be evident that Jeremiah voiced the deity's view, one may be inclined to read the story as an expression of Jeremiah's/Yahweh's ideology against which the others are to be judged, though that need not be the case. The text, however, does not offer that option. The king, along with the reader, must sift through the various ideologies to determine which, if any, represents the "truth."

The narrator's view, too, is "doubtful in principle." His assertion that Zedekiah and the people did not שׁמע to the voice of Yahweh spoken through Jeremiah is challenged by the events of the story; the repetition of the word שׁמע, with its multiple nuances and connotations, draws attention to this dubiousness. Readers are able to perceive that the narrator's perspective is too simplistic, too neat and clear-cut. It does not capture the intricate circumstances that confronted the king and city. In addition, the officials themselves noted that Jeremiah's words were influencing the people of Jerusalem (38:4), and Zedekiah himself appears favorably disposed to the prophet's message and seems periodically to be persuaded by his view—even if he is politically incapable of enacting it. The implied author employs the narrator, not as the controlling perspective against which all others are to be evaluated, but as another voice in the conversation. The narrator does not hold "ultimate semantic authority"; instead it is found in the intersection—the dialogue—of the various perspectives, including that of the narrator. The polyphonic nature of the text invites readers to judge the validity and the "doubtfulness" of the different views and to formulate their own opinions of the characters and events.

Adding to the richness and diversity of the voices presented are the text's connections to other passages both within and beyond the book of Jeremiah. The book of Jeremiah resists simple linear (consecutive) reading strategies. Voices, themes, and vocabulary emerge and resurface later; careful readers will discern the linkages and interplay. They will also hear echoes of many other texts, most notably, those of other prophet–kings narratives. These intertextual relations illumine elements of Jer 37–40. The light, however, will appear differently to different readers. As with the narratological features, particularly characterization, there is a wide range in which to interpret intertextual associations and a perhaps even wider range of potential resonances. The reverberations contribute to the complexity of Jeremiah's image. For example, he is cast in the role of the Rabshakeh and the medium at Endor; the comparisons to Daniel and Joseph depict him as a "Jew in the court of a foreign king"; he does not compare well to Micaiah in some respects; and he is portrayed as an anti-Moses figure. His ties with Samuel, Nathan, and the man of God from Judah evoke further questions about him and the prophetic office. Concerning Zedekiah, the intertextual links remind one, for instance, that although Jehoiachin had adopted a policy of submission to the Babylonians, it did not establish peace and security for the temple and the inhabitants of Jerusalem. Perhaps surrender was not the best option.

Zedekiah is analogous to Hezekiah, which fosters a sympathetic reading of Zedekiah, and his connections with Saul highlight the tragic nature of his reign. Further, the depictions of other characters in the story, such as Irijah and some of the officials, gain added dimensions by intertextual linkages created by their patronymics.

Although the story in Jer 37–40 is recounted from a temporal location after the fall of Jerusalem, it is narrated in such a way that readers appreciate the messiness of the predicament that Zedekiah faced. Surely this reflects the complexity and ambiguity of the circumstances in which the exiles found themselves. It is not difficult to imagine what may have prompted an exilic or early post-exilic (implied) author (final editor) to construct such a complex story. Bernard Paris, taking a psychoanalytic approach, offers one solution. He writes that authors' "conflicting trends will lead them to criticize each solution from the point of view of the others and to have toward their characters the mixed feelings that they have toward the aspects of themselves the characters embody."[16] It is easy to envision a post-587 author orchestrating a story with multiple points of view as he himself wrestled with the social, political, ideological, and theological intricacies of exilic and post-exilic life.[17] As the stories of Jeremiah and Zedekiah suggest, life is lived among ambiguous shades of gray where answers are rarely obvious, where competing views vie against one another, where truth is elusive.

The polyphonic and intertextual nature of the story furnishes an opportunity for readers to reflect on human life, to draw lines that stretch into the world of the reader. Closely related to Bakhtin's concept of polyphony is his notion of unfinalizability, which can briefly be mentioned here as a means to assist final reflections. Unfinalizability is tightly connected to a number of Bakhtin's other ideas: openness, potentiality, creativity, "surprisingness," and the authentically new.[18] He writes: "Nothing conclusive has taken place in the world, the ultimate word of the world and about the world has not yet been spoken, the world is free and open, everything is still in the future and will always be in the future."[19] For Bakhtin, freedom and openness characterize the unfinalized world in which genuine innovation remains a constant possibility. A polyphonic, multi-voiced work is characterized by its unfinalizability.

The author's position in a polyphonic work is discussed in terms of "surplus."[20] In monologic writing, authors have a surplus of vision or knowledge concerning their characters, but the characters do not have the same surplus with respect to the author. The author knows everything about the created character, while the

---

16. Bernard Paris, *Imagined Human Beings: A Psychological Approach to Character and Conflict in Literature* (New York: New York University Press, 1997), 264.

17. Similarly, Stipp asserts that "these texts are not about the last Judean king but about the writers themselves and their communities" ("Zedekiah in the Book of Jeremiah," 648).

18. Gary S. Morson and Caryl Emerson, *Mikhail Bakhtin: Creation of a Prosaics* (Stanford: Stanford University Press, 1990), 36–37. This (absurdly) brief discussion of Bakhtin is based on the work of Morson and Emerson.

19. Mikhail Bakhtin, *Problems in Dostoevsky's Poetics*, 166.

20. Cf. Morson and Emerson, *Mikhail Bakhtin*, 241–43, for a discussion of "surplus" and other terms in this paragraph.

character knows nothing about the author. This surplus of knowledge prohibits the author and character from dialoguing as equals. An author's surplus functions to finalize characters and to absolutize their identity. A polyphonic writer, in contrast, renounces the "essential surplus of meaning." There remains a surplus of knowledge necessary to create the characters, but this is only "information-based surplus" consisting of the required facts about the identity of the character. In addition, an author of a polyphonic text must endeavor to include what could be called an "addressive surplus." This involves an "active understanding, a willingness to listen." Characters in the text can employ this in relating to each other just as the author may use it in interacting with the characters. Characters and the author must be careful not to finalize others or definitively determine their identity. Instead, one should use one's "outsideness" to ask the apposite questions and to listen actively.

One must approach the "other" as a "personality," as someone who is capable of change, as someone who "has not yet uttered his ultimate word." For Bakhtin, as long as a person is alive he lives by the fact that he is not finalized, and ethically he must be treated accordingly. The heroes in a polyphonic work do not understand others "psychologically," but rather dialogically. They possess a "dialogic intuition" which permits them to see the unfinalizable inner dialogues of others and to participate in that dialogue while respecting its open-endedness. That is, a responsible participant converses in such a way as to contribute not only to the external conversation, but also to the dialogue that takes place within each person as he or she struggles slowly toward the truth.

It may be quite transparent how the unfinalizability of the characters in Jer 37:1–40:6 can be brought to bear on how one lives. The manner in which authors present and interact with the characters in their text can offer insight into how one treats the characters in one's own life. Undoubtedly, readers' personalities and the way in which they associate with "real people" influence their interpretation of characters in texts. But the influence can also move in the other direction—interaction with characters in literature may reshape one's approach toward interrelating with human beings. The (implied) author of Jer 37:1–40:6 has not finalized the characters; instead, they remain open-ended, genuine, and unique personalities who are in the process of becoming. In one's personal worlds, the story of Jeremiah and Zedekiah urge one not to finalize those people who inhabit one's life. They remind readers to listen actively, to use their "outsideness" to ask the right questions—questions that will not only productively move the dialogue forward, but ones that will assist others in their own inner conversations. The stories of Jeremiah and Zedekiah present a moment for reflection on the tensions and paradoxes within readers themselves and within life in general. In the current social and political climate, these stories exhort readers to be sensitive to the special challenges that confront national leaders. They point to the difficulties of navigating among competing ideologies—each claiming truth—and to the intricacies of national and international affairs and how they may intersect with personal interests. On the theological plain, these narratives remind readers of the difficulties of seeing the presence of God and hearing the voice of God. They encourage one to listen carefully to the message of those invoking the name of God. Indeed, Bakhtin's suggestion that truth emerges in the intersection of conversing voices is worth pondering deeply in a world replete with rival discourses each seeking to achieve hegemony.

Jeremiah 37–40 is not a "theological narrative" like Jonah or Job, but rather a story about "real life," about a prophet and king who lived and experienced Israel's greatest tragedy. A careful reading and contemplation of their story provides an occasion for reflection as one negotiates the complexities of "real life" today. The polyphonic and dialogic nature of the texts summons readers to enter the fray and to struggle to know the truth, to assess which views may contain at least partial truth, and to be sensitive to the difficulty of making such judgments. The intertextual threads spun by the story of Jeremiah, Zedekiah, and the fall of Jerusalem can be interwoven with contemporary human life. The specific ways in which that might be accomplished are best left to the reader.

BIBLIOGRAPHY

Abrams, Meyer H. *A Glossary of Literary Terms*. 5th ed.; Chicago: Holt, Rinehart & Winston, 1985.

Abrego, José M. *Jeremías y el Final del Reino: Lectura sincrónica de Jer 36–45*. Valencia: Institución san Jerónimo, 1983.

Ahlström, Gösta. *The History of Ancient Palestine from the Paleolithic Period to Alexander's Conquest*. Journal for the Study of the Old Testament: Supplement Series 146. Sheffield: JSOT Press, 1993.

Aiken, Kenneth. "The Oracles against Babylon in Jeremiah 50–51: Structures and Perspectives." *Tyndale Bulletin* 35 (1984): 25–63.

Alter, Robert. *The Art of Biblical Narrative*. New York: Basic Books, 1981.

—*The World of Biblical Literature*. New York: Basic Books, 1992.

Applegate, John. "The Fate of Zedekiah: Redactional Debate in the Book of Jeremiah." *Vetus Testamentum* 48 (1998): 137–60.

Bakhtin, Mikhail. *Problems of Dostoevsky's Poetics*. Translated by C. Emerson. Minneapolis: University of Minnesota Press, 1984.

Bal, Mieke. *Narratology: Introduction to the Theory of Narrative*. Toronto: University of Toronto Press, 1997.

Balentine, Samuel E. "The Prophet as Intercessor: A Reassessment." *Journal of Biblical Literature* 103 (1984): 161–73.

Barthes, Roland. *Image–Music–Text*. Glasgow: Fontana, 1977.

Barton, John. *Reading the Old Testament: Method in Biblical Study*. Philadelphia: Westminster, 1984.

Bar-Efrat, Shimon. *Narrative Art in the Bible*. Journal for the Study of the Old Testament: Supplement Series 70. Sheffield: Almond, 1989.

Begg, Christopher. "Josephus' Zedekiah." *Ephemerides theologicae lovanienses* 65 (1989): 96–104.

Bergen, Wesley. *Elisha and the End of Prophetism*. Journal for the Study of the Old Testament: Supplement Series 286. Sheffield: Sheffield Academic Press, 1999.

Berger, Benjamin L. "Picturing the Prophet: Focalization in the Book of Jonah." *Studies in Religion* 29 (2000): 55–68.

Berlin, Adele. *Poetics and Interpretation of Biblical Narrative*. Bible and Literature Series 9. Sheffield: Almond, 1983.

Berquist, Jon. "Prophetic Legitimation in Jeremiah." *Vetus Testamentum* 39 (1989): 129–39.

Biddle, Mark. *Polyphony and Symphony in Prophetic Literature*. Macon: Mercer University Press, 1996.

Boadt, Lawrence. *Jeremiah 26–52, Habakkuk, Zephaniah, Nahum*. Wilmington, Del.: Michael Glazier, 1982.

Bodner, Keith. "Nathan: Prophet, Politician and Novelist?," *Journal for the Study of the Old Testament* 95 (2001): 43–54.

Boecker, Hans J. *Law and the Administration of Justice in the Old Testament and Ancient East*. Minneapolis: Augsburg, 1980.

Boyle, Brian. "Narrative as Ideology: Synchronic (Narrative Critical) and Diachronic Readings of Jeremiah 37–38." *Pacifica* 12 (1999): 293–312.

—"Ruination in Jerusalem: Narrative Technique and Characterisation in Jeremiah 37–38." *Compass* 32 (1998): 38–45.

Bovati, Pietro. *Re-Establishing Justice: Legal Terms, Concepts and Procedures in the Hebrew Bible*. Translated by M. J. Smith. Journal for the Study of the Old Testament: Supplement Series 105. Sheffield: JSOT Press, 1994.

Bracke, John. *Jeremiah 30–52 and Lamentations*. Louisville, Ky.: Westminster John Knox, 2000.

Brawley, Robert. *Text to Text Pours Forth Speech: Voices of Scripture in Luke–Acts*. Bloomington: Indiana University Press, 1995.

Brichto, Herbert C. *Toward a Grammar of Biblical Poetics*. New York: Oxford University Press, 1992.

Bright, John. *Jeremiah: A New Translation with Introduction and Commentary*. The Anchor Bible 21. New York: Doubleday, 1965.

Brueggemann, Walter. *A Commentary on Jeremiah: Exile and Homecoming*. Grand Rapids: Eerdmans, 1997.

—"Jeremiah's Use of Rhetorical Questions." *Journal of Biblical Literature* 92 (1973): 358–74.

—*To Build, to Plant: A Commentary on Jeremiah 26–52*. International Theological Commentary. Grand Rapids: Eerdmans, 1991.

Buber, Martin. *Kingship of God*. Translated by R. Scheimann. New York: Harper & Row, 1967.

Callaway, Mary. "Black Fire on White Fire: Historical Context and Literary Subtext in Jeremiah 37–38." Pages 171–78 in *Troubling Jeremiah*. Edited by A. R. P. Diamond, K. M. O'Connor, and L. Stulman. Journal for the Study of the Old Testament: Supplement Series 260. Sheffield: Sheffield Academic Press, 1999.

—"Telling the Truth and Telling Stories: An Analysis of Jeremiah 37–38." *Union Seminary Quarterly Review* 44 (1991): 253–65.

Calvin, John. *Commentaries on the Book of the Prophet Jeremiah and the Lamentations*. Edited and translated by John Owen; 5 vols. Grand Rapids: Eerdmans, 1950.

Campbell, Antony. *Of Prophets and Kings: A Late Ninth Century Document (1 Samuel 1– 2 Kings 10*. Washington: Catholic Biblical Association of America, 1986.

Canetti, Elias. *Crowds and Power*. New York: Continuum, 1981.

Carroll, Robert. "The Book of J: Intertextuality and Ideological Criticism." Pages 220–43 in *Troubling Jeremiah*. Edited by A. R. P. Diamond, K. M. O'Connor, and L. Stulman. Journal for the Study of the Old Testament: Supplement Series 260. Sheffield: Sheffield Academic Press, 1999.

—"Intertextuality and the Book of Jeremiah: Animadversions on Text and Theory." Pages 55– 78 in *The New Literary Criticism and the Hebrew Bible*. Edited by J. C. Exum and D. J. A. Clines. Journal for the Study of the Old Testament: Supplement Series 143. Sheffield: JSOT Press, 1993.

—*Jeremiah: A Commentary*. Old Testament Library. Philadelphia: Westminster, 1986.

—*When Prophecy Failed: Cognitive Dissonance in the Prophetic Tradition of the Old Testament*. New York: Seabury, 1979.

Chatman, Seymour. *Story and Discourse: Narrative Structure in Fiction and Film*. Ithaca, N.Y.: Cornell University Press, 1978.

Clements, Ronald. *Jeremiah: A Bible Commentary for Teaching and Preaching*. Interpretation: A Bible Commentary for Teaching and Preaching. Atlanta: John Knox, 1988.

Collins, John. *The Apocalyptic Vision of the Book of Daniel*. Missoula, Mont.: Scholars Press, 1977.

Conroy, Charles. *Absalom, Absalom! Narrative and Language in 2 Sam 13–20*. Rome: Biblical Institute, 1978.

Coxon, Peter. "Was Naomi a Scold? A Response to Fewell and Gunn." *Journal for the Study of the Old Testament* 45 (1989): 25–37.

Craig, Kenneth. "Rhetorical Aspects of Questions Answered with Silence in 1 Samuel 14:37 and 28:6." *Catholic Biblical Quarterly* 56 (1994): 221–39.

Crenshaw, James. *Prophetic Conflict: Its Effect Upon Israelite Religion*. Beihefte zur Zeitschrift für die alttestamentliche Wissenschaft 124. Berlin: de Gruyter, 1971.

Culler, Jonathan. *The Pursuit of Signs*. Ithaca, N.Y.: Cornell University Press, 1981.

Culley, Robert. *Themes and Variations*. Atlanta: Scholars Press, 1992.

Darr, John. *On Character Building: The Reader and the Rhetoric of Characterization in Luke–Acts*. Louisville, Ky.: Westminster, 1992.

Daube, David. *The Exodus Pattern in the Bible*. London: Faber & Faber, 1963.

Dearman, Andrew. "My Servants the Scribes: Composition and Context in Jeremiah 36." *Journal of Biblical Literature* 109 (1990): 403–21.

Derby, Josiah, "The Tragic King." *Jewish Bible Quarterly* 29 (2001): 181–85.

Diamond, A. R. Pete. "Introduction." Pages 15–32 in *Troubling Jeremiah*. Edited by A. R. P. Diamond, K. M. O'Connor, and L. Stulman. Journal for the Study of the Old Testament: Supplement Series 260. Sheffield: Sheffield Academic Press, 1999.

—"Portraying Prophecy: Of Doublets, Variants and Analogies in the Narrative Representation of Jeremiah's Oracles—Reconstructing the Hermeneutics of Prophecy." *Journal for the Study of the Old Testament* 57 (1993): 99–119.

Duhm, Bernard. *Das Buch Jeremia*. Kurzer Hand-Commentar zum Alten Testament 11. Tübingen: J. C. B. Mohr, 1901.

Eslinger, Lyle. *House of God or House of David: The Rhetoric of 2 Samuel 7*. Journal for the Study of the Old Testament: Supplement Series 164. Sheffield: JSOT Press, 1994.

—*Kingship of God in Crisis: A Close Reading of 1 Samuel 1–12*. Bible and Literature 10; Sheffield: Sheffield Academic Press, 1985.

—"Viewpoints and Point of View in 1 Samuel 8–12." *Journal for the Study of the Old Testament* 26 (1983): 61–76.

Evans, G. " 'Coming' and 'Going' at the City Gate—A Discussion of Professor Speiser's Paper." *Bulletin of the American Schools of Oriental Research* 150 (1958): 28–33.

Exum, Cheryl. *Tragedy and Biblical Narrative*. Cambridge: Cambridge University Press, 1992.

Fewell, Dana, ed. *Reading Between Texts: Intertextuality and the Hebrew Bible*. Louisville, Ky.: Westminster John Knox, 1992.

Fewell, Dana, and David Gunn. "Is Coxon a Scold? On Responding to the Book of Ruth." *Journal for the Study of the Old Testament* 45 (1989): 39–43.

—" 'A Son is Born to Naomi!': Literary Allusions and Interpretation in the Book of Ruth." *Journal for the Study of the Old Testament* 40 (1988): 99–108.

Fokkelman, Jan. *Reading Biblical Narrative: An Introductory Guide*. Louisville, Ky.: Westminster John Knox, 1999.

Forster, Edward M. *Aspects of the Novel*. New York: Penguin Books, 1962.

Foucault, Michel. *Language, Counter-Memory, Practice: Selected Essays and Interviews*. Edited by D. Bouchard. Ithaca, N.Y.: Cornell University Press, 1977.

Frisch, Amos. "For I Feared the People and I Yielded to Them (1 Sam 15:24)—Is Saul's Guilt Attenuated or Intensified?," *Zeitschrift für die alttestamentliche Wissenschaft* 108 (1996): 98–104.

Galef, David. *The Supporting Cast: A Study of Flat and Minor Characters*. University Park: Pennsylvania State University Press, 1993.

Genette, Gérard. *Narrative Discourse: An Essay in Method*. Ithaca, N.Y.: Cornell University Press, 1980.

George, Mark K. "Yhwh's Own Heart." *Catholic Biblical Quarterly* 64 (2002): 442–59.

Ginzberg, Louis. *The Legends of the Jews*. Translated by H. Szold. 7 vols. Philadelphia: Jewish Publication Society, 1909–38.

Goldingay, John. *God's Prophet, God's Servant*. Greenwood, S.C.: Attic, 1984.

Graupner, Axel. *Auftrag und Geschick des Propheten Jeremia: Literarische Eigenart, Herkunft und Intention vordeuteronomistischer Prosa im Jeremiabuch*. Neukirchen–Vluyn: Neukirchener Verlag, 1991.

Green, Barbara. "The Determination of Pharaoh: His Characterization in the Joseph Story (Genesis 37–50)." Pages 150–71 in *The World of Genesis: Persons, Places, Perspectives*. Edited by P. R. Davies and D. J. A. Clines. Journal for the Study of the Old Testament: Supplement Series 257. Sheffield: Sheffield Academic Press, 1998.

—*How Are the Mighty Fallen? A Dialogical Study of King Saul in 1 Samuel*. Journal for the Study of the Old Testament: Supplement Series 365. London: Sheffield Academic Press, 2003.

—*Mikhail Bakhtin and Biblical Scholarship: An Introduction*. Atlanta: Society of Biblical Literature, 2000.

Gunn, David. *The Fate of King Saul*. Journal for the Study of the Old Testament: Supplement Series 14. Sheffield: JSOT Press, 1980.

—"Narrative Criticism." Pages 201–29 in *To Each its Own Meaning*. Edited by S. McKenzie and S. Haynes. Louisville, Ky.: Westminster John Knox, 1999.

—"New Directions in the Study of Biblical Hebrew Narrative." *Journal for the Study of the Old Testament* 39 (1987): 65–75.

—*The Story of King David*. Journal for the Study of the Old Testament: Supplement Series 6. Sheffield: JSOT Press, 1978.

Gunn, David and Dana Fewell. *Narrative in the Hebrew Bible*. Oxford: Oxford University Press, 1993.

Hardmeier, Christof. *Prophetie im Streit vor dem Untergang Judas: Erzählkommunikative Studien zur Entstehungssituation der Jesaja- und Jeremiaerzählungen in II Reg 18–20 und Jer 37–40*. Beihefte zur Zeitschrift für die alttestamentliche Wissenschaft 187. Berlin: de Gruyter, 1990.

Hawk, L. Daniel. "Saul as Sacrifice: The Tragedy of Israel's First Monarch." *Bible Review 12* (Dec 1996): 20–25, 56.

Hays, Richard. *Echoes of Scripture in the Letters of Paul*. New Haven: Yale University Press, 1989.

Hermann, Siegfried. "Overcoming the Israelite Crisis." Pages 299–311 in *A Prophet to the Nations*. Edited by L. Perdue and B. Kovacs. Winona Lake, Ind.: Eisenbrauns, 1984.

Hochman, Baruch. *Character in Literature*. Ithaca, N.Y.: Cornell University Press, 1985.

Holladay, William. "The Background of Jeremiah's Self-Understanding: Moses, Samuel, and Psalm 22." *Journal of Biblical Literature* 83 (1964): 153–64.

—*Jeremiah 1: A Commentary on the Book of the Prophet Jeremiah, Chapters 1–25*. Hermeneia. Philadelphia: Fortress, 1986.

—*Jeremiah 2: A Commentary on the Book of the Prophet Jeremiah, Chapters 26–52*. Hermeneia. Philadelphia: Fortress, 1989.

—"Jeremiah and Moses: Further Observations." *Journal of Biblical Literature* 85 (1966): 17–27.

Holt, Else. "The Potent Word of God: Remarks on the Composition of Jeremiah 37–44." Pages 161–70 in *Troubling Jeremiah*. Edited by A. R. P. Diamond, K. M. O'Connor and L. Stulman. Journal for the Study of the Old Testament: Supplement Series 260. Sheffield: Sheffield Academic Press, 1999.

Huey, F. B. *Jeremiah, Lamentations*. The New American Commentary 16. Nashville: Broadman, 1993.

Isbell, Charles. "2 Kings 22:3–23:4 and Jeremiah 36: A Stylistic Comparison." *Journal for the Study of the Old Testament* 8 (1978): 33–45.

Iser, Wolfgang. *The Act of Reading: A Theory of Aesthetic Response.* Baltimore: The Johns Hopkins University Press, 1978.

Ishida, Tomoo. *The Royal Dynasties in Ancient Israel.* Beihefte zur Zeitschrift für die alttestamentliche Wissenschaft 142. Berlin: de Gruyter, 1976.

Janzen, J. Gerald. "Withholding the Word." Pages 97–114 in *Traditions in Transformation: Turning Points in Biblical Faith.* Edited by B. Halpern and J. D. Levenson. Winona Lake, Ind.: Eisenbrauns, 1981.

Jones, Doug R. *Jeremiah.* New Century Bible Commentary. Grand Rapids: Eerdmans, 1992.

Jones, Gwilym. *The Nathan Narratives.* Journal for the Study of the Old Testament: Supplement Series 80. Sheffield: JSOT Press, 1990.

Keown, Gerald, Thomas Smothers, and Pamela Scalise. *Jeremiah 26–52.* Word Biblical Commentary 27. Dallas: Word Books, 1995.

Kessler, Martin. "Form Critical Suggestions on Jer. 36." *Catholic Biblical Quarterly* 28 (1966): 389–401.

—"Jeremiah Chapters 26–45 Reconsidered." *Journal of Near Eastern Studies* 27 (1968): 81–88.

Kissling, Paul. *Reliable Characters in the Primary History.* Journal for the Study of the Old Testament: Supplement Series 224. Sheffield: Sheffield Academic Press, 1996.

Klein, Ralph W. *1 Samuel.* Word Biblical Commentary 10. Waco, Tex.: Word Books, 1983.

Kremers, H., "Leidensgemeinschaft mit Gott im Alten Testament: Eine Untersuchung der 'biographischen' Berichte im Jeremiabuch." *Evangelische Theologie* 13 (1953): 122–40.

Kristeva, Julia. *Desire in Language: A Semiotic Approach to Literature and Art.* Edited by L. S. Roudiez. Translated by T. Gora, A. Jardine, and L. S. Roudiez. New York: Columbia, 1980 [Fr. 1969].

—"Word, Dialogue and Novel." Pages 34–61 in *The Kristeva Reader.* Edited by T. Moi. Oxford: Basil Blackwell, 1986.

Kugler, Jürgen. "The Prophetic Discourse and Political Praxis of Jeremiah: Observations on Jeremiah 26 and 36." Pages 47–56 in *God of the Lowly: Socio-Historical Interpretations of the Bible.* Edited by E. W. Schottroff and W. Stegemann. Maryknoll, N.Y.: Orbis Books, 1984.

Lalleman-deWinkel, Hetty. *Jeremiah in Prophetic Tradition.* Leuven: Peeters, 2000.

Landsberger, Franz. "The House of the People." *Hebrew Union College Annual* 22 (1949): 149–55.

Lanser, Susan S. *The Narrative Act: Point of View in Prose Fiction.* Princeton: Princeton University Press, 1981.

Lasine, Stuart. *Knowing Kings: Knowledge, Power, and Narcissism in the Hebrew Bible.* Atlanta: Society of Biblical Literature, 2001.

Lemche, Niels Peter. "What if Zedekiah had Remained Loyal to His Master?" *Biblical Interpretation* 8 (2000): 115–28.

Licht, Jacob. *Storytelling in the Bible.* Jerusalem: Magnes, 1978.

Lohfink, Norbert. "Die Gattung der 'Historischen Kurzgeschichte' in den letzen Jahren von Juda und in der Zeit des Babylonischen Exils." *Zeitschrift für die alttestamentliche Wissenschaft* 90 (1978): 319–47.

Long, Burke O. "Social Dimensions of Prophetic Conflict." *Semeia* 21 (1981): 31–53.

Lotman, Jurij. *The Structure of the Artistic Text.* Translated by R. Vroon. Ann Arbor: University of Michigan Press, 1977.

Love, Mark. *The Evasive Text: Zechariah 1–8 and the Frustrated Reader.* Journal for the Study of the Old Testament: Supplement Series 296. Sheffield: Sheffield Academic Press, 1999.

Macholz, George C. "Jeremia in der Kontinuität der Prophetie." Pages 306–34 in *Probleme biblischer Theologie.* Edited by H. W. Wolff. Munich: Kaiser, 1971.

Magonet, Jonathan. "Character/Author/Reader: The Problem of Perspective in Biblical Narrative." Pages 3–12 in *Literary Structure and Rhetorical Strategies in the Hebrew Bible*. Edited by L. J. Regt, J. de Waard, and J. P Fokkelman. Winona Lake, Ind.: Eisenbrauns, 1996.

Malamat, Abraham. "Jeremiah and the Last Two Kings of Judah." *Palestine Exploration Quarterly* 83 (1951): 81–87.

Mandell, Sara R. "Reading Samuel as Saul and Vice Versa." Pages 13–32 in *Approaches to Ancient Judaism*. Edited by J. Neusner. Atlanta: Scholars Press, 1996.

Marcus, David. "Elements of Ridicule and Parody in the Story of the Lying Prophet from Bethel." *Proceedings of the Eleventh World Congress of Jewish Studies, Div A* (1994): 67–74.

—*From Balaam to Jonah: Anti-Prophetic Satire in the Hebrew Bible*. Atlanta: Scholars Press, 1995.

Martens, Elmer A. "Narrative Parallelism and Message in Jeremiah 34–38." Pages 33–49 in *Early Jewish and Christian Exegesis: Studies in Memory of William Hugh Brownlee*. Edited by C. A. Evans and W. F. Stinespring. Atlanta: Scholars Press, 1987.

Matthews, Victor. "The Unwanted Gift: Implications of Obligatory Gift Giving in Ancient Israel." *Semeia* 87 (1999): 91–104.

McEvenue, Sean. "The Composition of Jeremiah 37.1 to 44.30." Pages 59–67 in *Studies in Wisdom Literature*. Edited by W. C. van Wyk. Pretoria: Society for the Study of the Old Testament, 1972.

McKane, William. *A Critical and Exegetical Commentary on Jeremiah I–XXV*. International Critical Commentary. Edinburgh: T&T Clark, 1986.

—*A Critical and Exegetical Commentary on Jeremiah XXVI–LII*. International Critical Commentary. Edinburgh: T&T Clark, 1996.

—"Jeremiah and the Wise." Pages 142–51 in *Wisdom in Ancient Israel: Essays in Honour of J. A. Emerton*. Edited by J. Day, R. P. Gordon, and H. G. M. Williamson. Cambridge: Cambridge University Press, 1995.

Mead, James K. "Kings and Prophets, Donkeys and Lions: Dramatic Shape and Deuteronomistic Rhetoric in 1 Kings XIII." *Vetus Testamentum* 49 (1999): 191–205.

Meier, Samuel. *Speaking of Speaking: Marking Direct Discourse in the Hebrew Bible*. Leiden: Brill, 1992.

Migsch, Herbert. *Gottes Wort über das Ende Jerusalems: Eine literar-, stil- und gattungskritische Untersuchung des Berichtes Jeremia 34, 1–7; 32, 2–5; 37,3–38,28*. Klosterneuburg: Österreichisches Katholisches Bibelwerk, 1981.

Miller, J. Hillis, "Narrative." Pages 66–79 in *Critical Terms for Literary Study*. Edited by F. Lentricchia and T. McLaughlin. Chicago: University of Chicago Press, 1995.

Miller, Owen. "Intertextual Identity." Pages 19–40 in *Identity of the Literary Text*. Edited by M. J. Valdes and O. Miller. Toronto: University of Toronto Press, 1985.

Mills, Mary. *Biblical Morality: Moral Perspectives in Old Testament Narratives*. Burlington, Vt.: Ashgate, 2001.

Miscall, Peter. "Isaiah: The Labyrinth of Images." *Semeia* 54 (1991): 103–21.

—"The Jacob and Joseph Stories as Analogies." *Journal for the Study of the Old Testament* 6 (1978): 28–40.

—*The Workings of Old Testament Narrative*. Philadelphia: Fortress, 1983.

Montgomery, James. *Critical and Exegetical Commentary on the Books of Kings*. International Critical Commentary. New York: Scribner, 1951.

Morgan, Thais. "The Space of Intertextuality." Pages 239–79 in *Intertextuality and Contemporary American Fiction*. Edited by P. O'Donnell and R. C. Davis. Baltimore: The Johns Hopkins University Press, 1989.

Morson, Gary S., and Caryl Emerson. *Mikhail Bakhtin: Creation of a Prosaics*. Stanford: Stanford University Press, 1990.

Murray, Donald. "Of All the Years the Hopes—Or Fears? Jehoiachin in Babylon (2 Kings 25:27–30)." *Journal of Biblical Literature* 120 (2001): 245–65.

Nash, Stanley. "Y.L. Gordon: Zedekiah in the Prison House." *Central Conference of American Rabbis: A Reform Jewish Quarterly* (Spring 2003): 33–48.

Nasuti, Harry. "A Prophet to the Nations: Diachronic and Synchronic Readings of Jeremiah 1." *Hebrew Annual Review* 10 (1986): 249–66.

Newsom, Carol A. "Bakhtin, the Bible, and Dialogic Truth." *The Journal of Religion* 76 (1996): 290–306.

Nicholson, Ernest W. *The Book of Jeremiah Chapters 26–52.* Cambridge Bible Commentary. Cambridge: Cambridge University Press, 1975.

—*Preaching to the Exiles: A Study of the Prose Tradition in the Book of Jeremiah.* New York: Schocken Books, 1970.

Nickelsburg, George W. *Resurrection, Immortality, and Eternal Life in Intertestamental Judaism.* Cambridge, Mass.: Harvard University Press, 1972.

O'Brien, Mark. "The Portrayal of Prophets in 2 Kings 2." *Australian Biblical Review* 46 (1998): 1–16.

Overholt, Thomas. *The Threat of Falsehood: A Study in the Theology of the Book of Jeremiah.* Naperville, Ill.: Alec R. Allenson, 1970.

Paris, Bernard. *Imagined Human Beings: A Psychological Approach to Character and Conflict in Literature.* New York: New York University Press, 1997.

Park-Taylor, Geoffrey H. *The Formation of the Book of Jeremiah: Doublets and Recurring Phrases.* Atlanta: Society of Biblical Literature, 2000.

Perdue, Leo G. *The Collapse of History.* Overtures to Biblical Theology. Minneapolis: Fortress, 1994.

Person, Raymond. *Structure and Meaning in Conversation and Literature.* Lanham, Md.: University Press of America, 1999.

Phelan, James. *Reading People, Reading Plots: Character, Progression and the Interpretation of Narrative.* Chicago: University of Chicago Press, 1989.

Pohlmann, Karl-Friedrich. *Studien zum Jeremiabuch: Ein Beitrag zur Frage nach der Entstehung des Jeremiabuches.* Göttingen: Vandenhoeck & Ruprecht, 1978.

Polzin, Robert. *David and the Deuteronomist.* Bloomington: Indiana University Press, 1993.

—*Moses and the Deuteronomist.* Bloomington: Indiana University Press, 1980.

—*Samuel and the Deuteronomist.* Bloomington: Indiana University Press, 1989.

Preston, T. R. "The Heroism of Saul: Patterns of Meaning in the Narrative of Early Kingship." *Journal for the Study of the Old Testament* 24 (1982): 27–46.

Prince, Gerald. *Narratology: The Form and Function of Narrative.* New York: Mouton, 1982.

Rad, Gerhard von. *Old Testament Theology.* 2 vols. New York: Harper & Row, 1965.

Ramsey, George. "Samuel." Pages 954–57 in vol. 5 of the *Anchor Bible Dictionary.* Edited by D. N. Freedman. 6 vols. New York: Doubleday, 1992.

Redford, Donald. *A Study of the Biblical Story of Joseph (Gen 37–50).* Leiden: Brill, 1970.

Reis, Pamela Tamarkin. "Vindicating God: Another Look at 1 Kings xiii." *Vetus Testamentum* 44 (1994): 376–86.

Reventlow, Henning G. *Liturgie und prophetisches Ich bei Jeremia.* Gütersloh: Gütersloher Verlag, 1963.

Riffaterre, Michael. *Semiotics of Poetry.* Bloomington: Indiana University Press, 1978.

—*Text Production.* Translated by T. Lyons. New York: Columbia University Press, 1983.

Rimmon-Kenan, Shlomith. *Narrative Fiction: Contemporary Poetics.* London: Methuen, 1983.

Roberts, J. J. M. "Prophets and Kings: A New Look at the Royal Persecution of Prophets against its Near Eastern Background." Pages 341–54 in *A God So Near.* Edited by B. A. Strawn and N. R. Bowen. Winona Lake, Ind.: Eisenbrauns, 2003.

Rofé, Alexander. *The Prophetical Stories.* Jerusalem: Magnes, 1988.

Roncace, Mark. "Elisha and the Woman of Shunem: 2 Kings 4.8–37 and 8.1–6 Read in Conjunction." *Journal for the Study of the Old Testament* 91 (2000): 109–27.

Rudolph, W. *Jeremia.* 3d ed.; Tübingen: Handbuch zum Alten Testament 12. J. C. B. Mohr, 1958.

Sanders, Jose. *Perspective in Narrative Discourse.* Tilburg: Proefschrift Katholieke Universiteit Brabant, 1994.

Savran, George W. *Telling and Retelling: Quotation in Biblical Narrative.* Bloomington: Indiana University Press, 1988.

Scheffler, Eben. "Saving Saul from the Deuteronomist." Pages 263–71 in *Past, Present, Future: The Deuteronomistic History and the Prophets.* Edited by J. C. de Moor and H. F. Van Rooy. Leiden: Brill, 2000.

Schökel, L. Alonso. "Jeremías como anti-Moisés." Pages 245–54 in *De la Tôrah au Messie: Etudes d'exégèse et herméneutique bibliques offertes à Henri Cazelles pur ses 25 années d'enseignement à l'Institut Catholique de Paris.* Edited by M. Carrez, J. Doré, and P. Grelot. Paris: Desclée, 1981.

Seitz, Christopher. "The Prophet Moses and the Canonical Shape of Jeremiah." *Zeitschrift für die alttestamentliche Wissenschaft* 101 (1989): 3–27.

—*Theology in Conflict: Reactions to the Exile in the Book of Jeremiah.* Beihefte zur Zeitschrift für die alttestamentliche Wissenschaft 176. Berlin: de Gruyter, 1989.

Simon, Uriel. "I Kings 13: A Prophetic Sign—Denial and Persistence." *Hebrew Union College Annual* 47 (1976): 81–117.

—*Reading Prophetic Narratives.* Translated by L. J. Schramm. Bloomington: Indiana University Press, 1997.

Sisson, Jonathan P. "Jeremiah and the Jerusalem Conception of Peace." *Journal of Biblical Literature* 105 (1986): 429–42.

Speiser, E.A. " 'Coming' and 'Going' at the City Gate." *Bulletin of the American Schools of Oriental Research* 144 (1952): 20–23.

Springer, Mary D. *A Rhetoric of Literary Character.* Chicago: University of Chicago Press, 1978.

States, Bert O. *Hamlet and the Concept of Character.* Baltimore: The Johns Hopkins University Press, 1992.

Sternberg, Meir. *The Poetics of Biblical Narrative.* Bloomington: Indiana University Press, 1985.

Stipp, Hermann-Josef. *Jeremia im Parteienstreit: Studien zur Textentwicklung von Jer 26, 36–43 und 45 als Beitrag zur Geschichte Jeremias, seines Buches und judäischer Parteien im 6. Jahrhundert.* Frankfurt am Main: Anton Hain, 1992.

——"Zedekiah in the Book of Jeremiah: On the Formation of a Biblical Character." *Catholic Biblical Quarterly* 58 (1996): 627–48.

Streete, Gail. "Redaction Criticism." Pages 105–21 in *To Each its Own Meaning.* Edited by S. L. McKenzie and S. R. Haynes. Louisville, Ky.: Westminster John Knox, 1999.

Thiel, Winfried. *Die deuteronomistische Redaktion von Jeremia 1–25.* Neukirchen–Vluyn: Neukirchener Verlag, 1973.

Thompson, John. *The Book of Jeremiah.* New International Commentary on the Old Testament. Grand Rapids: Eerdmans, 1980.

Tolmie, Donald F. *Narratology and Biblical Narratives: A Practical Guide.* San Francisco: International Scholars Publications, 1999.

Tull, Patricia. "Intertextuality and the Hebrew Scriptures." *Currents in Research: Biblical Studies* 8 (2000): 59–90.

—"Rhetorical Criticism and Intertextuality." Pages 156–80 in *To Each its Own Meaning.* Edited by S. L. McKenzie and S. R. Haynes. Louisville, Ky.: Westminster John Knox, 1999.

Uspensky, Boris. *Poetics of Composition*. Berkeley: University of California Press, 1973.

Volz, Paul. *Der Prophet Jeremia*. Leipzig: Deichert, 1928.

Vorster, Willem. "Intertextuality and Redaktionsgeschichte." Pages 15–26 in *Intertextuality in Biblical Writings: Essays in Honor of Bas van Iersel*. Edited by S. Draisma. Kampen: Kok, 1989.

Walcutt, Charles. *Man's Changing Mask: Modes and Methods of Characterization in Fiction*. Minneapolis: University of Minnesota Press, 1966.

Wanke, Gunther. *Untersuchungen zur sogenannten Baruchschrift*. Beihefte zur Zeitschrift für die alttestamentliche Wissenschaft 122. Berlin: de Gruyter, 1971.

Weinfeld, Moshe. *Social Justice in Ancient Israel and the Ancient Near East*. Jerusalem: Magnes, 1995.

Weippert, Helga. *Die Prosareden des Jeremiabuches*. Beihefte zur Zeitschrift für die alttestamentliche Wissenschaft 132. Berlin: de Gruyter, 1973.

Westermann, Claus. *Genesis 12–36: A Commentary*. Translated by J. Scullion. Minneapolis: Augsburg Fortress, 1986.

White, Hayden. *Tropics of Discourse: Essays in Cultural Criticism*. Baltimore: The Johns Hopkins University Press, 1978.

Willis, Timothy M. "'They Did Not Listen to the Voice of the Lord': A Literary Analysis of Jeremiah 37–45." *Restoration Quarterly* 42 (2000): 65–84.

Wills, Lawrence. *The Jew in the Court of the Foreign King: Ancient Jewish Court Legends*. Minneapolis: Fortress, 1990.

Wilson, Rawdon. "The Bright Chimera: Character as a Literary Term." *Critical Inquiry* 7 (1979): 725–49.

Wilson, Robert. *Prophecy and Society in Ancient Israel*. Philadelphia: Fortress, 1980.

Wolde, Ellen van. "Trendy Intertextuality." Pages 43–49 in *Intertextuality in Biblical Writings: Essays in Honor of Bas van Iersel*. Edited by S. Draisma. Kampen: Kok, 1989.

INDEXES

INDEX OF REFERENCES

INDEX OF AUTHORS